Middle Range Theory
for Nursing

Mary Jane Smith, PhD, RN, earned her bachelor's and master's degrees from the University of Pittsburgh and her doctorate from New York University. Her majors at the master's level include medical-surgical nursing and mental-health nursing; and nursing science while in the doctoral program. She has held faculty positions at the following nursing schools: University of Pittsburgh, Duquesne University, Cornell University–New York Hospital, and Ohio State University; and is currently Professor and Associate Dean for Graduate Academic Affairs at West Virginia University School of Nursing. She has been teaching nursing theory to master's students for over 25 years.

Patricia R. Liehr, PhD, RN, graduated from Ohio Valley Hospital, School of Nursing in Pittsburgh, Pennsylvania. She completed her baccalaureate degree in nursing at Villa Maria College, her master's in family health nursing at Duquesne University, and her doctorate at the University of Maryland—Baltimore, School of Nursing, with an emphasis on psychophysiology. She did postdoctoral education at the University of Pennsylvania as a Robert Wood Johnson scholar. Dr. Liehr is a professor of nursing at the University of Texas, Health Science Center—Houston, School of Nursing, where she has taught nursing theory to master's and doctoral students for the past 14 years.

Middle Range Theory
for Nursing

Mary Jane Smith, PhD, RN
Patricia R. Liehr, PhD, RN
Editors

 Springer Publishing Company

Springer Publishing Company, Inc.
536 Broadway
New York, NY 10012-3955

Acquisitions Editor: Ruth Chasek
Production Editor: Pamela Lankas
Cover design by Joanne Honigman

03 04 05 06 07 / 5 4 3 2

Library of Congress Cataloging-in-Publication Data

Middle range theory for nursing / Mary Jane Smith, Patricia R. Liehr.
    p. ; cm.
    Includes bibliographical references and index.
    ISBN 0-8261-1915-8 (alk. paper)
    1. Nursing—Philosophy.   2. Nursing models.   3. Information science.   I. Smith, Mary Jane, 1938– II. Liehr, Patricia R.
    [DNLM: 1. Nursing Theory.   2. Nursing Research.   WY 86 M627 2003]
    RT84.5.M537 2003
    610.73'01—dc21

                                                                    2003041526

Printed in the United States of America by Maple-Vail Book Manufacturing Group.

Contents

Contributors

Margaret F. Clayton, RN, MSN, FNP
Doctoral Candidate
School of Nursing
The University of North
 Carolina at Chapel Hill
Chapel Hill, NC

Eugenie Hildebrandt, PhD, RN, CS-ANP
Associate Professor
University of Wisconsin-
 Milwaukee
School of Nursing
Milwaukee, WI

Elizabeth R. Lenz, PhD, RN, FAAN
Dean and Professor
The Ohio State University
School of Nursing
Columbus, OH

Geri LoBiondo-Wood, PhD, RN, FAAN
Associate Professor
University of Texas Health
 Sciences Center-Houston
School of Nursing
Nursing Systems & Technology
Houston, TX

Merle H. Mishel, PhD, RN, FAAN
Kenan Professor of Nursing
School of Nursing
The University of North
 Carolina at Chapel Hill
Chapel Hill, NC

Cynthia Armstrong Persily, PhD, RN
Associate Professor and
 Associate Dean Southern
 Region
West Virginia University School
 of Nursing
Charleston Division
Charleston, WV

Linda C. Pugh, PhD, RNC
Associate Professor
Johns Hopkins School of
 Nursing
Baltimore, MD

Pamela G. Reed, PhD, RN, FAAN
Professor and Associate Dean
The University of Arizona
 College of Nursing
Tucson, AZ

Barbara Resnick, PhD, RN, FAAN
Associate Professor
University of Maryland
School of Nursing
Baltimore, MD

Marlaine C. Smith, RN, PhD, HNC
Associate Professor and
  Associate Dean for Academic
  Affairs
University of Colorado School
  of Nursing
Denver, CO

Patricia L. Starck, DSN, RN, FAAN
Dean and Professor
University of Texas Health
  Sciences Center-Houston
School of Nursing
Houston, TX

Foreword

T his book, *Middle Range Theory for Nursing*, is the first collection of its kind. It is a significant contribution to the development of nursing knowledge. The editors have selected eight middle range nursing theories that have been developed over the past two decades for inclusion in this first definitive work on the topic. One of the primary considerations made in the selection of these theories is that they conformed to the definition of nursing science explicated by Newman and colleagues (1991) that nursing is "caring in the human health experience." By setting this definition as a key parameter, the editors have targeted their work primarily to theories that fit within two of the three nursing paradigms previously identified by Newman and her colleagues. Five of the eight theories fall within the interactive/integrative paradigm and three fall within the unitary/transformative paradigm.

Smith and Liehr have organized the book so that each middle range theorist presents her theory in the same manner. Key components included in relation to each theory include the purpose of the theory, foundational literature, key concepts embedded in the theory, relationships among concepts, use of the theory in nursing research, and use of the theory in nursing practice. The ladder concept is used throughout each theory to demonstrate the movement from the more abstract concepts to the more specific ones. Each of these ladder diagrams helps the reader to understand the specific theory and to compare the theories to each other.

Another significant inclusion in relation to these theories is the authors' personal experiences in developing the theories. One of the fascinating components of this book is thus a view of the sociology of knowledge development in nursing from the perspective of the development of these eight middle range nursing theories. The authors trace their own scholarship and relate it to the contributions of their mentors and those who have been mentored by them. Thus, the reader is given a glimpse into the development of scholars in several doctoral programs in nursing where the key authors of the theories were faculty members who worked with other colleagues and doctoral students to initiate research to test and refine their theories. In one instance it is even possible to trace the relationship between two of the middle range theories. Both Reed (theory of self-transcendence) and Starck (theory of meaning) identify the relationship of their own theoretical work to the research contributions of Coward, who was Reed's doctoral advisee at the University of Arizona. In another instance there is a glimpse of the global perspective that recently has emerged in nursing theory development. The theory of community empowerment has been collaboratively developed by Persily and Hildebrandt from research based in both the United States and South Africa. This sociological perspective is further enhanced when one takes into account the references that are supplied in relation to each of the theories. The final chapter by Marlaine Smith presents a historical view of the evaluation process that can be used for these and other theories. Smith first recognizes the classic work of Kaplan (1964) in theory evaluation. Then she traces the nursing theory evaluation literature. The criteria that she proposes for theory evaluation is drawn primarily from the work of Kaplan, but is modified, based on the substantive work that has been done through the past two and a half decades in nursing. Each of the dimensions for evaluation is explained in detail by the chapter author.

All in all, this is a most welcome addition to the nursing science literature. It fills a substantial gap in theory development in nursing with the content of the discipline. For many years doctoral programs in nursing have focused on the process of theory development, including the development of middle range theory. Now, nurse educators and scholars will have the content to match the process and to guide their research.

JOYCE J. FITZPATRICK, PhD, MBA, RN, FAAN

REFERENCES

Kaplan, A. (1964). *The conduct of inquiry*. San Francisco: Chaldler.
Newman, M. A., Sime, A. M., & Corcoran-Perry, S. A. (1991). The focus of the discipline of nursing. *Advances in Nursing Science, 14*(1), 1–6.

Preface

Over the last several years, we have noticed an increasing interest in middle range theory as demonstrated by the number of published theories as well as through conversations with faculty in master's and doctoral programs across the country who are teaching middle range theories in their courses. We pondered the question: Why is there no book on middle range theory? This question led us to mobilize resources needed to put together this book. The book is based on the premise that students come to know and understand a theory as the meaning of concepts are made clear and as they experience the way a theory informs practice in the everyday world of nursing. Students and faculty need a reference if middle range theory is going to move to the forefront of research and practice.

Middle range theory can be defined as a set of related ideas that are focused on a limited dimension of the reality of nursing. These theories are composed of concepts and suggested relationships among the concepts that can be depicted in a model. Middle range theories are developed and grow at the intersection of practice and research to provide guidance for everyday practice and scholarly research rooted in the discipline of nursing.

The middle range theories chosen for presentation in this book cover a broad spectrum—from ones that were proposed decades ago and have been used extensively to those that are newly developed and just beginning to be used. Some of the theories were originated by the primary nurse-author who wrote the chapter, and some were originally created by persons outside of nursing. After much thought and discussion with colleagues and students, we have come to the conclusion that theories for nursing are ones that apply to the unique perspective of the discipline, regardless of origin, as long as they are consistent with one of the paradigms presented by Newman and colleagues (Newman, Sime, & Corcoran-Perry, 1991). These paradigms, which are recognized philosophical perspectives unique to the discipline, present an ontological grounding for the middle range theories in this book. By connecting each theory with a paradigmatic perspective, we offer a view of the middle range theory's place within the larger scope of nursing science. This view was included to create a context for considering theories, beyond those developed by nurses.

Each chapter addressing a middle range theory follows a standard format. This includes: purpose and evolution of the theory, foundational literature, major concepts, relationships among the concepts, a model, use of the theory in practice, use of the theory in research, and conclusions. We believe this standard format will facilitate a complete understanding of the theory and enable a comparison of the theories presented in the book. Each chapter includes a ladder of abstraction that offers a clear and formal way of presenting the theories. The ladders found in the Appendix of the book were created by the editors. So, the ladders represent the editors' view of the philosophical grounding of the theory rather than the chapter authors' view. We have found that a ladder of abstraction can guide students' thinking when they are trying to make sense of a theory. In addition, moving ideas up and down the ladder of abstraction generates scholarly dialogue. The more dialogue we have on theory dimensions, the more likely it will be that theory will be understood, valued, and used as a guide for nursing practice and research.

MARY JANE SMITH, PhD, RN
PATRICIA R. LIEHR, PhD, RN

REFERENCE

Newman, M. A., Sime, A. M., & Corcoran-Perry, S. A. (1991). The focus of the discipline of nursing. *Advances in Nursing Science, 14,* 1–6.

Acknowledgment

An endeavor like this book is always the work of many. We are grateful to our students, who have prodded us with thought-provoking questions; our colleagues, who have challenged our thinking and writing; our contributors, who gave willingly of their time and effort; our publishers, who believed that we had something to offer; and our families, who have provided a base of love and support that makes anything possible.

1

Introduction: Middle Range Theory and the Ladder of Abstraction

Mary Jane Smith and Patricia Liehr

Every discipline has a process of reasoning that is rooted in the philosophy, theories, and empirical generalizations that define it. The reasoning process is logical when all elements come together and make sense in an orderly and coherent manner. This book uses a "ladder of abstraction" as a tool for helping readers understand and use middle range theory. The ladder of abstraction is a way to visualize three different and distinct levels of discourse: philosophical, theoretical, and empirical. The purpose of this chapter is to describe the ladder of abstraction as central to understanding and using middle range theory in research and practice. The philosophical, theoretical, and empirical underpinnings of recently published middle range theories of nursing will be evaluated, and the middle range theories presented in this book will be considered relative to the ladder of abstraction.

Picture a ladder with three rungs. The highest rung stands for the philosophical, the middle for the theoretical, and the lowest for the empirical (See Figure 1.1). These rungs represent differing ways of describing ideas, or levels of discourse. The ladder illustrates the connection between these levels of discourse. The philosophical level is the highest and represents beliefs and assumptions that are accepted as true and fundamental to a theory. This level represents the belief systems essential to the reasoning in the other rungs.

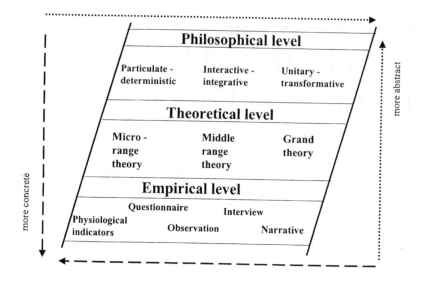

FIGURE 1.1 Ladder of abstraction.

The theoretical rung represents abstraction, which consists of symbols, ideas, and concepts. Many of the theories in this book have a central abstraction. For instance: self-transcendence, uncertainty, and self-efficacy are some of the theoretically abstract ideas that will be discussed in this book. Implicit in abstraction is some vagueness, which enables the ongoing development of the idea. This bit of vagueness can throw one off guard and cause confusion about the meaning of an idea. However, the abstract level is not intended to be confusing. In deciphering the abstract one figures out meaning and comes to know what is explicit about an abstract idea.

The empirical is the lowest rung on the ladder and is at a concrete level of discourse. For instance, if ideas are expressed as practice stories, they are low on the ladder of abstraction. The empirical represents what can be observed by the senses. It includes perceptions, descriptions of symbolic meanings, self-reports, observable behavior, biological indicators, and personal stories (Ford-Gilboe, Campbell, & Berman, 1995; Reed, 1995).

The levels of discourse on the ladder of abstraction are differing ways of expressing, defining, and specifying an idea. If one idea is more abstract than another, then it is more encompassing, enveloping a broader scope. On the other hand, if an idea is less abstract, then it is more concrete. The notion of levels of abstraction can be key to understanding and making sense of the theoretical. Each rung of the ladder relates to the others. When one is grappling with understanding the theoretical or middle level on the ladder, it can help to move the idea up to evaluate its philosophical premise and move it down to evaluate its empirical indicators (where the theory connects to the world of practice and research). The concepts that define the structure of the theory are learned by thinking through their meaning in the context of nursing practice and research. To have a complete understanding one can move the theoretical idea back and forth, along and within the rungs of the ladder. For example, start at the middle rung of the ladder. Ask the question: How is this theory defined conceptually, what are the concepts, and what do the concepts mean? Then move to the lower rung and ask: What does this mean to me and how does it connect with what I already know, namely my experience? How does my personal experience fit with the description of the theorist? Move to the highest rung and ask: What values and beliefs are included in the assumptions of the theory? The point is that in coming to know the realm of the theoretical, one can think through the theory by moving up and down the rungs of the ladder. The theory can also become understandable through discussion with colleagues and the theorist, through reading and thinking, and in talking with others about the theory. Such discourse is always both tacit and explicit. This means that a person can begin to describe in words the meaning of an abstract idea and at the same time hold more knowledge about the idea than can be made explicit. Each time the idea is described through talking, writing, and discussion, a greater grasp is achieved.

It should be pointed out that staying on one rung deters understanding and limits ability to use the theory in practice or research. Persons may choose to stay on the rung that is most comfortable. For example, theorists may stay at the theoretical, researchers may stay at the empirical, and metatheorists may be more comfortable at the philosophical. It is a premise of this work on middle range theory that in order to move nursing science to the front lines of practice and research, it is essential that nurses be skilled in moving up and down and back and forth on the ladder of abstraction when studying, practicing, and researching the science of nursing.

The ladder supplies a logical process that provides clarity and facilitates understanding and use of the theory in research and practice.

To understand a theory at all levels of abstraction requires a process of reasoning. By moving from the lower rung of the ladder to the middle and then the upper rung, one is making sense of phenomena through inductive reasoning. And conversely, movement from the upper philosophical rung to the theoretical and then to the empirical is deductive reasoning. This logical structure guides thinking through nursing research and nursing practice, flying in the face of the notion that theory is bewildering logic, abstruse and incomprehensible. In this book, each level of the ladder will be used to understand selected middle range theories.

PHILOSOPHICAL LEVEL

The philosophical level includes assumptions, beliefs, paradigmatic perspectives, and points of view. Reasoning through a nursing situation for practice and for research is based on assumptions. Assumptions are beliefs accepted as true about what constitutes reality. Assumptions about how individuals change are at the backbone of nursing theory. A paradigm is a world-view that includes disciplinary values and perspectives that are at the philosophical level. Several descriptions of paradigms in nursing have been developed. One of the first world-view offerings in nursing was the totality paradigm and the simultaneity paradigm (Parse, Coyne, & Smith, 1985). In the totality paradigm, health is a norm-based continuum, and persons are viewed as biopsychosocial beings separate from the environment. In the simultaneity paradigm, health is quality of life and persons are viewed as unitary and integrated with their environment. Newman, Sime, and Corcoran-Perry (1991) distinguished nursing paradigms from nursing focus. They identified caring in the human health experience as the focus of the discipline of nursing. Then they identified three paradigms, which guide the discipline: the particulate-deterministic, the interactive-integrative, and the unitary-transformative. Each paradigm incorporates unique values about health and caring and how change comes about. In the particulate-deterministic paradigm, the person is viewed as an isolated entity, change is primarily linear and causal, and the knowledge base is grounded in the perspective of the biophysical sciences. The interactive-integrative paradigm values persons as reciprocal interacting entities, with change as probabilistic and related to multiple factors. The knowledge base of this paradigm is grounded in the perspective of the social sciences. In the unitary-transformative paradigm, the person is viewed as unitary, evolving in a simultaneous process of creative and non-predictable change, and the knowledge base is grounded in the human sciences. One can clearly see that the three paradigms all hold assumptions, values, and a point of view at differing levels of abstraction. The most abstract is the unitary-transformative, next is the interactive-integrative, and lowest in level of abstraction is the particulate-deterministic. Although theorists may not explicate their assumptions or paradigmatic perspective, a careful reading of the theory will lead one to know where the theorist stands in relation to a point of view and what makes up the philosophical underpinnings of the proposed theory. The ladder of abstraction (Figure 1.1) depicts the highest level of abstraction as the philosophical level, including the particulate-deterministic, inter-active-integrative, and unitary-transformative paradigms. Recently published middle range theories and middle range theories presented in this book have been placed by the editors in one of these paradigms on the philosophical rung of the ladder. This was a judgment that reflects the view of two people (Smith & Liehr) and evolved through scholarly discourse. It is important for the reader to understand that different judgments will be made by different people who have a different understanding of the theory and the paradigms. There isn't a right way to link a theory with a paradigm but there are always substantiated reasons for the linking decisions. The editors made the decision about theory-paradigm link based on the knowledge roots of the middle range theories. The middle range theories of Community Empowerment, Family Stress and Coping, Self-Efficacy, Uncertainty, and Unpleasant Symptoms are rooted primarily in the social sciences and relate to a multidimensional and contextual reality. These five theories have substantiated links to the interactive-integrative para-digm. The middle range theories of Attentively Embracing Story, Meaning, and Self-Transcendence are primarily rooted in the human sciences and relate to reality as a process of person-environment mu-tual and creative unfolding. These three theories espouse values consis-tent with the unitary-transformative paradigm. Understanding the paradigmatic perspective of a theory helps one lay out a starting point for the theory by establishing its philosophical foundation, which has meaning for the theory's content, structure, and use in practice and research.

THEORETICAL LEVEL

The reader will note that the middle range theories presented in this book all comply with the focus of nursing as presented by Newman and colleagues (1991). They state, "We submit that nursing is the study of *caring in the human health experience*" (p. 3). They go on to say "A body of knowledge that does not include caring and human health experience is not nursing knowledge" (p. 3). Caring is described as a moral imperative having a service identity. All eight middle range theories described in this work have a focus of caring in the human health experience. Application of any one of these theories enables a change in the human health experience. The human health experience is explicit in each of the theories as: the human story, community power, family coping, pursuit of life meaning, believing in self and deciding how to behave, transcending self, uncertainty, and unpleasant symptom experience. Caring in the human health experience requires consideration of how the nurse lives relationships with people regarding their health. According to these theories, some of the ways that caring occurs are through engaged dialogue, involvement with community, managing crisis, attending to suffering, using information sources, supporting inner resources, promoting structure and order, and considering multidimensional experience (Table 1.1). These theories add to the body of knowledge about nursing regardless of their discipline origination. All of the theories have been applied in nursing practice and research to enhance caring in the human health experience. Theories belong to many disciplines, and what is important to nursing science is that the research and practice based on a theory can be grounded in the focus and paradigmatic perspective of the discipline of nursing.

The theoretical rung on the ladder of abstraction includes concepts, frameworks, and theories. A theoretical concept is different from an everyday concept because it is a mental image of an aspect of reality that is put into words in order to describe and explain the meaning of a phenomenon significant to the discipline of nursing. A theoretical framework is a structure of interrelating concepts that describes and explains the meaning of a phenomenon significant to the discipline of nursing. What, then, is a theory? Theory is described in the literature at all levels of abstraction. The accepted definition of a theory rests in the perspective of a critiquer. Chinn and Kramer (1999, p. 258) define theory as "a creative and rigorous structuring of ideas that

TABLE 1.1   Description of Caring in the Human Health Experience for Eight Middle Range Theories

Theory	Description
Attentively Embracing Story	Engaged dialogue about the human health story
Community Empowerment	Involvement with community to enhance community power
Family Stress and Adaptation	Managing crisis by supporting family coping with stress
Meaning	Attending to suffering to create life meaning and find purpose
Self-Efficacy	Using information sources to foster belief in self and behavior decisions
Self-Transcendence	Supporting inner resources to enable transcending self
Uncertainty	Promoting structure and order to reframe uncertainty
Unpleasant Symptoms	Considering multidimensional experience to manage unpleasant symptoms

project a tentative, purposeful and systematic view of phenomena." Im and Meleis (1999, p. 11) define theory as "an organized, coherent and systematic articulation of a set of statements related to significant questions in a discipline that are communicated in a meaningful whole to describe or explain a phenomena or set of phenomena." McKay (1969) on the other hand, describes theory as a logically interrelated set of confirmed hypotheses. Chinn and Kramer's definition of theory is at the highest level of abstraction; next is Im and Meleis's, and at the lowest level is McKay's. Given this array of theory definitions it is easy to understand why one could argue several ways about whether a particular theory is indeed a theory. It all depends on the way theory is defined.

Furthermore, there are levels of theory within the theoretical rung of the ladder. At the most abstract level there are the grand theories. These are theories that have a very broad scope. The conceptual focus of some of these grand theories includes goal attainment, self-care, adaptation, becoming, and unitary human field processes (King, 1996; Orem, 1971; Parse, 1992; Rogers, 1994; Roy & Andrews, 1991). Each of these grand theories offers a structure, which enables description and explanation of essential conceptualizations of nursing.

Middle range theories, the subject of this book, are described by Merton (1968, p. 39) as those "that lie between the minor but necessary working hypotheses that evolve in abundance during day-to-day research and the all-inclusive systematic efforts to develop unified theory." He goes on to say that the principal ideas of middle range theories are relatively simple. Simple, here, means rudimentary, straightforward ideas that stem from the focus of the discipline. Thus middle range theory is a basic, usable structure of ideas, less abstract than grand theory and more abstract than empirical generalizations or microrange theory.

Microrange theories, described as situation-specific theories by Im and Meleis (1999, p. 13), are theories that focus on "specific nursing phenomena that reflect clinical practice and that are limited to specific populations or to particular fields of practice." These theories "offer a blue print that is more readily operational and or has more accessible utility in clinical situations" (p. 19). It can be seen that this level of theory is lower on the ladder of abstraction than middle range theory. Examples of situation-specific theories are menopausal transition of Korean immigrant women, learned response to chronic illness of patients with rheumatoid arthritis, and women's responses when dealing with their multiple roles (Im & Meleis). The Ladder of Abstraction depicts microrange theory, middle range theory and grand theory on ascending levels of discourse.

The ladders in the Appendix at the end of the book show the concepts of the theory as described in each chapter. The authors for each chapter of this book have specifically identified theory concepts; therefore the inclusion of concepts on the ladder was a straightforward process. This may not always be true; sometimes the authors of published articles don't consistently identify concepts. In these instances, the reader is left to figure out what the concepts of the theory are and how they are defined. For some of the recent middle range theories in Table 1.3 it was necessary to decide upon concepts by careful reading of the manuscript and examination of the model. When this interpretative process is needed, there is always a risk that the identified concepts aren't exactly what the author of the theory intended.

THE EMPIRICAL LEVEL

The empirical level represents discourse that brings the theory to research and practice. Empirics include physiologic indicators, what can be obtained from questionnaires, observation, interview, and narrative (See Ladder of Abstraction). Like other rungs on the ladder, the empirical level of discourse moves from the most concrete (physiologic indicators) to the most abstract (narrative). Even at this lowest level of discourse there is a range of abstraction.

Whether doing practice or research, the nurse connects with the empirical level. The advanced practice nurse may use physiologic indicators, interview, and observation while applying theory to caring in the human health experience. The nurse researcher may use observation and narrative in a single study while applying theory to examine caring in the human health experience. Decisions about empirics are guided by philosophy and theory. It is important that the nurse choose empirics that fit with philosophic and theoretical perspectives.

RECENTLY PUBLISHED MIDDLE RANGE THEORY

Before addressing the middle range theories published in this book, we will review the most recently published middle range theories. In 1999, we reviewed a decade of nursing literature to identify a foundation of middle range nursing theory (Liehr & Smith, 1999). To locate this literature, CINAHL (Cumulative Index of Nursing and Allied Health Literature) was searched using the terms middle range theory, mid-range theory and nursing. All articles written in English were evaluated according to four inclusion criteria:

1. The theory's author identified it as middle range in the paper.
2. The theory name was accessible in the paper.
3. Concepts of the theory were explicitly or implicitly identified.
4. The development of the theory was the major focus of the paper (Liehr & Smith, 1999).

Twenty-two theories, published from 1988 to 1998, met these criteria and were addressed in the paper (see Table 1.2). A recent CINAHL search using the 1999 search terms plus midrange theory, and the same criteria for inclusion resulted in identification of fourteen new middle range theories published from 1998 through 2001. Table 1.3 lists the fourteen theories, classifying them according to paradigmatic perspective, conceptual base, and application in practice and research. We linked each theory with one of the paradigms (particulate-deterministic, interactive-integrative, unitary-transformative). The cited

TABLE 1.2   Names of Middle Range Theories Published from 1988 to 1998

- Uncertainty in illness (Mishel, 1988)
- Nurse-midwifery care (Thompson, Oakley, Burke, Tay, & Konklin, 1989)
- Facilitating growth and development (Kinney, 1990)
- Self-transcendence (Reed, 1991)
- Hazardous secrets and reluctantly taking charge (Burke, Kauffmann, Costello, & Dillon, 1991)
- Women's anger (Thomas, 1991)
- Caring (Swanson, 1991)
- Negotiating partnership (Powell-Cope, 1994)
- Cultural brokering (Jezewski, 1995)
- Homelessness/helplessness (Tollett & Thomas, 1995)
- Chronotherapeutic intervention for post-surgical pain (Auvil-Novak, 1997)
- Nurse-expressed empathy and patient distress (Olson & Hanchett, 1997)
- Interpersonal perceptual awareness (Brook & Thomas, 1997)
- Resilience (Polk, 1997)
- Individualized music intervention for agitation (Gerdner, 1997)
- Affiliated individuation as a mediator for stress (Acton, 1997)
- Unpleasant symptoms (Lenz, Pugh, Milligan, Gift, & Suppe, 1997)
- Balance between analgesia and side effects (Good, 1998)
- Chronic sorrow (Eakes, Burke, & Hainsworth, 1998)
- Acute pain management (Huth & Moore, 1998)
- Psychological adaptation (Levesque, Ricard, Ducharme, Duquette, & Bonin, 1998)
- Peaceful end of life (Ruland & Moore, 1998)

See Liehr & Smith (1999) for complete references.

manuscripts were used to identify individual concepts of each theory, and ways the concepts have been applied in research or used in practice are noted on the table.

The majority (71%) of these fourteen theories emerged from the interactive–integrative paradigm. One was from the particulate-deterministic paradigm and three were from the unitary-transformative paradigm. By looking closely at the match between the paradigm, concepts, and application, it is reasonable to expect that information across columns of the table will be consistent. For instance, urine control theory comes from the particulate-deterministic paradigm: the concepts include input stimuli, coping mechanisms, and adaptive modes, and the empirical indicators include urination records and mobility scores. There is consistency across these levels of discourse.

TABLE 1.3 Recently Published Middle Range Theories

Year	Author/s & journal	Theory name	Paradigm	Concepts	Application
2001	J. Engebretson & L. Littleton *Nursing Outlook*	Cultural negotiation	Interactive-integrative	• Nurse • Client/family • Interacting nursing process • Health care system • Ecological context	Nursing Process • Knowledge exchange • Information interpretation • Joint decision making • Mutual plan of action • Outcome appraisal
2001	R. G. S. Hills & E. Hanchett *Visions*	Enlightenment	Unitary-transformative	• Awareness • Wakefulness • Human field motion • Well-being	• Awareness subscale • Energy factor • Assessment of dream experience • Altered experience & state of awareness • Field dynamics index • Cantril ladder for well being

(continued)

11

TABLE 1.3 *(continued)*

Year	Author/s & journal	Theory name	Paradigm	Concepts	Application
2001	K. Kolcaba *Nursing Outlook*	Comfort	Interactive-integrative	• Health care needs • Nursing interventions • Intervening variables • Patient comfort • Health-seeking behavior • Institutional integrity	• Comfort care survey • Functional status • Care recipient satisfaction
2001	J. Wuest *Health Care for Women International*	Precarious ordering: Theory of women's caring	Interactive-integrative	• Environmental context • Competing & changing caring demands • Fraying connections ◆ Setting boundaries ◆ Negotiating ◆ Repatterning	• Interview and participant observation analyzed using grounded theory

TABLE 1.3 *(continued)*

Year	Author/s & journal	Theory name	Paradigm	Concepts	Application
2000	R. C. Sanford *Advances in Nursing Science*	Caring through relation and dialogue for patient education	Unitary-transformative	• Caring relation • Dialogue ♦ Engrossment ♦ Receptivity ♦ Mutual trust	• Dialogue • Interview • Narrative • Participant observation • Case study
2000	M. August-Brady *Journal of Advanced Nursing*	Prevention as intervention	Interactive-integrative	• Flexible and normal lines of defense • Created environment • Interrelatedness of core system variables	• Spielberger state-trait anxiety scale • Coping behavior
2000	A. I. Meleis, L. M. Sawyer, E. Im, D. K. H. Messias, & K. Schumacher *Advances in Nursing Science*	Experiencing transitions	Interactive-integrative	• Nature of transition • Transition conditions: facilitators & inhibitors • Patterns of response	• Skill behavior mastery • Self-identity

(continued)

TABLE 1.3 *(continued)*

Year	Author/s & journal	Theory name	Paradigm	Concepts	Application
2000	M. H. Leenerts & J. K. Magilvy *Advances in Nursing Science*	Investing in self-care	Interactive-integrative	• Focusing self • Fitting resources • Feeling emotions • Finding meaning	• Interview and participant observation analyzed using grounded theory
2000	M. M. Doornbos *Journal of Theory Construction and Testing*	Family health	Interactive-integrative	• Stressors • Coping • Perception of client's health • Time since diagnosis • Family health	• McCubbin family stress and coping scales (see family stress and adaptation chapter)
1999	M. J. Smith & P. Liehr *Scholarly Inquiry for Nursing Practice*	Attentively embracing story	Unitary-transformative	• Intentional dialogue • Connecting with self-in-relation • Creating ease	• Health story analyzed through phenomenologic, linguistic, and case study analysis

TABLE 1.3 *(continued)*

Year	Author/s & journal	Theory name	Paradigm	Concepts	Application
1999	A. A. Smith & M. Friedemann *Journal of Advanced Nursing*	Family dynamics of persons with chronic pain	Interactive-integrative	• Balancing autonomy & connectedness ◦ Obligations & mutual concerns ◆ Extreme closeness	• Interview with family about pain experience • Family cohesion measures

(continued)

TABLE 1.3 *(continued)*

Year	Author/s & journal	Theory name	Paradigm	Concepts	Application
1999	M. M. Jirovec, J. Jenkins, M. Isenberg, & J. Baiardi *Nursing Science Quarterly*	Urine control theory	Particulate-deterministic	• Input stimuli including bladder distention, accessible facilities, mobility skills, and socialization of sanitary habits • Coping mechanisms including spinal reflex, detrusor contraction, sphincter relaxation; and, perception, learning, judgment and body awareness about need to empty bladder • Adaptive modes (physiologic, self-concept, role function, interdependence) important to urine control	• Urination records • Mobility score (measurement wheel and stopwatch)

TABLE 1.3 *(continued)*

Year	Author/s & journal	Theory name	Paradigm	Concepts	Application
1998	C. M. Burns *Archives of Psychiatric Nursing*	Pathway to chemical dependency in nurses	Interactive-integrative	• Health promoting & compromising behavior ◆ Psychological risks ◆ Physiological risks ◆ Social risks ◆ Professional risks	• Addiction knowledge questionnaire • Self-efficacy (see chapter in this book) • Perceived health status
1998	M. H. Kearney	Truthful self-nurturing	Interactive-integrative	• Painful shift in awareness • Work of recovery ◆ Abstinence ◆ Self ◆ Connection	• Interview and participant observation through grounded theory approach used in 10 studies

According to the paradigm assignment, concrete concepts related to the biophysical sciences and indicators that are readily measured are expected. In comparison, the middle range theory of comfort comes from the interactive-integrative paradigm and the concepts of the theory (health care needs, nursing interventions, intervening variables, patient comfort, health-seeking behavior, institutional integrity) occur in an interactive complex context, which reflects social science knowledge and values. Application is expected to capture these interaction and multifactor complex qualities. Finally, a theory coming from the unitary-transformative paradigm, such as enlightenment, is focused on unitary person–environment movement through time. The concepts of awareness, wakefulness, human field motion, and well-being are measured with discrete indicators, which are consistent with the human sciences (see Table 1.3).

Two of the theories on the list of fourteen (Precarious ordering: theory of women's caring and Experiencing transitions) are referred to as "emerging" by their authors, indicating that they are in early stages of development. Wuest (2001) discussed the caring theory as emerging because she was reluctant to accept it as a formal theory prior to "more theoretical sampling and data collection using interviews and participant observation" (p. 171). Although Meleis and colleagues (2000) are not as specific as to why they believe theirs is an emerging theory, they identified the emergent quality of the theory in the title of their paper. Before beginning to read the paper, the reader knows it is a work in progress. In fact, all middle range theories are works in progress that are expected to change over time. Theories are published so that others can critique them, test them, revise them, and use them as a source of scholarly productivity in research and practice.

Four of the theories (Enlightenment, Family health, Urine control, and Pathway to chemical dependency) were derived from grand theories of nursing or other middle range theories. Burns (1998) linked her theory of a pathway to chemical dependency in nurses to Pender's health promotion model and Bandura's social learning theory. The middle range theory of enlightenment (Hills & Hanchett, 2001) emerged from Rogers' Science of Unitary Human Beings; family health (Doornbos, 2000) was derived from King's interacting systems framework: urine control theory (Jirovec, Jenkins, Isenberg, & Baiardi, 1999) is derived from Roy's adaptation model. Woods and Isenberg (2001) propose that they are testing one aspect of a middle range theory synthesized from the Roy adaptation model, which considered adaptation as a mediator of abuse and stress in battered women. Their work is not listed on Table 1.3 with the other fourteen theories because it did not meet the inclusion criterion of naming the middle range theory distinct from Roy's model. In our 1999 manuscript we discussed the importance of naming a middle range theory: "Theory, especially at the middle range, is known to practitioners and researchers by the way it is named. It is essential that theories at the middle range be named in the context of the disciplinary perspective and at the appropriate level of discourse" (Liehr & Smith, p. 86).

Each of the theories in the following chapters has been named. Some, like the theory of meaning, were named in the process of doing the scholarly work of preparing the chapter. The theories in these chapters are offered as starting points for nurses wishing to structure their practice and research. With these theories comes a challenge to stretch the boundaries of thinking, consider the rub between each theory and what is known from experience, and apply the theories so that the body of nursing knowledge remains a vibrant, relevant foundation for guiding practice and research.

MIDDLE RANGE THEORIES ON THE LADDER OF ABSTRACTION

There are eight middle range theories presented in the book. The first middle range theory encompasses the Uncertainty in Illness and Reconceptualized Uncertainty in Illness middle range theories. Mishel and Clayton address both of these theories in the chapter. The original uncertainty theory pertains to acute illness and the reconceptualized theory pertains to the continual uncertainty experienced in chronic illness. On the ladder (Appendix, A), the reconceptualization is represented in bold print at the philosophical and theoretical levels. The theories are consistent with beliefs associated with the interactive-integrative paradigm. Persons experience uncertainty during diagnosis and treatment and when illness has a downward trajectory, and persons experience continual uncertainty in ongoing chronic illness and with the possibility of recurrence of an illness. Concepts at the theoretical level in both theories are antecedents of uncertainty, appraisal of uncertainty, and coping with uncertainty. Concepts added in the reconceptualized theory include self-organization and probabilistic thinking. Moving to the empirical level with practice is offering information and explanation, providing structure and order, and focusing on choices and alternatives. An instrument has been developed that is directly related to the theory, the Uncertainty in Illness Scale.

The second middle range theory is self-efficacy, addressed by Resnick, which is grounded in the assumptions of the interactive-integrative paradigm (Appendix, B). Persons change in a reciprocal, interactive process where they exercise influence over what they do and decide how to behave. Concepts at the theoretical level include self-efficacy expectations and self-efficacy outcomes. Practice applications used by Resnick include walking, addessing unpleasant sensations, learning about exercise, and cueing to exercise. Research based on this middle range theory uses self-efficacy scales.

The third middle range theory is Unpleasant Symptoms, presented by Lenz and Pugh. The theory is grounded in the beliefs and assumptions associated with the interactive-integrative paradigm (Appendix, C). Specific beliefs of the theory are that there are commonalities across different symptoms experienced by persons in varied situations, and symptoms are subjective phenomena occurring in family and community contexts. Concepts at the theoretical level include symptoms, influencing factors, and performance. Practice applications at the empirical level include assessment of the symptom, symptom management, and relief intervention. Empirical measurements are gathered through scales and observations, which capture the symptom experience.

The fourth middle range theory, Family Stress and Adaptation, addressed by LoBiondi-Wood (Appendix, D), is grounded in the interactive-integrative paradigm. Families change through reciprocal interactive processes that are related to multiple factors. Beliefs about family stress and adaptation are that hardship is natural and predictable, basic competencies foster family growth, families give to and take from a relationship network, and families facing crisis work together. Concepts of this theory include stressor, existing resources, perception of the stressor, crisis, pile-up, existing and new resources, perception, coping, and adaptation. Empirics related to this theory include practice interventions based on illness trajectories and research measures of stress and adaptation.

The fifth middle range theory, Community Empowerment, is presented by Persily and Hildebrandt (Appendix, E). This theory is grounded in the beliefs of the interactive-integrative paradigm in which change is an interactive process related to multiple factors in the community. Communities are empowered through an interactive-integrative reciprocal process. Specific assumptions for this theory are that communities are complex, experience can be generalized, and answers to health problems lie in and with the community. Theoretical concepts are involvement, lay workers, and reciprocal health, which is the outcome of community involvement with lay workers. Practice and research at the empirical level includes lay workers at the interface with traditional health care providers in the community.

The sixth middle range theory is a theory of Meaning presented by Starck (Appendix, F). This theory is grounded in the unitary-transformative paradigm. It is assumed that through a transformative process persons find meaning. When one is confronted with a hopeless situation, meaning can be freely and responsibly realized in every moment. Concepts at the theoretical level include life purpose, freedom to choose, and suffering. Practice approaches at the empirical level include dereflection, paradoxical intention, and Socratic dialogue. Empirical indicators for research include questionnaires, interviews, and other narrative approaches.

The seventh middle range theory, Self-Transcendence, developed by Reed, is grounded in assumptions of the unitary transformative paradigm (Appendix, G). Self-transcendence is a unitary process. The theory assumes that persons are integral and coextensive with their environment and capable of an awareness that extends beyond physical and temporal dimensions. Concepts at the theoretical level of discourse include vulnerability, self-transcendence, and well-being. Taking the theory to the empirical level with practice includes integrative spiritual care; support of inner resources; and expansion of intrapersonal, interpersonal, temporal, and transpersonal boundaries. A research instrument, the self-transcendence scale, has been developed that is directly related to the theory.

The eighth middle range theory presented is Attentively Embracing Story (Smith and Liehr, Appendix, H). This theory is grounded in the assumptions of the unitary-transformative paradigm in which change is viewed as creative and unpredictable. Attentively embracing story is a transformative experience in the unitary nurse–person process. The specific assumptions of the theory include that person's change in interrelationship with his or her world as he or she lives an expanded present and experiences meaning. There are three concepts at the theoretical level, which are intentional dialogue, connecting with self-in-relation, and creating ease. At the empirical level the health story is the basis for both practice and research. Examples of empirical approaches in practice include creation of a story path and family tree. Health story data may be analyzed using phenomenological, linguistic or case study methods.

There is one final ladder in this book in the evaluation chapter by Marlaine Smith. In this chapter, Smith offers a process for understanding and evaluating middle range theory based on postmodern beliefs. Overall, the ladders of abstraction provide a structure to guide the reader in deciphering theory so that it can be used productively in nursing practice and research. So, we urge you to begin climbing the ladders. Stay long enough on each rung to get comfortable and be sure to spend time on all three rungs to get the whole picture of any theory. Also, expect to be uncomfortable when a rung is new to you. Discomfort is a space for growing and connecting what you know with what you are learning.

REFERENCES

August-Brady, M. (2000). Prevention as intervention. *Journal of Advanced Nursing*, *31*, 1304–1308.

Burns, C. M. (1998). A retroductive theoretical model of the pathway to chemical dependency in nurses. *Archives of Psychiatric Nursing, 12*, 59–65.

Chinn, P., & Kramer, M. K. (1999). *Theory and nursing: Integrated knowledge development*. St. Louis: Mosby.

Doornbos, M. M. (2000). King's systems framework and family health: The derivation and testing of a theory. *Journal of Theory Construction & Testing, 4*(1), 20–26.

Engebretson, J., & Littleton, L. (2001). Cultural negotiation: A constructivist-based model for nursing practice. *Nursing Outlook, 49*, 223–230.

Ford-Gilboe, M., Campbell, J., & Berman, H. (1995). Stories and numbers: Coexistence without compromise. *Advances in Nursing Science, 18*(1), 14–26.

Hills, R. G. S., & Hanchett, E. (2001). Human change and individuation in pivotal life situations: Development and testing the theory of enlightenment. *Visions, 9*(1), 6–19.

Im, E., & Meleis, A. I. (1999). Situation-specific theories: Philosophical roots, properties, and approach. *Advances in Nursing Science, 22*(2), 11–24.

Jirovec, M. M., Jenkins, J., Isenberg, M., & Baiardi, J. (1999). Urine control theory derived from Roy's conceptual model. *Nursing Science Quarterly, 12*, 251–255.

Kearney, M. H. (1998). Truthful self-nurturing: A grounded formal theory of women's addiction recovery. *Qualitative Health Research, 8*(4), 495–512.

King, I. (1996). The theory of goal attainment in research and practice. *Nursing Science Quarterly, 9*, 61–66.

Kolcaba, K. (2001). Evolution of the mid range theory of comfort. *Nursing Outlook, 49*, 86–92.

Leenerts, M. H., & Magilvy, J. K. (2000). Investing in self-care: A midrange theory of self-care grounded in the lived experience of low-income HIV-positive white women. *Advances in Nursing Science, 22*(3), 58–75.

Liehr, P., & Smith, M. J. (1999). Middle range theory: Spinning research and practice to create knowledge for the new millennium. *Advances in Nursing Science, 21*(4), 81–91.

McKay, R. P. (1969). Theories, models, and systems for nursing. *Nursing Research, 18*, 393–399.

Meleis, A. I., Sawyer, L. M., Im, E., Messias, D. K. H., & Schumacher, K. (2000). Experiencing transitions: An emerging middle range theory. *Advances in Nursing Science, 23*(1), 12–28.

Merton, R. K. (1968). *Social theory and social structure.* New York: Free Press.

Newman, M., Sime, A. M., & Corcoran-Perry, S. A. (1991). The focus of the discipline of nursing. *Advances in Nursing Science, 14*(1), 1–6.

Orem, D. (1971). *Nursing: Concepts of practice.* New York: McGraw-Hill.

Parse, R. R. (1992). Human becoming: Parse's theory of nursing. *Nursing Science Quarterly, 5*(1), 35–42.

Parse, R. R., Coyne, B., & Smith, M. J. (1985). *Nursing research: Qualitative methods.* Bowie, MD: Brady.

Reed, P. (1995). A treatise on nursing knowledge development for the 21st century: Beyond postmodernism. *Advances in Nursing Science, 17*, 70–84.

Rogers, M. E. (1994). The science of unitary human beings: Current perspectives. *Nursing Science Quarterly, 7*, 33–35.

Roy, C., & Andrews, H. A. (1991). *The Roy adaptation model: The definitive statement.* Norwalk, CT: Appleton & Lange.

Sanford, R. C. (2000). Caring through relation and dialogue: A nursing perspective for patient education. *Advances in Nursing Science, 22*(3), 1–15.

Smith, A. A., & Friedemann, M. (1999). Perceived family dynamics of persons with chronic pain. *Journal of Advanced Nursing, 30*(3), 543–551.

Smith, M. J., & Liehr, P. (1999). Attentively Embracing Story: A middle-range theory with practice and research implications. *Scholarly Inquiry for Nursing Practice, 13*, 187–204.

Woods, S. J., & Isenberg, M. A. (2001). Adaptation as a mediator of intimate abuse and traumatic stress in battered women. *Nursing Science Quarterly, 14*(3), 215–221.

Wuest, J. (2001). Precarious ordering: Toward a formal theory of women's caring. *Health Care for Women International, 22*, 167–193.

2

Theories of Uncertainty in Illness

Merle H. Mishel and
Margaret F. Clayton

I n this chapter, two theories of uncertainty in illness will be described. The original uncertainty in illness theory was developed
to address uncertainty during the diagnostic and treatment phases
of an illness or an illness with a determined downward trajectory. This
theory will be referred to by the acronym UIT (Mishel, 1988). The
reconceptualized uncertainty in illness theory was developed to address the experience of living with continuous uncertainty in either a
chronic illness requiring ongoing management or an illness with the
possibility of recurrence. This reconceptualized theory will be referred
to by the acronym RUIT (Mishel, 1990). The acronyms will be used
to discuss each theory in the remainder of the chapter.

The uncertainty in illness theory (UIT) proposes that uncertainty
exists in illness situations that are ambiguous, complex, unpredictable,
and when information is unavailable or inconsistent. Uncertainty is
defined as the inability to determine the meaning of illness-related
events. It is a cognitive state created when the individual cannot
adequately structure or categorize an illness event because of insuffi-
cient cues (Mishel, 1988). The theory explains how patients cognitively
structure a schema for the subjective interpretation of uncertainty in
illness, treatment, and outcome. The theory is composed of three
major themes. These are (1) antecedents of uncertainty, (2) appraisal

of uncertainty, and (3) coping with uncertainty. Uncertainty and cognitive schema are the major concepts of the theory.

The reconceptualized theory of uncertainty (RUIT) retains the definition of uncertainty and major themes as in the UIT. The two concepts of self-organization and probabilistic thinking are added. The RUIT addresses the process that occurs when a person lives with unremitting uncertainty found in chronic illness or in illness with a potential for recurrence. The desired outcome from the RUIT is growth to a new value system, whereas the outcome of the UIT is a return to the previous level of adaptation or functioning (Mishel, 1990).

PURPOSE OF THE THEORIES AND HOW THE THEORIES WERE DEVELOPED

The purpose of the theories is to describe and explain uncertainty as a basis for practice and research. The UIT applies to the prediagnostic, diagnostic, and treatment phases of acute and chronic illness, and the RUIT applies to enduring uncertainty in chronic illness or illness with the possibility of recurrence and where self-management is the primary focus for treatment. The theories focus on the individual in the context of illness or a treatable condition, and to the family or parent of an ill individual. Use with groups or communities is not consistent with the conceptualization of either theory.

The finding that uncertainty was reported to be a common experience of people experiencing illness or receiving medical treatment led to the creation of the UIT (Mishel, 1988). Although the concept was cited in the literature, there was no substantive exploration of how uncertainty developed or was resolved by ill individuals. It was a personal experience with my (M. M.) ill father that catalyzed the concept for me. He was dying from colon cancer, and his body was swollen in some places and emaciated in others. He didn't understand what was happening to him to cause these diverse physiological responses, so he focused on whatever he could control to provide some degree of predictability for himself. The effort he spent on achieving some understanding brought the significance of uncertainty home to me. Although I explored the work on the concept of uncertainty, it was not until I entered doctoral study in psychology that I focused on the concept in earnest.

Developing the UIT included a synthesis of the research on uncertainty, cognitive processing, and managing threatening events, as well as clinical data and discussion with colleagues. The UIT was revised from the original measurement model published in 1981 to the theory published in 1988. During my doctoral study, I focused my dissertation on the development and testing of a measure of uncertainty. At that time, I was influenced by the literature on stress and coping that discussed uncertainty as one type of stressful event (Lazarus, 1974). As I began to explore the literature, I discovered the work of Norton (1975), who identified eight dimensions of uncertainty. His work, along with that of Moos and Tsu (1977), formed the framework for interviews leading to the development of the Mishel Uncertainty in Illness Scale.

My early ideas were further influenced by Bower (1978) and Shalit (1977), who described uncertainty as a complex cognitive stressor, along with Budner (1962), who considered ambiguous stimuli that are novel or complex as a source for uncertainty. These cognitive psychologists did not apply their work to a specific context; however their ideas about uncertainty influenced me to view uncertainty as a cognitive state instead of an emotional response. This was an important distinction that directed ongoing theory development. Uncertainty as a stressor or threat was reinforced by the work of both Shalit (1977) and Lazarus (1974). Coping resulting from primary appraisal of the uncertainty and secondary appraisal of the response to uncertainty was adapted from the work of Lazarus (1974). The measurement model of uncertainty (Mishel, 1981) incorporated the work of these primary sources to conceptualize uncertainty in illness and to develop the Uncertainty in Illness Scale.

Once the Uncertainty in Illness Scale was published, a body of findings on uncertainty quickly emerged in the nursing literature (Mishel, 1983, 1984; Mishel & Braden, 1987, 1988; Mishel, Hostetter, King, & Graham, 1984; Mishel & Murdaugh, 1987). The findings on uncertainty flushed out the antecedents of uncertainty presented in the measurement model. The stimuli frame variable, composed of familiarity of events and congruence of events, was formed from a combination of research on uncertainty in illness and research in cognitive psychology. The third component of stimuli frame, which is symptom pattern, was developed from qualitative studies (Mishel & Murdaugh, 1987) describing the importance of consistency and predictability of symptoms to form a symptom pattern. Following this mode for theory development, the antecedent of cognitive capacities was based on cognitive psychology (Mandler, 1979) and practice knowledge about instructing patients when cognitive processing abilities are compromised. The final antecedent of structure providers was developed from research on uncertainty in illness.

The appraisal section of the theory was developed using sources from the 1981 model, and was expanded based on clinical data and discussions with colleagues. Colleagues identified the need to consider personality variables in the evaluation of uncertainty, and clinical data indicated that uncertainty could be a preferred state under specific circumstances. This led to include inference and illusion as two phases of appraisal and to support and define these phases using research from nursing and psychology. Expanding on the process of appraisal and coping included in the 1981 measurement model, the coping strategies were developed from research in nursing and psychology (Mishel & Braden, 1987; Mishel & Murdaugh, 1987).

The RUIT was developed through discussion with colleagues, qualitative data from chronically ill individuals, and an awareness of the limitations of the UIT theory. There was the need to rethink the theory for application with the chronically ill. The UIT explained uncertainty in the acute and treatment phases of illness, but did not address life changes expressed by persons with chronic illness. Furthermore, the UIT was linear and did not incorporate change over time. Qualitative interviews with chronically ill individuals revealed that many acknowledged continuous uncertainty and a new view of life that incorporated uncertainty. Furthermore, questions emerged from an examination of the role of uncertainty in Western society. From the perspective of critical social theory (Allen, 1985), the patient's desire for certainty may reflect the goals of control and predictability that form the socio-historic values of Western society (Mishel, 1990). Clinical data revealed that those who chose to incorporate uncertainty into their lives were living a value system on the edge of mainstream ideas. In order to explain the clinical data, a framework that conceptualized uncertainty as a preferred state was needed. Using the process of theory derivation described by Walker and Avant (1989), chaos theory was chosen as the parent theory to reconceptualize the uncertainty theory. The reconceptualization was compatible with the parent theory and advanced the understanding of uncertainty in a new light. Chaos theory emphasizes disorder, instability, diversity, disequilibrium, and restructuring as the healthy variability of a system. The reconceptualized theory included ideas of disorganization and reformulation of a new stability to explain how a person with enduring uncertainty emerges with a new view of life.

Drawing from the concepts in chaos theory (Prigogine & Stengers, 1984), uncertainty is viewed as a force that spreads from illness to other areas of a person's life and competes with the person's previous mode of functioning. As uncertain areas of life increase, they can disrupt ongoing life patterns. Pattern disruption occurs as uncertainty feeds back on itself and generates more uncertainty such as questions about the ability to meet desired goals and to maintain desired relationships. When uncertainty persists, the concentration of uncertainty increases and exceeds a person's level of tolerance. There is a sense of disorganization that promotes personal instability. With a high level of disorganization comes a loss of a sense of coherence (Antonovsky, 1987). A system in disorganization begins to reorganize at an imperceptible level. This reorganization represents a gradual transition from a perspective of life oriented to predictability and control to a new view of life in which multiple contingencies are preferable.

MAJOR CONCEPTS OF THE THEORIES

The UIT theory is organized around three major themes: antecedents of uncertainty, appraisal of uncertainty, and coping with uncertainty. Uncertainty is the central concept in the theory and is defined as the inability to determine the meaning of illness-related events occurring when the decision maker is unable to assign definite value to objects or events and/or is unable to accurately predict outcomes. Another concept central to the uncertainty theory is cognitive schema, which is defined as the person's subjective interpretation of illness-related events (see Figure 2.1).

The ideas included in the antecedent theme of the theory include stimuli frame, cognitive capacity, and structure providers. Stimuli frame is defined as the form, composition, and structure of the stimuli that the person perceives. The stimuli frame has three components: symptom pattern, event familiarity, and event congruence. Symptom pattern refers to the degree to which symptoms are present with sufficient consistency to be perceived as having a pattern or configuration. Event familiarity is the degree to which the situation is habitual, repetitive, or contains recognized cues. Event congruence refers to the consistency between the expected and the experienced illness-related events. Cognitive capacity and structure providers influence the three components of the stimuli frame. Cognitive capacity is the informa-

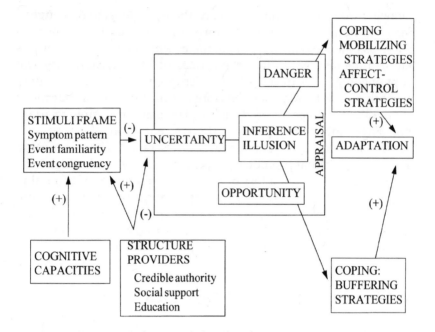

FIGURE 2.1   Model of perceived uncertainty in illness.

Note: Reprinted with permission from: Mishel, M. H. (1988). Uncertainty in illness. *Image: The Journal of Nursing Scholarship, 20*(4), 225–232.

tion-processing ability of the individual. Structure providers are the resources available to assist the person in the interpretation of the stimuli frame. Structure providers include education, social support, and credible authority.

The second major theme in the UIT is appraisal of uncertainty, which is defined as the process of placing a value on the uncertain event or situation. There are two components of appraisal: inference or illusion. Inference refers to the evaluation of uncertainty using related examples and is built on personality dispositions, general experience, knowledge, and contextual cures. Illusion refers to the construction of beliefs formed from uncertainty that have a positive outlook. The result of appraisal is the valuing of uncertainty as a danger or an opportunity.

The third theme in the UIT is coping with uncertainty, and the concepts include danger, opportunity, coping, and adaptation. Danger is the possibility of a harmful outcome. Opportunity is the possibility of a positive outcome. Coping with a danger appraisal is defined as activities directed toward reducing uncertainty and managing the emotion generated by a danger appraisal. Coping with an opportunity appraisal is defined as activities directed toward maintaining uncertainty. Adaptation is defined as biopsychosocial behavior occurring within the person's individually defined range of usual behavior.

The RUIT includes the antecedent theme in the UIT and adds the two concepts of self-organization and probabilistic thinking. Self-organization is the reformulation of a new sense of order, resulting from the integration of continuous uncertainty into one's self-structure in which uncertainty is accepted as the natural rhythm of life. Probabilistic thinking is a belief in a conditional world in which the expectation of certainty and predictability is abandoned. The RUIT proposes four factors that influence the formation of a new life perspective. These are prior life experience, physiological status, social resources, and health care providers. In the process of reorganization, the person evaluates uncertainty by gradual approximations, from an aversive experience to one of opportunity. Thus uncertainty becomes the foundation of a new sense of order and is accepted as the natural rhythm of life. There is a new ability to focus on multiple alternatives, choices, and possibilities; reevaluate what is important in life; consider variation in personal investment; and appreciate the impermanence and fragility of life. The theory identifies conditions under which the new ability is maintained or is blocked.

The concepts of both theories tie clearly to nursing by describing and explaining human responses to illness situations. Uncertainty crosses all phases of illness from prediagnosis symptomatology to diagnosis, treatment, treatment residuals, recovery, potential recurrence, and exacerbation. Thus the theories are pertinent to the health experience for all age groups. Uncertainty is experienced by ill persons, caregivers, and parents of ill children.

The theories incorporate a consideration of the health care environment as a component of the stimuli frame as well as the broader support network. Nursing care is represented under the concept of structure providers. Since an important part of nursing involves explaining and providing information, nursing actions are interventions to help patients manage uncertainty. The outcomes of both theories are directly related to health. The health outcome is either to regain personal control, as in adaptation in the UIT, or consciousness expansion, as in the RUIT.

RELATIONSHIPS AMONG THE CONCEPTS:
THE MODEL

As seen in Figure 2.1, the UIT is displayed as a linear model with no feedback loops. According to the model, uncertainty is the result of antecedents. The major path to uncertainty is through the stimuli frame variables. Cognitive capacities influence stimuli frame variables. If the person has a compromised cognitive capacity due to fever, infection, pain, or mind altering medication, the clarity and definition of the stimuli frame variables are likely to be reduced, resulting in uncertainty. In such a situation, it is assumed that stimuli frame variables are clear, patterned, and distinct, and only become less so because of limitations in cognitive capacity. However, when cognitive capacity is adequate, stimuli frame variables may still lack a symptom pattern or be unfamiliar and incongruent due to lack of information, complex information, information overload, or conflicting information. The structure provider variables then come into play to alter the stimuli frame variables by interpreting, providing meaning, and explaining. These actions serve to structure the stimuli frame, thereby reducing or preventing uncertainty. Structure providers may also directly impact uncertainty. The health care provider can offer explanations or use other approaches that directly reduce uncertainty. Similarly, uncertainty can be reduced by one's level of education and resultant knowledge. Social support networks also influence the stimuli frame by providing information from similar others, providing examples, and offering supportive information.

Uncertainty is viewed as a neutral state and is not associated with emotions until evaluated. During the evaluation of uncertainty, inference and illusion come into play. Inference and illusion are based on beliefs and personality dispositions that influence whether uncertainty is appraised as a danger or an opportunity. Because uncertainty renders a situation amorphous and ill defined, positively oriented illusions can be generated from uncertainty, leading to an appraisal of uncertainty as an opportunity. Uncertainty appraised as an opportunity implies a positive outcome and buffering coping strategies are used to maintain it. In contrast, beliefs and personality dispositions can result in uncertainty appraised as danger. Uncertainty evaluated as danger implies harm. Problem-focused coping strategies are employed to reduce it. If problem-focused coping cannot be used, then emotional coping strategies are used to respond to the uncertainty. If the coping strategies are effective, adaptation occurs. Difficulty in adapting indicates inability to manipulate uncertainty in the desired direction.

The RUIT (Figure 2.2) represents the process of moving from uncertainty appraised as danger to uncertainty appraised as an opportunity and resource for a new view of life. As noted earlier in this chapter, the reconceptualized theory builds on the original theory at the appraisal portion. The RUIT describes enduring uncertainty that is initially viewed as danger due to its invasion into broader areas of life resulting in instability. The jagged line within the arrow represents both the invasion of uncertainty and the growing instability. The patterned circular portion of the line represents the repatterning and reorganization resulting in a revised view of uncertainty. The bottom arrow indicates that this is a process that evolves over time.

USE OF THE THEORY IN NURSING RESEARCH

Beginning with the publication of the Uncertainty in Illness Scale (Mishel, 1981), there has been extensive research into experiences with uncertainty in both acute and chronic illnesses. Several comprehensive reviews of research have summarized and critiqued the current state of the knowledge on uncertainty in illness (Mast, 1995; Mishel, 1997, 1999; Stewart & Mishel, 2000). In this chapter, the research review will be limited to studies that directly support elements of the UIT and the RUIT.

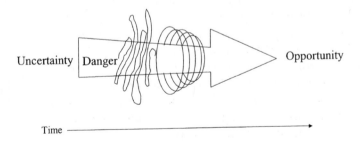

FIGURE 2.2   Uncertainty in chronic illness.

Note: Reprinted with permission from: Bailey, D. E. Jr., & Stewart, J. L. (2001). Mishel's Theory of Uncertainty in Illness. In A. M. Mariner-Tomey & M. R. Alligood (Eds.), *Nursing theorists and their work* (5th ed,, pp. 560–583). St. Louis, MO: Mosby.

Many studies have focused on the antecedents of stimuli frame and structure providers. Three aspects of illness have been found to cause uncertainty: (1) severity of illness, (2) erratic nature of symptoms, and (3) ambiguity of symptoms. Severity of illness and ambiguity of symptoms correspond to the stimuli frame component of symptom pattern, while the erratic nature of symptoms corresponds to the stimuli component of event congruence.

Studies that focus on severity of illness and uncertainty are classified as those that address the theoretical link between symptom pattern and uncertainty. Severity of illness refers to symptoms with such intensity that they do not clearly reflect a discernable, understandable pattern. Several studies have shown that severity of illness is a predictor of uncertainty, although the indicators of severity of illness have varied across studies (Mishel, 1997). Among patients in the acute or treatment phase of illnesses such as cardiovascular disease (Christman et al., 1988), cancer (Galloway & Graydon, 1996; Hilton, 1994), and parenting of critically ill children, severity of illness was positively associated with uncertainty (Tomlinson, Kirschbaum, Harbaugh, & Anderson, 1996). According to the UIT, the nature of the severity presents difficulty delineating a symptom pattern about the extent of the disease, resulting in uncertainty.

STIMULI FRAME: SYMPTOM PATTERN

Studies that address the process of identifying symptoms of a disease or condition and reaching a diagnosis are classified as addressing symptom pattern. The process of receiving a diagnosis requires that a symptom pattern exist and can be labeled as an illness or condition. In the UIT, absence of the symptom pattern is associated with uncertainty. Uncertainty levels have been reported to be highest in those without a diagnosis and undergoing diagnostic examinations (Hilton, 1993; Mishel, 1981). In studies where patients' symptoms are not clearly distinguishable from those of other comorbid conditions or where symptoms of recurrence can be confused with signs of aging or other natural processes and not recognizable as signs of disease, such as in lupus, survivors of breast cancer, and cardiac disease, these symptoms are associated with uncertainty (Hilton, 1988; Mishel & Murdaugh, 1987; Nelson, 1996; Winters, 1999).

SYMPTOM PATTERN: EVENT CONGRUENCE

The erratic nature of symptom onset and disease progression is the major antecedent of uncertainty in chronic illness (Mishel, 1999). Symptoms that occur unpredictably fit the description of the stimuli frame component of event incongruence because there is no congruity between the cue and the outcome. The timing and nature of symptom onset, duration, intensity and location are unforeseeable, characterized by periods of stability and erratic flares of exacerbation or unpredictable recurrence resulting in uncertainty (Brown & Powell-Cope, 1991; Mast, 1998; Mishel & Braden, 1988; Sexton, Calcasola, Bottomley, & Funk, 1999). Among parents of ill children, unpredictable trajectories with few markers of illness are also positively associated with uncertainty (Cohen, 1993b). Determining the cause of an illness is another example of cue–outcome congruence. If a specific cause can be identified, the cause functions as the cue with illness as the outcome. Difficulty in determining cause of illness has been found to be associated with uncertainty (Cohen, 1993a; Sharkey, 1995; Turner, Tomlinson, & Harbaugh, 1990).

STIMULI FRAME: EVENT FAMILIARITY

Studies that focus on the health care or home environment for treatment of illness fit under the stimuli frame component of event familiarity. Although fewer studies have addressed this component of stimuli frame, the studies that have been conducted support that unfamiliarity with health care environment, organization and expectations is associated with uncertainty. Health care environments characterized by novelty and confusion where the rules and routines are unknown and equipment and treatments are unfamiliar are associated with uncertainty (Horner, 1997; Stewart & Mishel, 2000; Turner, Tomlinson, & Harbaugh, 1990).

STRUCTURE PROVIDERS: SOCIAL SUPPORT

In the UIT, social support from friends, family, and those with similar experiences are proposed to reduce uncertainty directly, and indirectly by influencing the stimuli frame. Those with similar experience have been found to influence the stimuli frame by providing information about illness-related events and symptom pattern (van Riper & Selder, 1989; White & Frasure-Smith, 1995). There are a number of studies that support the role of social support in reducing uncertainty among parents of ill children, adult and adolescent patients, and their care providers (Bennett, 1993; Davis, 1990; Mishel & Braden, 1987; Neville, 1998; Tomlinson et al., 1996). However, when the illness is stigmatized, the questionable acceptance by others limits the use of social support to manage uncertainty (Brown & Powell-Cope, 1991; Weitz, 1989). Social interaction also may not always be supportive. Unsupportive interactions serve to heighten uncertainty (Wineman, 1990). Family members have been found to experience high levels of uncertainty, which may impair their ability to provide support for the patient (Brown & Powell-Cope, 1991; Mishel & Murdaugh, 1987; Wineman, O'Brien, Nealon, & Kaskel, 1993). Current research supports the theoretical relationship between social support and uncertainty and provides information on factors that influence effective social support.

STRUCTURE PROVIDERS: CREDIBLE AUTHORITY

Credible authority refers to health care providers who are seen as credible information givers by the patient or family member. As experts, health care providers have been proposed to reduce uncertainty by providing information and promoting confidence in their clinical judgment and performance. Trust and confidence in the health care provider's ability to make a diagnosis, to control the illness, and to provide adequate treatment has been reported to be related to less uncertainty across a variety of acute and chronic illnesses (Mishel & Braden, 1988; Santacroce, 2000). On the other hand, patients' lack of confidence in the provider's abilities increases uncertainty (Becker, Janson-Bjerklie, Benner, Slobin, & Ferdetich, 1993; Smeltzer, 1994). Uncertainty has also been found to increase when patients report that they are not receiving adequate information from health care providers (Galloway & Graydon, 1996; Hilton, 1988; Nyhlin, 1990; Small & Graydon, 1993; Weems & Patterson, 1989).

APPRAISAL OF UNCERTAINTY

According to the UIT, appraisal of uncertainty involves personality dispositions, attitudes and beliefs, which influence whether uncertainty is appraised as a danger or an opportunity. This area has received limited testing; however, there is support for the impact of uncertainty on reducing personality dispositions such as optimism, sense of coherence, and level of resourcefulness (Christman, 1990; Hilton, 1989; Mishel et al., 1984). Certain dispositions such as generalized negative outcome expectancies interact with uncertainty to predict psychological distress (Mullins et al., 1995). However, selected cognitive and personality factors have been reported to mediate the relationship between uncertainty and danger or opportunity. Mediators that decrease the impact of uncertainty on danger and adjustment include higher enabling skill, self-efficacy, mastery, hope, and existential well being (Braden, Mishel, Longman, & Burns, 1998; Landis, 1996; Mishel, Padilla, Grant, & Sorenson, 1991; Mishel & Sorenson, 1991; Wonghongkul, Moore, Musil, Schneider, & Deimling, 2000).

COPING WITH UNCERTAINTY

Numerous investigators who have studied the management of uncertainty have found that higher uncertainty is associated with danger and resultant emotion-focused coping strategies such as wishful thinking, avoidance, and fatalism (Christman, 1990; Hilton, 1989; Mishel & Sorenson, 1991; Mishel et al., 1991; Redeker, 1992; Webster & Christman, 1988). Others report more varied coping strategies for managing uncertainty including cognitive strategies such as downward comparison, constructing a personal scenario for the illness, use of faith or religion, and identifying markers and triggers (Baier, 1995; Mishel & Murdaugh, 1987; Wiener & Dodd, 1993). Mishel (1993) offered a review of major management methods; however there is little evidence for the use of any of these coping strategies mediating the relationship between uncertainty and emotional distress (Mast, 1998; Mishel & Sorenson, 1991; Mishel et al., 1991).

UNCERTAINTY AND ADJUSTMENT

According to the UIT, adjustment refers to returning to the individual's level of pre-illness functioning. However, most of the research has interpreted this as emotional stability or quality of life. Few studies have tested the complete outcome portion of the theory including uncertainty, appraisal, coping strategies, and adjustment. Most studies examine the relationship between uncertainty and an outcome and relate these findings to the theory. The findings from these studies have consistently shown positive relationships between uncertainty and negative emotional outcomes (Bennett, 1993; Mast, 1998; Mishel, 1984; Mullins et al., 2001; Sanders-Dewey, Mullins, & Chaney, 2001; Small & Graydon, 1993; Taylor-Piliae & Molassiotis, 2001; Wineman, Schwetz, Goodkin, & Rudick, 1996). Uncertainty has also been related to poorer psychosocial adjustment in the areas of less life satisfaction (Hilton, 1994), negative attitudes toward health care, family relationships, recreation and employment (Mishel et al., 1984; Mishel & Braden, 1987), less satisfaction with health care services (Green & Murton, 1996), and poorer quality of life (Carroll, Hamilton, & McGovern, 1999; Padilla, Mishel, & Grant, 1992).

There has been extensive study of uncertainty in illness based on the UIT and most of the research supports sections of the theory. Although some studies were not done to test theory, the findings are consistent with the UIT. Overall, the theory has been very useful in guiding research, and sections of the theory are well supported by published studies with a variety of clinical populations and caregivers.

RESEARCH ON THE RUIT

Less attention has been given to study of the RUIT, possibly due to the difficulty in studying a process that evolves over time. Support for the RUIT has been found in qualitative studies that favor a transition through uncertainty to a new orientation toward life with acceptance of uncertainty as a part of life (Mishel, 1999). The samples for these studies included long-term diabetic patients (Nyhlin, 1990), chronically ill men (Charmaz, 1994), HIV patients (Katz, 1996), persons with schizophrenia (Baier, 1995), spouses of heart transplant patients (Mishel & Murdaugh, 1987), family caregivers of AIDS patients (Brown & Powell-Cope, 1991), breast cancer survivors (Nelson, 1996; Pelusi, 1997), and women recovering from cardiac disease (Fleury, Kimbrell, & Kruszewski, 1995). The transition through uncertainty toward a new view of life was framed differently by each investigator and included themes such as a revised life perspective, new ways of being in the world, growth through uncertainty, new levels of self-organization, new goals for living, reevaluating what is worthwhile, redefining what is normal, and building new dreams (Bailey & Stewart, 2001). All of the investigators described the gradual acceptance of uncertainty and the restructuring of reality as major components of the process, both of which are consistent with the RUIT.

An instrument to measure growth through uncertainty toward a new view of life was developed by Mishel and Fleury and is being tested for construct validity. Initial use of the scale was reported by Mast (1998); however, further testing of the scale is necessary before it is available for general use.

INTERVENTIONS TO MANAGE UNCERTAINTY

An uncertainty management intervention has been developed and tested in four clinical trials for breast cancer patients and patients with localized or advanced prostate cancer (Braden et al., 1998; Mishel, 1997; Mishel et al., 2002). The intervention was structured to follow the theory of the UIT and was delivered by weekly phone calls to cancer patients. All studies included equal numbers of Caucasian and minority samples. The intervention has been shown to be effective in teaching patients skills to manage uncertainty including improvements in problem solving, cognitive reframing, and patient–provider communication. Improvement was also found for the ability to manage the uncertainty related to side effects from cancer treatment.

USE OF THE THEORIES IN NURSING PRACTICE

Nurses are included in the UIT as part of the antecedent variable of structure providers. The clinical literature supports delivery of information as the major method used to help patients manage uncertainty. Nurses provide information that helps patients develop meaning from the illness experience by providing structure to the stimuli frame.

Understanding the sources of patient uncertainty can help nurses plan for effective information giving. For example, Sexton and colleagues (1999) found that advanced practice nurses can help patients manage a diagnosis of asthma by implementing nursing actions that assist patients to predict and manage asthma attacks. Among cardiac patients, White and Frasure-Smith (1995) suggested that nurses promote the use of patient-solicited social support in order to manage uncertainty in percutaneous transluminal coronary angioplasty (PCTA) patients. The researchers suggested that the benefit from the social support received by PCTA patients was due to direct requests tailored to specific needs versus unsolicited social support due to simply being ill. Additionally, information from nurses about the potential long-term success of this procedure might help reduce the higher uncertainty found in PCTA patients three months after surgery.

Recognizing uncertainty and then providing contextual cues to reduce ambiguity and increase understanding explains how nurses communicate with patients. Contextual cues provide explanations of what patients will see, hear, and feel during procedures and tests, as well as what signs and symptoms they will experience at various points in their illness trajectory. Providing information and explanations about treatments and medications has been proposed to be important in reducing patient uncertainty (Wineman et al., 1996). Galloway and Graydon (1996), based on their findings from recently discharged colon cancer patients, noted that nurses could provide information to alleviate the uncertainty of being discharged to the home environment. Other effective methods for reducing patient uncertainty can include encouraging communication with patients who have successfully managed their uncertainties. Weems and Patterson (1989) suggest sharing the uncertainties of waiting for a renal transplant with someone who has already received a transplant, or sharing the uncertainties of how to live with chronic obstructive pulmonary disease (COPD) with someone who is successfully managing this chronic disease (Small & Graydon, 1993). This type of communication provides information to patients for structuring the stimuli and also functions as a source of social support.

Clinical journals are increasingly identifying patient uncertainty as an important part of the illness experience and provide suggestions for nursing actions to reduce patient uncertainty or facilitate a new outlook by focusing on choices and alternatives. Suggestions for managing uncertainty in clinical practice include work by Crigger (1996), who suggests that nurses can assist women to adapt positively to multiple sclerosis by shifting the emphasis from the management of physical disability to the management of uncertainty, thereby assisting women to achieve mastery over their daily lives. Similarly, Calvin and Lane (1999) suggested incorporating preoperative psychoeducational interventions to reduce uncertainty into orthopedic pre-admission visits. Other examples of using UIT to develop and implement nursing interventions in clinical settings are suggested by Allan (1990) for HIV-positive men, Sterken (1996) for fathers of pediatric cancer patients, Northouse, Mood, Templin, Mellon, and George (2000) for patients with colon cancer, and Sharkey (1995) for homebound pediatric oncology patients. Sterken (1996) found that younger fathers did not understand the information about their child's treatment and disease patterns as well as older fathers, illustrating how cognitive capacity influences uncertainty. Allan (1990) discussed promoting self-care activities to reduce uncertainty among seropositive gay men, helping them to regain a degree of control in their lives. Based on the antecedent variables of UIT, Northouse and colleagues (2000) suggested that health professionals should keep in mind individual characteristics of patients, social environments, and methods of illness appraisal when caring for patients with colon cancer. They suggested that nurses provide patients with a framework of expectations about the physical and emotional illness trajectory associated with the first year of managing this diagnosis. In one of the few articles to address the environmental component of the stimuli frame, Sharkey (1995) discussed how family coping could be enhanced by home care nurses normalizing health care into the familiar routines of families caring for a terminally ill child at home. These studies all illustrate how nurses can identify specific sources of uncertainty and implement nursing actions to assist patients to manage or reduce the uncertainty of the illness experience.

A few clinical articles have focused on explaining how the theory can be applied to understanding a clinical situation or used in clinical practice. Sorenson (1990) discusses the concepts of symptom pattern, event familiarity and congruency, cognitive capacity, structure providers, and credible authority, using examples from normal pregnancy in order to help nurses relate the theory to women who are experiencing difficulty adapting to the uncertainties of pregnancy. Lemaire and Lenz (1995) applied the UIT to the condition of menopause. The stimuli frame for menopause was defined as the symptoms that indicate menopause is approaching, including mood swings, hot flashes, dry skin, and memory changes. If women received factual information from a source that is deemed credible, such as nurses and health care providers, it was thought that familiarity with the event of menopause would be increased and that uncertainty about this normal life event would be decreased. Consistent with predictions of UIT, uncertainty declined after receipt of understandable information delivered by a credible source, allowing women to construct meaning from the ambiguity and unpredictability of their symptoms surrounding the normal process of menopause.

Righter (1995) used the UIT to describe the role of an enterostomal therapy (ET) nurse as a credible authority for the ostomy patient. She describes the ET nurse as providing structure and order to the experience of the new ostomy patient through clinical expertise and experience. The ET nurse reduces the ambiguity of the ostomy experience by providing information, counseling, and support. This facilitates ostomy patients' adaptation to their newly altered perception of themselves and helps them regain a sense of control and mastery by creating order and predictability. Further discussion of nursing intervention to manage uncertainty in clinical practice is the work reported by Ritz and colleagues (2000). These clinicians investigated the effect of follow-up nursing care by the advanced practice nurse after discharge of newly treated breast cancer patients. Six months after diagnosis, uncertainty was reduced and quality of life was improved. Other ideas on changing clinical practice to reduce patient uncertainty include educational interventions delivered by telephone and individualized patient information packets delivered through the mail (Calvin & Lane, 1999).

Another approach to improving patient care is recognizing the importance of professional education on uncertainty to effect change in clinical practice. Wunderlich, Perry, Lavin, and Katz (1999) suggested that critical care nurses would benefit from staff development sessions on how to address the uncertainty that patients experience during the process of weaning from mechanical ventilation. Dombeck (1996) commented that health care professionals need to increase their own tolerance for ambiguity and uncertainty to effectively listen to clients who are experiencing ambiguity and uncertainty. Similarly Light (1979) noted that health care professionals have been socialized to minimize uncertainty; this socialization may make it difficult to effectively address patient uncertainty until health care workers learn more about it (Baier, 1995). Recognizing the importance of integrating UIT into a management strategy for asthma patients, the American Nurses Credentialing Center's Commission on Accreditation offered 3 credit hours for successful completion of a continuing education unit (CEU) quiz following the published article (Sexton et al., 1999) about coping with uncertainty. Other CEU offerings incorporating uncertainty theory have been offered following a case study on spiritual disequilibrium (Dombeck, 1996), and an article on the process of weaning a patient from mechanical ventilation (Wunderlich et al., 1999).

The Uncertainty in Illness theories have been used in multiple ways to inform understanding of patients, families, and illness situations.

Clinical research guided by both the original UIT (1988) and the RUIT (1990) for those coping with chronic illnesses will continue to increase understanding of patients and families, helping to identify appropriate nursing interventions for many types of illnesses and patients. Ultimately the recognition of the importance of uncertainty can change clinical practice, allowing the development of nursing interventions that facilitate a positive patient adaptation to the illness experience.

CONCLUSIONS

The uncertainty theory and the reconceptualized uncertainty in illness theory are mature theories that have stimulated research, literature reviews, and practice-related investigations. As studies continue there is growing support for both theories. Both UIT and RUIT (Mishel, 1988, 1990) have been used to help nurses understand patient behaviors and change clinical practice. Uncertainty theories have also been used to guide research measuring clinical uncertainty and to inform the understanding of qualitative research. Development of the uncertainty scales has facilitated study and testing of sections of the theories. Further testing of growth through the Uncertainty Scale may enable research on the RUIT to increase and approximate the large body of research on the UIT. However, it is in the area of practice that more work on using the theory is needed. Planning care to address uncertainty, or attempting to use different approaches in the clinical setting to prevent uncertainty, would encourage the application of the theories to practice. Since uncertainty is a clinical phenomenon, it is in the clinical setting where it should be addressed. There is also need to teach about uncertainty in undergraduate nursing education so that it is recognized as a nursing component of patient care.

REFERENCES

Allan, J. D. (1990). Focusing on living, not dying: A naturalistic study of self-care among seropositive gay men. *Holistic Nursing Practice, 4*(2), 56–63.

Allen, D. G. (1985). Nursing research and social control: Alternative models of science that emphasize understanding and emancipation. *Image: Journal of Nursing Scholarship, 17,* 58–64.

Antonovsky, A. (1987). *Unraveling the mystery of health: How people manage stress and stay well.* San Francisco: Jossey-Bass.

Baier, M. (1995). Uncertainty of illness for persons with schizophrenia. *Issues in Mental Health Nursing, 16,* 201–212.

Bailey, D. E. Jr., & Stewart, J. L. (2001). Mishel's Theory of Uncertainty in Illness. In A. M. Mariner-Tomey & M. R. Alligood (Eds.), *Nursing theorists and their work* (5th ed., pp. 560–583). St. Louis, MO: Mosby.

Becker, G., Janson-Bjerklie, S., Benner, P., Slobin, K., & Ferdetich, S. (1993). The dilemma of seeking urgent care: Asthma episodes and emergency service use. *Social Science and Medicine, 37,* 305–313.

Bennett, S. J. (1993). Relationships among selected antecedent variables and coping effectiveness in postmyocardial infarction patients. *Research in Nursing and Health, 16,* 131–139.

Bower, G. H. (1978). *The psychology of learning and motivation: Advances in research and theory.* New York: Academic Press.

Braden, C. J., Mishel, M. H., Longman, A. J., & Burns, L. (1998). Self-Help Intervention Project: Women receiving breast cancer treatment. *Cancer Practice, 6*(2), 87–98.

Brown, M. A., & Powell-Cope, G. M. (1991). AIDS family caregiving: Transitions through uncertainty. *Nursing Research, 40,* 337–345.

Budner, S. (1962). Intolerance of ambiguity as a personality variable. *Journal of Personality, 30,* 29–50.

Calvin, R., & Lane, P. (1999). Perioperative uncertainty and state anxiety of orthopaedic surgical patients. *Orthopedic Nursing, 18*(6), 61–66.

Carroll, D., Hamilton, G., & McGovern, B. (1999). Changes in health status and quality of life and the impact of uncertainty in patients who survive life-threatening arrhythmias. *Heart and Lung, 28*(4), 251–260.

Charmaz, K. (1994). Identity dilemmas of chronically ill men. *Sociological Quarterly, 35*(2), 269–288.

Christman, N. J. (1990). Uncertainty and adjustment during radiotherapy. *Nursing Research, 39*(1), 17–20.

Christman, N. J., McConnell, E. A., Pfeiffer, C., Webster, K. K., Schmitt, M., & Ries, J. (1988). Uncertainty, coping, and distress following myocardial infarction: Transition from home to hospital. *Research in Nursing and Health, 11,* 71–82.

Cohen, M. H. (1993a). Diagnostic closure and the spread of uncertainty. *Issues in Comprehensive Pediatric Nursing, 16,* 135–146.

Cohen, M. H. (1993b). The unknown and the unknowable—managing sustained uncertainty. *Western Journal of Nursing Research, 15*(1), 77–96.

Crigger, N. J. (1996). Testing an uncertainty model for women with multiple sclerosis. *Advances in Nursing Science, 18*(3), 37–47.

Davis, L. L. (1990). Illness uncertainty, social support, and stress in recovering individuals and family caregivers. *Applied Nursing Research, 3*(2), 69–71.

Dombeck, M. (1996). Chaos and self-organization as a consequence of spiritual disequilibrium. *Clinical Nurse Specialist, 10*(2), 69–73; quiz 74–75.

Fleury, J., Kimbrell, L. C., & Kruszewski, M. A. (1995). Life after a cardiac event: Women's experience in healing. *Heart and Lung, 24,* 474–482.

Galloway, S., & Graydon, J. (1996). Uncertainty, symptom distress, and information needs after surgery for cancer of the colon. *Cancer Nursing, 19*, 112–117.

Green, J., & Murton, F. (1996). Diagnosis of Duchenne muscular dystrophy: Parents' experiences and satisfaction. *Child: Care, Health & Development, 22*, 113–128.

Hilton, B. A. (1988). The phenomenon of uncertainty in women with breast cancer. *Issues in Mental Health Nursing, 9*, 217–238.

Hilton, B. A. (1989). The relationship of uncertainty, control, commitment, and threat of recurrence to coping strategies used by women diagnosed with breast cancer. *Journal of Behavioral Medicine, 12*(1), 39–54.

Hilton, B. A. (1993). Issues, problems, and challenges for families coping with breast cancer. *Seminars in Oncology Nursing, 9*(2), 88–100.

Hilton, B. A. (1994). The uncertainty stress scale: Its development and psychometric properties. *Canadian Journal of Nursing Research, 26*(3), 15–30.

Horner, S. (1997). Uncertainty in mothers' care for their ill children. *Journal of Advanced Nursing, 26*, 658–663.

Katz, A. (1996). Gaining a new perspective on life as a consequence of uncertainty in HIV infection. *Journal of the Association of Nurses in AIDS Care, 7*(11), 51–60.

Landis, B. J. (1996). Uncertainty, spirituality, well-being, and psychosocial adjustment to chronic illness. *Issues in Mental Health Nursing, 17*, 217–231.

Lazarus, R. S. (1974). Psychological stress and coping in adaptation and illness. *International Journal of Psychiatry in Medicine, 5*, 321–333.

Lemaire, G. S., & Lenz, E. R. (1995). Perceived uncertainty about menopause in women attending an educational program. *International Journal of Nursing Studies, 32*(1), 39–48.

Light, D. (1979). Uncertainty and control in professional training. *Journal of Health and Social Behavior, 20*, 310–322.

Mandler, G. (1979). Thought processes, consciousness and stress. In V. Hamilton & D. M. Warburton (Eds.), *Human stress and cognition: An information processing approach* (pp. 179–201). New York: Wiley.

Mariner-Tomey, A. M., & Alligood, M. R. (Eds.). (2001). *Nursing theorists and their work.* St. Louis: Mosby.

Mast, M. E. (1995). Adult uncertainty in illness: A critical review of research. *Scholarly Inquiry for Nursing Practice, 9*(1), 3–24.

Mast, M. E. (1998). Survivors of breast cancer: Illness uncertainty, positive reappraisal, and emotional distress. *Oncology Nursing Forum, 25*, 555–562.

Mishel, M. H. (1981). The measurement of uncertainty in illness. *Nursing Research, 30*, 258–263.

Mishel, M. H. (1983). Parents' perception of uncertainty concerning their hospitalized child. *Nursing Research, 32*, 324–330.

Mishel, M. H. (1984). Perceived uncertainty and stress in illness. *Research in Nursing and Health, 7*, 163–171.

Mishel, M. H. (1988). Uncertainty in illness. *Image: Journal of Nursing Scholarship, 20*, 225–231.

Mishel, M. H. (1990). Reconceptualization of the Uncertainty in Illness Theory. *Image: Journal of Nursing Scholarship, 22*, 256–262.

Mishel, M. H. (1993). Living with chronic illness: Living with uncertainty. In S. G. Funk, E. M. Tornquist, M. T. Champagne, & R. A. Wiese (Eds.), *Key aspects of caring for the chronically ill: Hospital and home* (pp. 46–58). New York: Springer.

Mishel, M. H. (1997). Uncertainty in acute illness. In J. J. Fitzpatrick (Ed.), *Annual review of nursing research* (Vol. 15, pp. 57–80). New York: Springer.

Mishel, M. H. (1999). Uncertainty in chronic illness. In J. J. Fitzpatrick (Ed.), *Annual review of nursing research* (Vol. 17, pp. 269–294). New York: Springer.

Mishel, M. H., Belyea, M., Germino, B., Stewart, J., Bailey, D., Robertson, C., et al. (2002). Helping patients with localized prostate cancer manage uncertainty and treatment side effects: Nurse delivered psycho-educational intervention via telephone. *Cancer, 94,* 1854–1866.

Mishel, M. H., & Braden, C. J. (1987). Uncertainty: A mediator between support and adjustment. *Western Journal of Nursing Research, 9,* 43–57.

Mishel, M. H., & Braden, C. J. (1988). Finding meaning: Antecedents of uncertainty in illness. *Nursing Research, 37,* 98–127.

Mishel, M. H., Hostetter, T., King, B., & Graham, V. (1984). Predictors of psychosocial adjustment in patients newly diagnosed with gynecological cancer. *Cancer Nursing, 7,* 291–299.

Mishel, M. H., & Murdaugh, C. L. (1987). Family adjustment to heart transplantation: Redesigning the dream. *Nursing Research, 36,* 332–336.

Mishel, M. H., Padilla, G., Grant, M., & Sorenson, D. S. (1991). Uncertainty in illness theory: A replication of the mediating effects of mastery and coping. *Nursing Research, 40,* 236–240.

Mishel, M. H., & Sorenson, D. S. (1991). Uncertainty in gynecological cancer: A test of the mediating functions of mastery and coping. *Nursing Research, 40,* 167–171.

Moos, R., & Tsu, V. (1977). The crisis of physical illness: An overview. In R. Moos (Ed.), *Coping with physical illness* (pp. 3–25). New York: Plenum.

Mullins, L. L., Cheney, J. M., Hartman, V. L., Albin, K., Miles, B., & Roberson, S. (1995). Cognitive and affective features of postpolio syndrome: Illness uncertainty, attributional style, and adaptation. *International Journal of Rehabilitation and Health, 1,* 211–222.

Mullins, L., Cote, M., Fuemmeler, B., Jean, V., Beatty, W., & Paul, R. (2001). Illness intrusiveness, uncertainty, and distress in individuals with multiple sclerosis. *Rehabilitation Psychology, 46,* 139–153.

Nelson, J. P. (1996). Struggling to gain meaning: Living with the uncertainty of breast cancer. *Advances in Nursing Science, 18*(3), 59–76.

Neville, K. (1998). The relationships among uncertainty, social support, and psychological distress in adolescents recently diagnosed with cancer. *Journal of Pediatric Oncology Nursing, 15*(1), 37–46.

Northouse, L., Mood, D., Templin, T., Mellon, S., & George, T. (2000). Couples' patterns of adjustment to colon cancer. *Social Science and Medicine, 50,* 271–284.

Norton, R. (1975). Measurement of ambiguity tolerance. *Journal of Personal Assessment, 39,* 607–619.

Nyhlin, K. T. (1990). Diabetic patients facing long-term complications: Coping with uncertainty. *Journal of Advanced Nursing, 15,* 1021–1029.

Padilla, G., Mishel, M., & Grant, M. (1992). Uncertainty, appraisal and quality of life. *Quality of Life Research, 1,* 155–165.

Pelusi, J. (1997). The lived experience of surviving breast cancer. *Oncology Nursing Forum, 24*(8), 1343–1353.

Prigogine, I., & Stengers, I. (1984). *Order out of chaos: Man's new dialogue with nature.* New York: Bantam.

Redeker, N. S. (1992). The relationship between uncertainty and coping after coronary bypass surgery. *Western Journal of Nursing Research, 14,* 48–68.

Righter, B. (1995). Ostomy care: Uncertainty and the role of the credible authority during an ostomy experience. *Journal of Wound and Ostomy Care Nursing, 22,* 100–104.

Ritz, L., Nissen, M., Swenson, K., Farrell, J., Sperduto, P., Sladek, M., et al. (2000). Effects of advanced nursing care on quality of life and cost outcomes of women diagnosed with breast cancer. *Oncology Nursing Forum, 27,* 923–932.

Sanders-Dewey, N., Mullins, L., & Chaney, J. (2001). Coping style, perceived uncertainty in illness, and distress in individuals with Parkinson's disease and their caregivers. *Rehabilitation Psychology, 46,* 363–381.

Santacroce, S. (2000). Support from health care providers and parental uncertainty during the diagnosis phase of perinatally acquired HIV infection. *Journal of the Association of Nurses in AIDS Care, 11*(2), 63–75.

Sexton, D. L., Calcasola, S. L., Bottomley, S. R., & Funk, M. (1999). Adults' experience with asthma and their reported uncertainty and coping strategies. *Clinical Nurse Specialist, 13*(1), 8–17.

Shalit, B. (1977). Structural ambiguity and limits to coping. *Journal of Human Stress, 3,* 32–45.

Sharkey, T. (1995). The effects of uncertainty in families with children who are chronically ill. *Home Healthcare Nurse, 13*(4), 37–42.

Small, S. P., & Graydon, J. E. (1993). Uncertainty in hospitalized patients with chronic obstructive pulmonary disease. *International Journal of Nursing Studies, 30,* 239–246.

Smeltzer, S. C. (1994). The concerns of pregnant women with multiple sclerosis. *Qualitative Health Research, 4,* 497–501.

Sorenson, D. L. S. (1990). Uncertainty in pregnancy. *NAACOG Clinical Issues in Perinatal and Women's Health Nursing, 1,* 289–296.

Sterken, D. J. (1996). Uncertainty and coping of fathers of children with cancer. *Journal of Pediatric Oncology Nursing, 13,* 81–90.

Stewart, J. L., & Mishel, M. H. (2000). Uncertainty in childhood illness: A synthesis of the parent and child literature. *Scholarly Inquiry for Nursing Practice, 17,* 299–319.

Taylor-Piliae, R., & Molassiotis, A. (2001). An exploration of the relationships between uncertainty, psychological distress and type of coping strategy among Chinese men after cardiac catheterization. *Journal of Advanced Nursing, 33*(1), 79–88.

Tomlinson, P., Kirschbaum, M., Harbaugh, B., & Anderson, K. (1996). The influence of illness severity and family resources on maternal uncertainty during critical pediatric hospitalization. *American Journal of Critical Care, 5,* 140–146.

Turner, M., Tomlinson, P., & Harbaugh, B. (1990). Parental uncertainty in critical care hospitalization of children. *Maternal-Child Nursing Journal, 19*, 45–62.

van Riper, M., & Selder, F. E. (1989). Parental responses to birth of a child with Down syndrome. *Loss, Grief and Care: A Journal of Professional Practice, 3*(3–4), 59–76.

Walker, L. O., & Avant, K. C. (1989). *Strategies for theory construction in nursing.* Norwalk, CT: Appleton-Century-Crofts.

Webster, K. K., & Christman, N. J. (1988). Perceived uncertainty and coping post myocardial infarction. *Western Journal of Nursing Research, 10*, 384–400.

Weems, J., & Patterson, E. T. (1989). Coping with uncertainty and ambivalence while awaiting a cadaveric renal transplant. *ANNA Journal, 16*(1), 27–32.

Weitz, R. (1989). Uncertainty and the lives of persons with AIDS. *Journal of Health and Social Behavior, 30*, 270–281.

White, R. E., & Frasure-Smith, N. (1995). Uncertainty and psychologic stress after coronary angioplasty and coronary bypass surgery. *Heart & Lung, 24*(1), 19–27.

Wiener, C. L., & Dodd, M. J. (1993). Coping amid uncertainty: An illness trajectory perspective. *Scholarly Inquiry for Nursing Practice, 7*(1), 17–31.

Wineman, N. M. (1990). Adaptation to multiple sclerosis: The role of social support, functional disability, and perceived uncertainty. *Nursing Research, 39*, 294–299.

Wineman, N. M., O'Brien, R. A., Nealon, N. R., & Kaskel, B. (1993). Congruence in uncertainty between individuals with multiple sclerosis and their spouses. *Journal of Neuroscience Nursing, 25*, 356–361.

Wineman, N. M., Schwetz, K. M., Goodkin, D. E., & Rudick, R. A. (1996). Relationships among illness uncertainty, stress, coping, and emotional well-being at entry into a clinical drug trial. *Applied Nursing Research, 9*(2), 53–60.

Winters, C. A. (1999). Heart failure: Living with uncertainty. *Progress in Cardiovascular Nursing, 14*, 85–91.

Wonghongkul, T., Moore, S., Musil, C., Schneider, S., & Deimling, G. (2000). The influence of uncertainty in illness, stress appraisal, and hope on coping in survivors of breast cancer. *Cancer Nursing, 23*, 422–429.

Wunderlich, R., Perry, A., Lavin, M., & Katz, B. (1999). Patients' perceptions of uncertainty and stress during weaning from mechanical ventilation. *Dimensions of Critical Care Nursing, 18*(1), 8–12.

3

The Theory of Self-Efficacy

Barbara Resnick

S elf-efficacy is defined as an individual's judgment of his or her capabilities to organize and execute courses of action. At the core of self-efficacy theory is the assumption that people can exercise influence over what they do. Through reflective thought, generative use of knowledge and skills to perform a specific behavior, and other tools of self-influence, a person will decide how to behave (Bandura, 1995). To determine self-efficacy an individual must have the opportunity for self-evaluation or the ability to compare individual output to some sort of evaluative criterion. It is this comparison process that enables an individual to judge performance capability and establish self-efficacy expectation.

PURPOSE OF THE THEORY AND HOW IT WAS CREATED

Self-efficacy theory is based on social cognitive theory and conceptualizes person-behavior-environment interaction as triadic reciprocality, the foundation for reciprocal determinism (Bandura, 1977, 1986). Triadic reciprocality is the interrelationship among person, behavior, and environment; reciprocal determinism is the belief that behavior, cognitive and other personal factors, and environmental influences all operate interactively as determinants of each other. Reciprocality does not mean that the influence of behavioral, personal factors and environmental influences are equal. Depending on the situation, the influence of one factor may be stronger than another, and these influences may vary over time.

Cognitive thought, which is a critical dimension of the person-behavior-environment interaction, does not arise in a vacuum. Bandura (1977, 1986, 1995) suggested that individuals' thoughts about themselves are developed and verified through four different processes: (1) direct experience of the effects produced by their actions, (2) vicarious experience, (3) judgments voiced by others, and (4) derivation of further knowledge of what they already know by using rules of inference. External influences play a role in activation and continuous development of cognitive thought processes. These ideas about cognitive thought are central to self-efficacy expectations, having relevance for use of the theory in practice and research.

Initial Theory Development and Research

The early research using the theory of self-efficacy was done to test the assumption that exposure to treatment conditions could result in behavioral change by altering an individual's level and strength of self-efficacy. In the initial study (Bandura, Adams, & Beyer, 1977) 33 subjects with snake phobias were randomly assigned to three different treatment conditions: (1) enactive attainment, which included actually touching the snakes, (2) role modeling, or seeing others touch the snakes, and (3) the control group. Results suggested that self-efficacy was predictive of subsequent behavior, and enactive attainment resulted in stronger and more generalized (to other snakes) self-efficacy expectations.

Expansion of the early research included three additional studies (Bandura, Reese, & Adams, 1982): (1) ten subjects with snake phobias, (2) fourteen subjects with spider phobias, and (3) twelve subjects with spider phobias. Similar to the initial self-efficacy study, enactive attainment and role modeling were effective interventions for strengthening self-efficacy expectations and impacting behavior. The study of 12 subjects with spider phobias also considered the physiological arousal component of self-efficacy. Pulse and blood pressure were measured as indicators of fear arousal when interacting with spiders. After interventions to strengthen self-efficacy expectations (enactive attainment and role modeling), heart rate decreased and blood pressure stabilized.

This early self-efficacy research used an ideal controlled setting in that the individuals with snake phobias were unlikely to seek out opportunities to interact with snakes when away from the laboratory setting. Therefore, there was controlled input of efficacy information. While this ideal situation is not possible in the clinical setting, the theory of self-efficacy has been used to study and predict health behavior change and management in a variety of settings.

I came to use the theory as I reviewed the literature, exploring factors that influenced the willingness of older adults to participate in functional activities and exercise. There was a recurring theme that suggested that self-efficacy and outcome expectations mattered to an individual's willingness. It seemed appropriate, therefore, to use the theory to help understand behavior and guide the development of interventions to change behavior.

CONCEPTS OF THE THEORY

Bandura, a social scientist, differentiated between two components of self-efficacy theory: self-efficacy expectations and outcome expectations. These two components are the major ideas of the theory. Self-efficacy expectations are judgments about personal ability to accomplish a given task. Outcome expectations are judgments about what will happen if a given task is successfully accomplished. Self-efficacy and outcome expectations were differentiated because individuals can believe that a certain behavior will result in a specific outcome; however, they may not believe that they are capable of performing the behavior required for the outcome to occur. For example, Mrs. White may believe that rehabilitation will result in her being able to go home independently; however, she may not believe she is capable of ambulating across the room. Therefore Mrs. White may not participate in the rehabilitation program or be willing to practice ambulation.

Bandura (1977, 1986, 1997) suggests that outcome expectations are based largely on the individual's self-efficacy expectations. The types of outcomes people anticipate generally depend on their judgments of how well they will be able to perform the behavior. Those individuals who consider themselves to be highly efficacious in accomplishing a given behavior will expect favorable outcomes for that behavior. Expected outcomes are dependent on self-efficacy judgments. Therefore, Bandura postulated that expected outcomes may not add much on their own to the prediction of behavior.

Bandura (1986) does state, however, that there are instances when outcome expectations can be dissociated from self-efficacy expectations. This occurs either when no action will result in a specific outcome, or the outcome is loosely linked to the level or quality of the performance. For example, if Mrs. White knows that *even if* she regains functional independence by participating in rehabilitation she will still be discharged to a skilled nursing facility rather than back home, her behavior is likely to be influenced by her outcome expectations (discharge to the skilled nursing facility). In this situation no matter what Mrs. White's performance, the outcome is the same; thus outcome expectancy may influence her behavior independent of her self-efficacy beliefs.

Expected outcomes are also partially separable from self-efficacy judgments when extrinsic outcomes are fixed. For example, when a nurse provides care to six patients during an eight-hour shift the nurse receives a certain salary. When the same nurse cares for ten patients during that shift, she receives the same salary. This could negatively impact performance. It is also possible for an individual to believe he or she is capable of performing a specific behavior, but not believe that the outcome of performing that behavior is worthwhile. For example, older adults in rehabilitation may believe that they are capable of performing the exercises and activities involved in the rehabilitation process, but they may not believe that performing the exercises will result in improved functional ability. Some older adults believe that resting rather than exercising will lead to recovery. In this situation outcome expectations may have a direct impact on performance.

Some researchers have found that perceived self-efficacy expectations predicted behavior much better than outcome expectations, while others have found that outcome expectations were more important for predicting behavior. Stanley and Maddux (1986) included both outcome expectations and outcome value, or a more general consideration of the outcome, in an investigation of participation in health-promoting behaviors. The results suggest that self-efficacy and outcome expectations both significantly predicted behavior ($R^2 = .17$ and .26, respectively). However, outcome value did not add significantly to the model. In both quantitative and qualitative research Resnick (1994, 1996, 1998a, 1998b, 2001, 2002; Resnick & Spellbring, 2000) has demonstrated that, with regard to older adults, outcome expectations explain behavior beyond the influence of self-efficacy expectations. It is likely that outcome and self-efficacy expectations are both important determinants of health behavior. Which one is more important in any given situation may depend on the features of the situation, such as the cost of performing the activity or the perceived certainty of its benefit or outcome.

Sources of Self-Efficacy Judgment

Bandura (1986) suggested that judgment about one's self-efficacy is based on four informational sources: (1) enactive attainment, which is the actual performance of a behavior; (2) vicarious experience or visualizing other similar people perform a behavior; (3) verbal persuasion or exhortation; and (4) physiological state or physiological feedback during a behavior, such as pain or fatigue. The cognitive appraisal of these factors results in a perception of a level of confidence in the individual's ability to perform a certain behavior. The positive performance of this behavior reinforces self-efficacy expectations (Bandura, 1995).

Enactive Attainment

Enactive attainment has been described as the most influential source of self-efficacy information (Bandura, 1986; Bandura & Adams, 1977). There has been repeated empirical verification that actually performing an activity strengthens self-efficacy beliefs. Specifically, the impact of enactive attainment has been demonstrated with regard to snake phobias, smoking cessation, exercise behaviors, performance of functional activities, and weight loss. Enactive attainment generally results in greater strengthening of self-efficacy expectations than do informational sources. However, performance alone does not establish self-efficacy beliefs. Other factors, such as preconceptions of ability, the perceived difficulty of the task, the amount of effort expended, the external aid received, the situational circumstance, and past successes and failures all impact the individual's cognitive appraisal of self-efficacy (Bandura, 1995). An older adult who strongly believes he or she is able to bathe and dress independently because he or she has been doing so for 90 years will not likely alter self-efficacy expectations if he or she wakes up with severe arthritic changes one morning and is consequently unable to put on a shirt. However, repeated failures to perform the activity will impact self-efficacy expectations. The relative stability of strong self-efficacy expectations is important; otherwise an occasional failure or setback could severely impact both self-efficacy expectations and behavior.

Vicarious Experience

Self-efficacy expectations are also influenced by vicarious experiences or seeing other similar people successfully perform the same activity (Bandura, Adams, Hardy, & Howells, 1980). There are some conditions, however, which impact the influence of vicarious experience. If the individual has not been exposed to the behavior of interest, or has had little experience with it, vicarious experience is likely to have a greater impact. Additionally, when clear guidelines for performance are not explicated, self-efficacy will be more likely to be impacted by the performance of others.

Verbal Persuasion

Verbal persuasion involves telling an individual that he or she has the capabilities to master the given behavior. Empirical support for the influence of verbal persuasion has been documented since Bandura's early research of phobias (Bandura & Adams, 1977). Verbal persuasion has proven effective in supporting recovery from chronic illness and in health promotion research. Persuasive health influences lead people with a high sense of self-efficacy to intensify efforts at self-directed change of risky health behavior. For example, in post-myocardial infarction patients, verbal persuasion by a physician and a nurse resulted in enhanced self-efficacy expectations in regard to sexual activity, lifting, and general exertion (Meyerowitz & Chaiken, 1987). The verbal persuasion had the greatest impact on the activities that were not actually performed while in the hospital.

Physiological Feedback

Individuals rely in part on information from their physiological state in order to judge their abilities. Physiological indicators are especially important in relation to coping with stressors, physical accomplishments, and health functioning. Individuals evaluate their physiological state, or arousal, and if aversive, they may avoid performing the behavior. For example, if the older adult has a fear of falling or getting hurt when walking, a high arousal state associated with the fear can limit performance, and decrease the individual's confidence in ability to perform the activity. Likewise if the rehabilitation activities result in fatigue, pain, or shortness of breath, these symptoms may be interpreted as physical inefficacy, and the older adult may not feel capable of performing the activity.

Interventions can be used to alter the interpretation of physiological feedback and help individuals cope with physical sensations, enhancing self-efficacy and resulting in improved performance. Interventions include (1) visualized mastery, which eliminates the emotional reactions to a given situation (Bandura & Adams, 1977), (2) enhancement of physical status (Bandura, 1995), and (3) altering the interpretation of bodily states (Meichenbaum, 1974).

RELATIONSHIPS AMONG THE CONCEPTS: THE MODEL

The theory of self-efficacy was derived from Social Cognitive Theory and must be considered within the context of reciprocal determinism. The four sources of experience (direct experience, vicarious experience, judgments by others, derivation of knowledge by inference) that can potentially influence self-efficacy and outcome expectations interact with characteristics of the individual and the environment. Ideally, self-efficacy and outcome expectations are strengthened by these experiences and subsequently moderate behavior. Since self-efficacy and outcome expectations are influenced by performance of a behavior, it is likely that there is a reciprocal relationship between performance and efficacy expectations (see Figure 3.1).

USE OF THE THEORY IN NURSING RESEARCH

The theory of self-efficacy has been used in nursing research, focusing on clinical aspects of care, education, nursing competency, and professionalism. Over the past ten years there have been approximately 400 articles in nursing journals that focus on the measurement and use of self-efficacy expectations and/or outcome expectations to predict

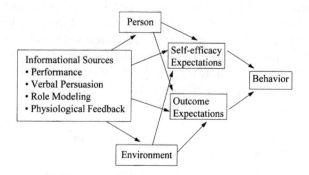

FIGURE 3.1   Self-efficacy theory.

behavior. While the focus of the articles ranges from management of chronic illnesses to education of nurses and parental training, the majority have been related to chronic health problems and participation in health-promoting activities such as exercise, smoking cessation, and weight loss. The majority of these studies are descriptive in nature, exploring the relationship between self-efficacy expectations and behavior. A smaller number, however, have tested interventions developed to strengthen efficacy expectations related to the behavior of interest. What is most important with regard to the use of the theory of self-efficacy in nursing research is that the researcher maintains the behavioral specificity by developing a specific fit between the behavior that is being considered and efficacy and outcome expectations. If the behavior of interest is walking for 20 minutes every day, the self-efficacy measure should focus on the challenges related to this specific behavior (time, fatigue, pain, or fear of falling).

Self-Efficacy Studies Related to Managing Chronic Illness

Building on Bandura's self-efficacy work with cardiac patients (Taylor, Bandura, Ewart, Miller, & DeBusk, 1985), Gortner and colleagues were some of the first nurses to initiate self-efficacy intervention research (Gortner, Rankin, & Wolfe, 1988). Jenkins, whose work with Gortner began during post-doctoral study, added to these self-efficacy intervention studies with an experimental study of the recovery of 156 patients following cardiac surgery (Gortner & Jenkins, 1990). During the acute hospital stay, participants were randomized to receive routine information about recovery after cardiac surgery or an intervention that included routine information plus a slide/tape program on family coping and conflict resolution, a brief counseling session, and a weekly follow-up telephone call to monitor recovery. Efficacy expectations and behaviors focused on walking, climbing, lifting, and general activity, and follow-up measures were done at 4, 8, 12, and 24 weeks by telephone. Based on repeated measures analyses, main effects of treatment were significant for increasing self-efficacy expectations for walking ($p = .013$), and actual walking performance ($p = .01$). Post hoc analyses demonstrated significantly higher levels of lifting ($p = .001$) and general activity ($p = .003$) between 4 and 8 weeks. Significant main effects of time were noted across all aspects of self-efficacy expectations, although there was little increase after the eighth week. Overall, this study provided support for the impact of intervention to strengthen self-efficacy expectations regarding walking. The intervention also influenced self-reported behavioral outcomes following cardiac surgery.

Allen, Becker, and Swank (1990) considered the impact of self-efficacy expectations on 125 male cardiac patients following cardiac surgery. Patients were tested on the fifth post operative day and then 4 weeks and 6 months after discharge. Self-efficacy related to performance of activities of daily living at discharge was the best predictor of six-month functional status.

Schuster and Waldron (1991) studied the impact of self-efficacy expectations on attendance in a cardiac rehabilitation program. The sample included 101 participants followed over a 4-week period. On admission to rehabilitation, the men were significantly better able to tolerate physical activity, had stronger self-efficacy expectations, and were less anxious than the women. Among nonbypass males, those with high self-efficacy and high activity tolerance had fewer days in attendance, and among nonbypass females, those with low self-efficacy had fewer days in attendance. There was no relationship between attendance and anxiety, self-efficacy, or activity tolerance in bypass patients of either sex. The findings from this study are different from what was anticipated based on the theory of self-efficacy (that increased self-efficacy would lead to increased attendance). However, it is possible that those with increased self-efficacy in this study felt they didn't need cardiac rehabilitation, and they simply resumed their normal activities.

Nurse researchers have also used self-efficacy expectations to increase physical activity for patients with heart failure (Borsody, Courtney, Taylor, & Jairath, 1999), and for patients who have had percutaneous transluminal coronary angioplasty (Perkins & Jenkins, 1998). There continue to be studies of the impact of self-efficacy expectations on participation in cardiac rehabilitation programs (Jeng & Braun, 1997).

Several studies have considered self-efficacy expectations in adults with diabetes. In a descriptive study of 142 inpatients with diabetes, Hurley and Shea (1992) reported that self-efficacy expectations about general management of diabetes predicted follow-up diabetic self-care behaviors 4 weeks after discharge. Other research in the area of diabetes management has focused on self-management and self-care issues (Bernal, Woolley, Schensul, & Dickinson, 2000; Bijl, Poelgeest-Eeltink, & Shortridge-Baggett, 1999; Lo, 1998). Specifically, consideration has been given to exploring the relationship between self-efficacy expectations and meal planning for adolescents (Remley & Cook-Newell, 1999), and maternal self-efficacy related to diabetes management in children (Leonard, Skay, & Rheinberger, 1998).

Building on early work by Kaplan, Atkins, and Reinsch (1984), nurse researchers have focused on managing chronic obstructive pulmonary disease (COPD) through self-efficacy intervention. In particular, research has explored the relationship between self-efficacy expectations and managing the associated shortness of breath in COPD and asthma. Interventions such as educational programs and rehabilitation for COPD have been implemented and tested to determine if they resulted in increased self-efficacy expectations and decreased symptomatology (Scherer & Schmieder, 1997; van der Palen, Klein, & Seydel, 1997; van der Palen, Klein, Zielhuis, Van Herwaarden, & Seydel, 2001). As with diabetes, consideration has also been given to the impact of parental self-efficacy expectations with regard to the management of childhood asthma (Sterling, 1999).

Self-efficacy theory has been used in nursing research to explore the relationship between self-efficacy expectations and management of chronic musculoskeletal problems, including osteoarthritis (Lorig & Holman, 1998), and chronic low back pain (Lin & Ward, 1996). In studies of mood and self-efficacy, Perraud (2000) examined self-efficacy expectations related to coping with depression. McDougall (2000) tested interventions to strengthen self-efficacy expectations related to cognition and improvement in cognitive ability.

Nurse researchers in the area of oncology identified relationships among self-efficacy, cancer prevention, and adaptation to cancer. Strong self-efficacy expectations predict behaviors, such as intention to quit smoking, increased participation in screening programs, and adjustment to cancer diagnosis (Boehm et al., 1995; Lev, 1997; Lev, Paul, & Owen, 1999). Increased self-efficacy is associated with increased adherence to treatment, increased self-care behaviors, and decreased physical and psychological symptoms.

Self-Efficacy for Exercise

Resnick (1994, 1996, 1998a, 1998b, 1999, 2000), using combined quantitative and qualitative approaches, demonstrated that self-efficacy expectations and outcome expectations influence older adults' participation in functional activities and exercise. Based on these findings, interventions were developed to strengthen self-efficacy and outcome expectations related to these activities (Resnick, 1998a, 1998b, 2002; Resnick, Zimmerman, Orwig, Furstenberg, & Magaziner, 2001). Overall, this is work that uses self-efficacy theory to encourage healthy behaviors such as engaging in regular exercise. The work was started by doing qualitative research to explore factors that influenced motivation to engage in such behaviors (Resnick, 1991, 1994; Resnick & Spellbring, 2000). Once identified through qualitative study, specific challenges and benefits of performing exercise were used to develop the self-efficacy and outcome expectation scales that were appropriate for this behavior (Resnick, 1999; Resnick & Fleishell, 1999; Resnick & Jenkins, 2000; Resnick, Zimmerman, Orwig, Furstenberg, & Magaziner, 2001; Resnick, 2002). Development of self-efficacy expectation measures was based on Bandura's (1977) early work with snake phobias. This approach included a paper and pencil measure that listed activities, from least to most difficult, in a specific behavioral domain. Respondents were given a 100-point scale, divided into 10-unit intervals ranging from 0, which is completely uncertain, to 10, which is completely certain, to identify the extent of confidence they had in performing a particular activity (strength of self-efficacy) given the existence of a challenge or benefit. An example of items on a self-efficacy scale for exercise follows:

How confident are you right now that you could exercise three times per week for 20 minutes if:

		Not confident								Very confident		
1.	the weather was bothering you	0	1	2	3	4	5	6	7	8	9	10
2.	you were bored by the program or activity	0	1	2	3	4	5	6	7	8	9	10

The development of appropriate self-efficacy and outcome expectation measures enables the testing of interventions designed to help participants believe in the benefits and overcome the challenges of performing selected activities. Examples of how this has been done are demonstrated in the WALC (**W**alk, **A**ddress unpleasant symptoms, **L**earn about exercise, **C**ueing to exercise) intervention and the Exercise Plus Program (Resnick, 2001, 2002; Resnick, Zimmerman, Orwig, Furstenberg, & Magaziner, 2001). Both of these interventions incorporate the four sources of information known to influence self-efficacy and outcome expectations. Specifically, they both use verbal encouragement, decreasing unpleasant sensations, cueing and role modeling, and the actual performance of the behavior.

Self-Efficacy for Health Promotion

Self-efficacy theory has directed research in nursing with regard to a variety of health promotion activities. These studies focus on (1) exercise in middle-aged adults (Fletcher & Banasik, 2001), older adults (Resnick, 2000, 2001; Resnick, Palmer, Jenkins, & Spellbring, 2000), and individuals with diabetes (Plotnikoff, Brez, & Holz, 2000); (2) smoking cessation (Kowalski, 1997; Macnee & Talsma, 1995); (3) cancer prevention, specifically related to breast cancer (Adderly-Kelly, Rabin, & Azulai, 1997); (4) safe sexual activity (Dilorio, Dudley, Soet, Watkins, & Maibach, 2000); (5) education related to pre- and post-op care for cardiac surgeries (Parent & Fortin, 2000) and orthopedic surgeries (Moon & Backer, 2000; Pellino et al., 1998); and (6) changing behavior related to drug dependence (Washington, 1999, 2001). The theory has likewise driven research in the area of maternal-child nursing related to childbirth activities (Sinclair & O'Boyle, 1999), breast feeding (Dennis & Faux, 1999), maternal self-efficacy related to care of toddlers (Gross, Conrad, Fogg, & Manteuffel, 1994), and care of children with asthma (Hanson, 1998).

In addition to a clinical focus, self-efficacy–based research has also guided the exploration of education techniques for nursing. Studies of undergraduates have focused on self-efficacy expectations related to academic performance (Andrew, 1998) and clinical skills (Ford-Gilboe, 1997; Madorin & Iwasiw, 1999). The impact of self-efficacy expectations for nurse practitioner students (Hayes, 1998) and new nurse educators (Nugent, Bradshaw, & Kito, 1999) has also been explored.

This report covers a wide array of topics and yet is only a small representation of the last decade of nursing research that used self-efficacy theory. Clearly, the theory is used extensively to guide nursing research, and the research has contributed to guidance for nursing practice.

USE OF THE THEORY IN NURSING PRACTICE

Translation of research findings into practice is not often done in a timely fashion. This is particularly true of research findings that focus on behavior change. There is, however, evidence to demonstrate that the theory of self-efficacy can help direct nursing care. The theory has been particularly helpful with regard to motivating individuals to participate in health-promoting activities such as regular exercise, smoking cessation, weight loss, and going for recommended cancer screenings. For example, Resnick (1999, 2001, 2002) has used self-efficacy theory as a foundation for programs that encourage exercise activity in older adults. The Seven Step Approach to Developing and Implementing an Exercise Program for community-dwelling older adults incorporates the theory of self-efficacy. The seven steps include (1) education, (2) exercise prescreening, (3) setting goals, (4) exposure to exercise, (5) role models, (6) verbal encouragement, and (7) verbal reinforcement/rewards, all of which are designed to strengthen self-efficacy and outcome expectations. Each of the steps will be briefly discussed.

Education about exercise can be done both formally and informally, incorporating written materials appropriate for the individual. For older patients routine health care visits offer opportunities for education as do periods of time during hospitalization. It is important that education be delivered with sensitivity to the unpleasant sensations associated with exercise, offering interventions to decrease unpleasantness. For instance, anticipating pain and fatigue, or identifying that the older adult fears getting hurt during exercise, the nurse can provide specific interventions to manage these problems. Exercise prescreening, the second step, is done using a simple prescreening form (Resnick, 1999), with the intent of assuring older individuals that it is safe for them to exercise at a moderate level. Next, it is useful to help patients identify appropriate short- and long-term exercise goals. The goals should be very specific. An example of a short-term goal might be walking three times per week for 10 minutes. The long-term goal might include being able to walk without an assistive device, going on a trip, or being able to get on the floor and play with a grandchild. The next steps focus on motivating the patient to actually begin exercising. Attempts should be made to get the individual to engage in the first exercise session. This exposure will help emphasize the benefits. Identifying role models such as a neighbor, friend, relative, or celebrity who exercise can be helpful, especially to get the individual to initiate the appropriate behavior. To be most effective the role models should be similar to the individual in terms of characteristics such as age and overall health status. Verbal encouragement to continue the exercise behavior, and positive reinforcement for any attempt at exercise is an ongoing necessity for the Program. When a patient comes back for a health care visit, the nurse must remember to ask about exercise activity, review how progress toward goals is occurring, and be enthusiastic with the patient regarding any progress. In many cases the reward is your support and excitement, the hug provided for work well done!

The theory of self-efficacy also guides the recommended steps for the development and implementation of restorative care nursing programs (Fleishell & Resnick, 1998). A 5-step approach is recommended as a practical way to implement a successful restorative care nursing program, and includes the following steps: (1) establishing an appropriate philosophy of care, (2) evaluating the resident, (3) motivating the resident to engage in functional activities, (4) getting to work: recognition, reinforcement, and reward, and (5) documentation, re-evaluation, and demonstrating outcomes. Steps 3 and 4, both of which focus on motivating the residents to participate in functional activities, are specifically geared toward strengthening self-efficacy and outcome expectations. Techniques such as verbal encouragement, performance accomplishment, role modeling, and decreasing the unpleasant sensations associated with performance are addressed. Similarly, self-efficacy theory has been used to guide the development of cardiac rehabilitation programs (Jeng & Braun, 1997). For patients to achieve the greatest benefit from such programs, nurses must help them to modify unhealthy behaviors. The theory of self-efficacy provides systematic guidance, which allows the nurse to interpret, modify, and predict the patient's behaviors. Changes in lifestyle are commonly needed for individuals who must learn to live with chronic illness. The ease with which such changes occur is affected by self-efficacy and outcome expectations. Self-efficacy theory has been especially useful in helping patients to manage chronic disease and to adopt healthy lifestyles.

CONCLUSIONS

The studies that nurse researchers have done using the theory of self-efficacy provide support for the importance of self-efficacy and outcome expectations with regard to behavior change. They also provide support for the effectiveness of specific interventions that have been tested to strengthen both self-efficacy and outcome expectations and thereby improve behavior. It is important to note, however, that these studies have also demonstrated that self-efficacy and outcome expectations may not be the only predictors of behavior. Other variables, such as tension/anxiety, barriers to behavior, and other psychosocial experiences impact behavior. Bandura (1986) recognized that expectations alone would not result in behavior change if there was no incentive to perform, or if there were inadequate resources or external constraints. Certainly, an individual may believe he or she can participate in a rehabilitation program, but may not have the resources (i.e., transportation or money) to do so.

Self-efficacy theory is situation-specific. It is difficult, therefore, to generalize an individual's self-efficacy from one type of behavior to another. If an individual has high self-efficacy with regard to diet management, this may or may not generalize to persistence in an exercise program. Future nursing research needs to focus on the degree to which specific self-efficacy behaviors can be generalized. To what degree is self-efficacy a dimension of individual humanness, distinct for each person, but consistent across a range of related behaviors for one person?

Measurement of self-efficacy and outcome expectations requires the development of situation-specific scales with a series of activities listed in order of increasing difficulty, or by a contextual arrangement in nonpsychomotor skills such as dietary modification (Gortner, Miller, & Jenkins, 1988). It is important to carefully construct these scales and establish evidence of reliability and validity. These scales, which are behavior-specific, can be used as the foundation for assessing an individual's self-care abilities in a particular area. Interventions can then be developed that are relevant for that individual.

A major problem with the use of the theory of self-efficacy in nursing research has been the lack of consideration of outcome expectations. In particular, with regard to exercise in older adults, outcome expectations have been noted to be better predictors of exercise behavior than self-efficacy expectations (Jette et al., 1998; Resnick, Palmer, Jenkins, & Spellbring, 2000). Consideration also needs to be given to the influence of self-efficacy expectations beyond incentive to initiate behavior. More important, how does self-efficacy influence behavior over time? Clearly, social cognitive theory and the theory of self-efficacy have helped guide nursing research related to behavior change. Ongoing studies are needed to continue to evaluate the impact of both self-efficacy and outcome expectations on behavior change, as well as develop and test interventions that strengthen these expectations.

REFERENCES

Adderly-Kelly, T., Rabin, S., & Azulai, S. (1997). Breast cancer education, self-efficacy, and screening in older African American women. *Journal of the National Black Nurses Association, 9*(1), 45–57.

Allen, J. K., Becker, D. M., & Swank, R. T. (1990). Factors related to functional status after coronary artery bypass surgery. *Heart & Lung, 19*, 337–343.

Andrew, S. (1998). Self-efficacy as a predictor of academic performance in science. *Journal of Advanced Nursing, 27*, 596–603.

Bandura, A. (1977). Self-efficacy: Toward a unifying theory of behavioral change. *Psychological Review, 84*, 191–215.

Bandura, A. (1986). *Social foundations of thought and action.* Englewood Cliffs, NJ: Prentice Hall.

Bandura, A. (1995). *Self-efficacy in changing societies.* New York: Cambridge University Press.

Bandura, A. (1997). *Self-efficacy: The exercise of control.* New York: W. H. Freeman.

Bandura, A., & Adams, N. (1977). Analysis of self-efficacy theory of behavioral change. *Cognitive Therapy and Research, 1,* 287–308.

Bandura, A., Adams, N., & Beyer, J. (1977). Cognitive processes mediating behavioral change. *Journal of Personality and Social Psychology, 35*(3), 125–149.

Bandura, A., Adams, N., Hardy, A., & Howells, G. (1980). Tests of the generality of self-efficacy theory. *Cognitive Therapy and Research, 4,* 39–66.

Bandura, A., Reese, L., & Adams, N. (1982). Microanalysis of action and fear arousal as a function of differential levels of perceived self-efficacy. *Journal of Personality and Social Psychology, 43,* 5–21.

Bernal, H., Woolley, S., Schensul, J., & Dickinson, J. (2000). Correlates of self-efficacy in diabetes self-care among Hispanic adults with diabetes. *Diabetes Educator, 26,* 673–680.

Bijl, J., Poelgeest-Eeltink, A., & Shortridge-Baggett, L. (1999). The psychometric properties of the diabetes management self-efficacy scale for patients with type 2 diabetes mellitus. *Journal of Advanced Nursing, 30,* 352–359.

Boehm, S., Coleman-Burns, P., Schlenk, E., Funnell, M. M., Parzuchowski, J., & Powel, I. J. (1995). Prostate cancer in African American men: Increasing knowledge and self-efficacy. *Journal of Community Health Nursing, 12,* 161–169.

Borsody, J., Courtney, M., Taylor, K., & Jairath, N. (1999). Using self-efficacy to increase physical activity in patients with heart failure. *Home Healthcare Nurse, 17,* 113–118.

Dennis, C., & Faux, S. (1999). Development and psychometric testing of the Breastfeeding Self-efficacy Scale. *Research in Nursing and Health, 22,* 399–409.

Dilorio, C., Dudley, W., Soet, J., Watkins, J., & Maibach, E. (2000). A social cognitive based model for condom use among college students. *Nursing Research, 49,* 208–214.

Fleishell, A., & Resnick, B. (1998). *Stayin alive: Minimizing loss and maximizing potential: Manual for restorative care nursing programs.* Laurel, MD: Joanne Wilson's Gerontological Nursing Ventures.

Fletcher, J., & Banasik, J. (2001). Exercise self-efficacy. *Clinical Excellence for Nurse Practitioners, 5*(3), 134–143.

Ford-Gilboe, M. (1997). Family strengths, motivation, and resources as predictors of health promotion behavior in single-parent and two-parent families. *Research in Nursing and Health, 20,* 205–217.

Gortner, S., & Jenkins, L. (1990). Self-efficacy and activity level following cardiac surgery. *Journal of Advanced Nursing, 15,* 1132–1138.

Gortner, S., Miller, N., & Jenkins, L. (1988). Self-efficacy: A key to recovery. In C. Jillings (Ed.), *Cardiac rehabilitation nursing* (pp. 84–102). Rockville, MD: Aspen.

Gortner, S., Rankin, S., & Wolfe, M. (1988). Elders' recovery from cardiac surgery. *Progress in Cardiovascular Nursing, 3*(2), 54–61.

Gross, D., Conrad, B., Fogg, L., & Manteuffel, B. (1994). A longitudinal model of maternal self-efficacy, depression, and difficult temperament during toddlerhood. *Research in Nursing and Health, 17,* 207–215.

Hale, P., & Trumbetta, S. (1996). Women's self-efficacy and sexually transmitted disease preventive behaviors. *Research in Nursing and Health, 19*(2), 101–110.

Hanson, J. (1998). Parental self-efficacy and asthma self-management skills. *Journal of Society of Pediatric Nurses, 3*(4), 146–154.

Hayes, E. (1998). Mentoring and nurse practitioner student self-efficacy. *Western Journal of Nursing Research, 20,* 521–535.

Hurley, D., & Shea, C. (1992). Self-efficacy: Strategy for enhancing diabetes self-care. *The Diabetes Educator, 18,* 146–150.

Jeng, C., & Braun, L. T. (1997). Bandura's self-efficacy theory: A guide for cardiac rehabilitation nursing practice. *Journal of Holistic Nursing, 12,* 425–436.

Jette, A. M., Rooks, D., Lachman, M., Lin, T. H., Levenson, C., Heislein, D., et al. (1998). Home-based resistance training: Predictors of participation and adherence. *Gerontologist, 38,* 412–421.

Kaplan, R., Atkins, C., & Reinsch, S. (1984). Specific efficacy experiences mediate exercise compliance in patients with COPD. *Health Psychology, 3,* 223–242.

Kowalski, S. (1997). Self-esteem and self-efficacy as predictors of success in smoking cessation. *Journal of Holistic Nursing, 15*(2), 128–142.

Leonard, B., Skay, C., & Rheinberger, M. (1998). Self-management development in children and adolescents with diabetes: The role of maternal self-efficacy and conflict. *Journal of Pediatric Nursing, 13,* 224–233.

Lev, E. L. (1997). Bandura's theory of self-efficacy: Applications to oncology. *Image: Journal of Nursing Scholarship, 11*(1), 21–37.

Lev, E., Paul, D., & Owen, S. (1999). Age, self-efficacy and change in patients' adjustment to cancer. *Cancer Practitioner, 7*(4), 170–176.

Lin, C., & Ward, S. (1996). Perceived self-efficacy and outcome expectancies in coping with chronic low back pain. *Research Nursing and Health, 19,* 299–310.

Lo, R. (1998). A holistic approach in facilitation adherence in people with diabetes. *Australian Journal of Holistic Nursing, 5*(1), 10–18.

Lorig, K., & Holman, H. (1998). Arthritis self-efficacy scales measure self-efficacy. *Arthritis Care Research, 11,* 155–157.

Macnee, C. L., & Talsma, A. (1995). Predictors of progress in smoking cessation. *Public Health Nursing, 12,* 242–248.

Madorin, S., & Iwasiw, C. (1999). The effects of computer-assisted instruction on the self-efficacy of baccalaureate nursing students. *Journal of Nurse Educators, 38,* 282–285.

McDougall, G. (2000). Memory improvement in assisted living elders. *Issues in Mental Health Nursing, 21,* 217–233.

Meichenbaum, D. (1974). Self-instructional strategy training: A cognitive prosthesis for the aged. *Human Development, 17,* 273–280.

Meyerowitz, C., & Chaiken, H. (1987). The impact of self-efficacy on risky health behaviors. *Behavioral Research and Therapy, 25*(5), 267–273.

Moon, L., & Backer, J. (2000). Relationships among self-efficacy, outcome expectancy, and postoperative behaviors in total joint replacement patients. *Orthopedic Nursing, 19*(2), 77–85.

Nugent, K., Bradshaw, M., & Kito, N. (1999). Teacher self-efficacy in new nurse educators. *Journal of Professional Nursing, 15,* 229–237.

Parent, N., & Fortin, F. (2000). A randomized, controlled trial of vicarious experience through peer support for male first time cardiac surgery patients: Impact on anxiety, self-efficacy expectation, and self-reported activity. *Heart & Lung, 29,* 389–400.

Pellino, T., Tluczek, A., Collins, M., Trimborn, S., Norwick, H., Engelke, Z., & Broad, J. (1998). Increasing self-efficacy through empowerment: Preoperative education for orthopedic patients. *Orthopedic Nursing, 17*(4), 48–51, 54–59.

Perkins, S., & Jenkins, L. (1998). Self-efficacy expectation, behavior performance and mood status in early recovery from percutaneous transluminal coronary angioplasty. *Heart & Lung, 27,* 37–46.

Perraud, S. (2000). Development of the Depression Coping Self-efficacy Scale (DCSES). *Archives of Psychiatric Nursing, 14,* 276–284.

Plotnikoff, R., Brez, S., & Holz, S. (2000). Exercise behavior in a community sample with diabetes: Understanding the determinants of exercise behavioral change. *Diabetes Educator, 26,* 450–459.

Remley, D., & Cook-Newell, M. (1999). Meal planning self-efficacy index for adolescents with diabetes. *Diabetes Educator, 25,* 883–886.

Resnick, B. (1991). Geriatric motivation: How to help the elderly comply. *Journal of Gerontological Nursing, 17,* 17–21.

Resnick, B. (1994). The wheel that moves. *Rehabilitation Nursing, 19,* 140.

Resnick, B. (1996). Motivation in geriatric rehabilitation. *Image: The Journal of Nursing Scholarship, 28,* 41–47.

Resnick, B. (1998a). Efficacy beliefs in geriatric rehabilitation. *Journal of Gerontological Nursing, 24,* 34–45.

Resnick, B. (1998b). Functional performance of older adults in a long-term care setting. *Clinical Nursing Research, 7,* 230–246.

Resnick, B. (1999). Reliability and validity testing of the self-efficacy for functional activities scale . . . three studies. *Journal of Nursing Measurement, 7,* 5–20.

Resnick, B. (2000). Functional performance and exercise of older adults in long-term care settings. *Journal of Gerontological Nursing, 26*(3), 7–16.

Resnick, B. (2001). Testing a model of exercise behavior in older adults. *Research in Nursing and Health, 24,* 83–92.

Resnick, B. (2002). Testing the impact of the WALC intervention on exercise adherence in older adults. *Journal of Gerontological Nursing, 28*(6), 40–49.

Resnick, B., & Fleishell, A. (1999). Restoring quality of life. *Advance for Nurses, 1,* 10–12.

Resnick, B., & Jenkins, L. (2000). Testing the reliability and validity of the self-efficacy for exercise scale. *Nursing Research, 49*(3), 154–159.

Resnick, B., Palmer, M. H., Jenkins, L., & Spellbring, A. M. (2000). Path analysis of efficacy expectations and exercise behavior in older adults. *Journal of Advanced Nursing, 31,* 1309–1315.

Resnick, B., & Spellbring, A. M. (2000). Understanding what motivates older adults to exercise. *Journal of Gerontologic Nursing, 26*(3), 34–42.

Resnick, B., Zimmerman, S., Orwig, D., Furstenberg, A. L., & Magaziner, J. (2001). Model testing for reliability and validity of the Outcomes, Expectations for Exercise Scale. *Nursing Research, 50,* 293–299.

Scherer, Y., & Schmieder, L. (1997). The effect of a pulmonary rehabilitation program on self-efficacy, perceptions of dyspnea, and physical endurance. *Heart & Lung, 26,* 15–22.

Schuster, P., & Waldron, J. (1991). Gender differences in cardiac rehabilitation patients. *Rehabilitation Nursing, 16,* 248–253.

Sinclair, M., & O'Boyle, C. (1999). The Childbirth Self-efficacy Inventory: A replication study. *Journal of Advanced Nursing, 30,* 1416–1423.

Stanley, M., & Maddux, J. (1986). Cognitive process in health enhancement: Investigation of a combined protection motivation and self-efficacy model. *Basic and Applied Social Psychology, 7,* 101–113.

Sterling, Y. (1999). Parental self-efficacy and asthma self-management. *Journal of Child and Family Nursing, 2,* 280–281.

Taylor, C., Bandura, A., Ewart, C., Miller, N., & DeBusk, R. (1985). Exercise testing to enhance wives confidence in their husbands' cardiac capability soon after clinically uncomplicated acute MIs. *American Journal of Cardiology, 55,* 635–638.

van der Palen, J., Klein, J. J., & Seydel, E. R. (1997). Are high generalised and asthma-specific self-efficacy predictive of adequate self-management behavior among adult asthma patients? *Patient Education and Counseling, 32,* S35–S41.

van der Palen, J., Klein, J., Zielhuis, G., Van Herwaarden, C., & Seydel, E. (2001). Behavioral effect of self-treatment guidelines in a self-management program for adults with asthma. *Patient Education Counseling, 43*(2), 161–169.

Washington, O. (1999). Effects of cognitive and experiential group therapy on self-efficacy and perceptions of employability of chemically dependent women. *Issues in Mental Health Nursing, 20*(3), 181–198.

Washington, O. (2001). Using brief therapeutic interventions to create change in self-efficacy and personal control of chemically dependent women. *Archives of Psychiatric Nursing, 15*(1), 32–40.

4

The Theory of Unpleasant Symptoms

Elizabeth R. Lenz and Linda C. Pugh

Symptom management is a central element of nursing practice and key to nursing science and the knowledge base of health care. With the notable exception of the Symptom Management Model developed and updated by faculty and students at the University of California, San Francisco (Dodd et al., 2001; Larson et al., 1994), most of the theoretical work that has been carried out to elucidate the experience of symptoms and to guide their management has been symptom or disease specific.

PURPOSE OF THE THEORY AND HOW IT WAS DEVELOPED

The Theory of Unpleasant Symptoms (TOUS) was designed to integrate existing knowledge about a variety of symptoms. It was based on the premise that there are commonalities across different symptoms experienced by a variety of clinical populations in varied situations. A framework that highlights common elements and dimensions has potential to be useful in both nursing practice and research. The TOUS was designed for clinical practice as well as research. The purpose of the theory is to improve understanding of the symptom experience in various contexts, and to provide information useful for designing effective means to prevent or ameliorate unpleasant symptoms and their negative effects. Because it is more general than a theory describing or explaining a specific symptom, the TOUS lacks some of the detail that may be useful in working with a particular symptom in a given clinical population. On the other hand, by highlighting dimensions and considerations that are common to many symptoms, it is at the middle range and encourages investigators and clinicians to think about aspects that are not readily apparent and to consider symptoms both alone and in combination. It provides an organizing schema and encourages thought about the interplay among the many aspects of the symptom experience.

A model such as the TOUS provides a framework within which multiple researchers can work simultaneously, ultimately combining the results of their many programs of research. The TOUS provides common definitions and dimensions for examining symptoms, ultimately enhancing the probability that the results from multiple studies can be combined to produce convincing evidence upon which to base practice.

Because the symptom experience, by definition, occurs at the level of individual perception, the theory is applicable at the level of the individual. However, the TOUS does not consider the individual in isolation. Rather, it positions the individual within the context of his or her family and community by taking into account situational factors in the environment that may influence the symptom experience. It also defines the outcome of the symptom experience in terms of performance, a notion that considers the impact of the symptom experience on the individual's interactions with others and his or her short- and long-term functioning.

The Middle Range Theory of Unpleasant Symptoms was developed by a group of four nurse researchers who shared interest in the nature and experience of different symptoms (specifically fatigue and dyspnea), and who were in the processes of concept and theory development. These individuals (Audrey Gift, Renee Milligan, Linda Pugh, and Elizabeth Lenz) had collaborated in dyads or triads on various empirical studies and theoretical articles. They shared geographic proximity, which facilitated collaboration, and, by virtue of their common association with one PhD program in nursing, they also shared exposure to the same philosophical and metatheoretical perspectives regarding the development and substance of nursing science. They had access to a philosopher of science colleague, Frederick Suppe, who played an important role in shaping their understanding of middle range theory and who assisted in the theory development process.

This is a theory that was developed from the bottom up. That is, it had its beginnings at the relatively narrow scope of a single symptom and in the concrete world of practice. Three of the theory's developers had conducted dissertation research regarding a specific symptom: Gift studied dyspnea, and Milligan and Pugh studied fatigue. At the time their initial studies about individual symptoms were carried out, they had no intention of developing a theory. The opportunity to do so evolved over time, as they began to realize that their work on individual symptoms represented concept development activity. It became apparent, as they continued to identify and discuss the elements that were common across the symptom experience in both ill and healthy populations, that their thinking was moving to the level of middle range theory.

The initial collaboration took place between Pugh and Milligan, who were both studying the symptom of fatigue during a different phase of the perinatal experience. Pugh (1990) studied correlates of fatigue during labor and delivery. Milligan (1989) had conducted qualitative and quantitative research about fatigue during the postpartum period and was also carrying out concept development and measurement studies (Milligan, Lenz, Parks, Pugh, & Kitzman, 1996). These two researchers, who were also engaged in clinical practice in labor and delivery and postpartum environments, combined their findings about the concept to develop a framework for the study of fatigue during childbearing (Pugh & Milligan, 1993).

Milligan's inductive analysis of fatigue during the postpartum period included clinical observations, interviews with postpartum mothers, and data from a quantitative measure of fatigue. Her work pointed out the importance of differentiating fatigue from related concepts, such as depression, and the desirability of differentiating different types of fatigue. From Pugh's deductive work, which was based on existing models of fatigue, came the identification of physiologic, psychological, and situational factors that influence fatigue during labor, and the recognition that fatigue is a multidimensional phenomenon. These two investigators recognized commonalities in their conceptualizations of and findings about fatigue at different stages in the childbearing process. Pugh and Milligan (1995) tested the framework in a study of pregnant women, examining fatigue longitudinally. Examples of the commonalities include the cumulative nature of the symptom experience and the importance of energy depletion. The framework that emerged from this collaboration incorporated a nursing diagnosis-based definition of fatigue and the results of empirical studies of fatigue from other disciplines, as well as theoretical models developed within nursing to explain fatigue in childbearing situations.

The second collaboration took place when Pugh began to discuss the model of fatigue with Gift (Gift, 1990; Gift & Cahill, 1990), who had conducted multiple studies of dyspnea in patients with chronic obstructive pulmonary disease and asthma. They realized that their conceptualizations were similar, and discovered a number of commonalities between dyspnea and fatigue. They developed a model combining elements of their previous work that was meant to be equally applicable to the two symptoms (Gift & Pugh, 1993).

Gift had carried out Wilsonian concept development activities, which clarified the nature and measurement of dyspnea as a subjective phenomenon. She used pain as an analog to develop a model of dyspnea as having physiological and psychological components, and as varying along such dimensions as the degree of distress experienced and the intensity and duration of the dyspnea. Her conceptualization bore similarities to Pugh and Milligan's framework for studying fatigue: for example, the respective symptom having both acute and chronic manifestations, being influenced by the same categories of factors, and affecting performance or functional ability.

Having developed the multiple-concept dyspnea/fatigue model, which was also potentially applicable to pain, the investigators went on to reason that they could develop a generic theory that was at an even higher level of abstraction and could be extended to encompass additional symptoms. Lenz was familiar with the work of all three researchers and had offered ongoing critique of their work. The decision to develop a middle range theory occurred in collaboration with her. Having made a commitment to develop a generic theory of the middle range, all four investigators then began to meet regularly to discuss and resolve differences in the models for individual symptoms and to reach agreement on the elements of a more inclusive theory. The resulting TOUS was introduced and described briefly in an article advocating the development of middle range theories to guide nursing practice (Lenz, Suppe, Gift, Pugh, & Milligan, 1995). It should be noted that the call for papers about middle range nursing theory by *Advances in Nursing Science* (*ANS*) served as an important stimulus to this theory development activity.

The TOUS generated considerable interest in the nursing academic community, as indicated by correspondence received by the authors, much of which came from graduate students who recognized its potential while seeking clinically relevant theories upon which to base their research. Its publication and more general exposure also pointed out some weaknesses of the theory, as well as some aspects that were unclear. As a result, the authors continued to work on refining it, and an updated, improved version was subsequently published (Lenz, Pugh, Milligan, Gift, & Suppe, 1997). Again, the prospect of an opportunity to publish the refinements in *ANS* served as a stimulus to the revision.

In considering the process by which the TOUS was developed, several observations should be made. First, it was not preplanned but occurred spontaneously, stimulated by shared interests and the opportunity for frequent communication. Proximity that allowed face-to-face meetings, a common background in philosophy and theory development acquired during doctoral study, and the ability to take the time required to debate difficult conceptual issues were facilitators of the collaborative efforts at all stages. Subsequent geographical moves by two of the theory developers have unfortunately slowed continued work on the theory. Second, forward movement on the development of the theory has tended to occur in spurts of activity, undertaken in response to external stimuli, primarily publication opportunities and explicit critiques. This seems to underscore the importance of nursing journal editors' willingness to publish the results of theoretical work as well as empirical research findings. It also reaffirms the value of scholarly dialogue and debate of ideas. Third, the development of the theory occurred in an inductive fashion, which contributed to its practice relevance. At every step concept analysis and clarification were grounded in nursing practice and in practice-related research. The theory was not conceived from armchair musings but was based on real-world observations and attempts to study and solve problems encountered in practice.

CONCEPTS OF THE THEORY

The TOUS has three major concepts: the symptom(s), influencing factors, and performance outcomes. The overall structure of the theory, which is portrayed in Figure 4.1, asserts that three interrelated categories of factors (physiologic, psychologic, and situational) influence predisposition to and manifestation of a given symptom or multi-

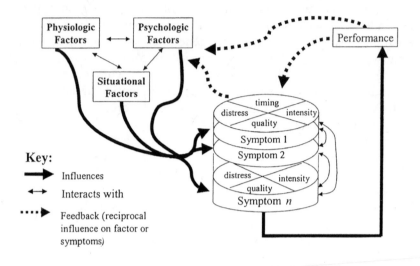

FIGURE 4.1   Theory of unpleasant symptoms.

Note: Reprinted with permission from: Lenz, E. R., Pugh, L. C., Milligan, R., Gift, A., & Suppe, F. (1997). The middle-range theory of unpleasant symptoms: An update. *Advances in Nursing Science, 19*(3), 14–27.

ple symptoms and the nature of the symptom experience. The symptom experience, in turn, affects the individual's performance, which encompasses cognitive, physical, and social functioning. The performance outcomes can feed back to influence the symptom experience itself, as well as to modify the influencing factors. Literature supporting the structure of the theory was cited in the published descriptions of the original theory (Lenz et al., 1995) and the updated version (Lenz et al., 1997).

Symptoms

Symptoms were the starting point for conceptualizing the theory, and hence should be considered its central concept. Thus far, the TOUS has focused on subjectively perceived symptoms rather than objectively observable signs. Symptoms are defined as "the perceived indicators of change in normal functioning as experienced by patients" (Rhodes & Watson, 1987, p. 242). The perception-based definition assumes awareness by the individual, that the nature of a symptom can be truly known and described only by the individual experiencing it, and that it is subjective. Therefore implications for measurement must be subjective. The extent to which objectively observable signs can be explained by the theory has not been examined to date, but clearly is an important question.

The TOUS asserts that symptoms can occur either in isolation—one at a time—or in combination with other symptoms. In many illness or stress-related situations multiple symptoms are experienced simultaneously. In postsurgical patients, for example, pain, nausea, and fatigue often occur together. Likewise, dyspnea and fatigue frequently occur together in COPD patients. In some situations, one symptom may precede and possibly give rise to another. For example, extreme fatigue may precipitate episodes of nausea and vertigo. When more than one symptom is experienced at the same time, the net effect can be greater than the sum of the parts. That is, when pain is accompanied by one or more other symptoms, such as fatigue and nausea, it tends to be perceived as considerably worse than when it occurs alone. Symptoms are conceptualized as manifesting multiple variables and measurable dimensions. It is asserted that all symptoms vary in intensity or severity, degree of associated distress, timing, and quality.

Intensity is the dimension that quantifies the degree, strength, or severity of the symptom, and is the most frequently measured aspect of the symptom experience. It is part of the routine assessment of postsurgical patients to ask them to quantify the intensity of their pain on a numerical rating scale or visual analog scale. Intensity is often the simplest characteristic for patients to rate. In pediatric practice, nonnumeric measures of pain are used to capture children's ratings of its intensity (e.g., the faces pain scale).

The distress dimension reflects an affective aspect of the symptom experience in that it refers to the degree to which the individual experiencing the symptom is bothered by it. Because of differences in pain threshold levels, for example, individuals exposed to the same intensity of pain-inducing stimuli can experience very different levels of distress. Clearly, the degree of distress experienced with a symptom is related to its intensity; however, it can also be moderated by other considerations, such as the meaning of the symptom to the individual. For example, a woman who has been treated for infertility may perceive nausea associated with pregnancy as a very welcome symptom and not be bothered at all by it, whereas a cancer patient could be bothered considerably by chemotherapy-induced nausea of the same severity because of its potentially negative connotations. Distress can also be influenced by the degree of focused attention that the individual directs toward the symptom. Symptom management strategies include diverting attention from the symptom (for example, in the breathing techniques practiced in the Lamaze method of childbirth to divert attention from pain) in order to lessen the resulting distress.

The time dimension qualifies the way symptoms vary in duration and frequency. First they vary in duration, the length of time they continue. It is common to differentiate acute from chronic symptom experiences because they tend to be different in nature and to be treated differently. Chronic symptoms are often remarkable due to their duration. Headaches, while often acute in nature, take on new meaning to the patient when they last for weeks or months. Strategies that are appropriate for acute pain, for example, are not necessarily useful in treating chronic pain. Secondly, intermittent symptoms vary in the frequency with which they occur; they can also vary in the degree to which their occurrence is regular or irregular, and/or periodic or sustained. Nausea that occurs every morning for three hours during the first trimester of pregnancy can be described, and hence measured, along several time-related dimensions.

The final dimension of the symptom experience incorporated in the TOUS is the quality of the symptom. This dimension refers to the nature of the symptom or the way in which it is manifested or experienced, that is, what it feels like to have the symptom. By including this dimension, the TOUS acknowledges that in addition to reflecting characteristics that are common across all symptoms, each symptom has unique aspects and characteristics. The descriptors that best characterize each symptom are highly specific. For example, pain is often characterized by the nature of the sensation: stinging, burning, stabbing, pounding, and so forth. Dyspnea can be characterized by the way the shortness of breath feels to the individual, for example, tightness versus suffocation. These descriptors are important because they differ systematically from one disease state to another, and so may provide valuable diagnostic clues. Moreover, changes in the nature of the pain may signal changes in disease progression. Hence they are incorporated in many of the widely used symptom-specific measures.

Describing and measuring the quality of specific symptoms depends on the patient's ability to articulate what he or she is experiencing. Individuals differ in the descriptors that they use and also in their ability for expression. Accordingly, qualitative research with a variety of patient populations is often valuable in describing the quality of the symptom experience. The measurement of the symptom(s) would be more descriptive when all four characteristics are included. However, measuring one, two, or three characteristics is still valid and informative for health care providers in managing the symptom(s).

Influencing Factors

Three categories of factors that influence the symptom experience (and can, in turn, be influenced by it) are identified in the TOUS: physiologic factors, psychologic factors, and situational factors. The specific factors that are most relevant in influencing a given symptom may be different from those that are most influential for another.

Physiologic factors include anatomical/structural, physiological, and genetic variables. Examples of variables in this category include the presence of structural anomalies, existence of pathology or disease states, inflammation due to infection or trauma, fluctuations in hormonal or energy levels, adequacy of hydration and nutrition, level of consciousness, and age. All may influence the occurrence of a symptom and how it is experienced. The interplay among different physiologic influencing factors can be quite complex. For example, breastfeeding mothers' experiences of fatigue are influenced by many physiologic factors, including the duration of labor, type of delivery, level of hydration, time since delivery, maternal age, and the presence of any infection. Symptoms are often the indicators that pathology exists, so clearly there is a reciprocal relationship between physiologic factors and symptoms.

Psychologic factors represent one of the more complex and controversial components of the model. They include both affective and cognitive variables. The individual's affective state or mood (e.g., level of anxiety or depression) at or preceding the time of the symptom experience, even if unrelated to the symptom, and his or her affective response to the illness or the symptom itself (e.g., anger, fear, anxiety) can serve to intensify the symptom. Cognitive variables that may impact the symptom experience include the degree of uncertainty surrounding it, the meaning it has for the individual experiencing it, the individual's level of knowledge about the illness or the symptom, and his or her cognitive coping skills. As psychobiological research underscores the physiological basis for mood, the psychologic and physiologic factors impacting the symptom experience become difficult to separate.

The third category of influencing factors is situational and encompasses the individual's environment, both social and physical. For instance, the experience of symptoms can vary by culture because there is a learned component to interpreting and expressing symptoms. Other situational factors that can influence the experience of symptoms include those that are associated with the individual's experiential background and access to resources, including the availability of emotional and instrumental help in dealing with the symptom. Examples are socioeconomic status, marital and family status, availability of social support, and access to health care. Lifestyle behaviors, such as smoking, can influence the occurrence and intensity of symptoms. The physical environment can also influence symptoms and includes altitude, temperature, humidity, noise level, light, and presence of pollutants or irritants in the air or water.

Performance Outcomes

The outcome concept in the TOUS is performance. It represents the consequences of the symptom experience. Quite simply, the theory asserts that the experience of symptoms can have an impact on the individual's ability to function, with function including motor skills, social behaviors, and cognition. The specification of performance as the key outcome of the model reflects a pragmatic orientation. It is also consistent with the genesis of the theory in maternal-infant and adult health nursing domains.

The concept of performance has several possible dimensions: physical activity and impairment; functional role performance, including activities of daily living; cognition, including comprehension, learning, concentration, and problem solving; and social interaction. A given symptom or set of symptoms may generate a number of different performance outcomes that may occur simultaneously but also can be time-ordered. Performance outcomes that are proximal in time to the symptom experience can influence more distal outcomes, particularly if the symptom is sustained in duration. An example would be a heart failure patient who suffers from extreme dyspnea. The symptom interferes with the ability to walk uphill, climb steps, and carry groceries. As a result of these more proximal functional limitations in performance, the more distal performance outcome is that the elderly, city-dwelling patient is unable to maintain previous patterns of socializing with friends, shopping independently for food, and ultimately living in an apartment that requires climbing a hill or climbing stairs.

RELATIONSHIPS AMONG CONCEPTS: THE MODEL

The relationships among the major concepts of the TOUS are depicted as lines in Figure 4.1. In the original version of the theory, simplifying assumptions were made, and the relationships between the influencing factors and the symptom experience, and, in turn, between the symptom experience and performance, were depicted as unidirectional. The revised version of the TOUS acknowledges the complexity of the symptom experience by depicting the relationships among the three major components as reciprocal. That is, the influencing factors are assumed to impact the nature of the symptom experience, which impacts performance. However, experiencing symptoms can also change the patient's psychological, physiological, or social status. For example, severe pain and severe dyspnea can negatively impact one's mood state (psychologic influencing factor). Likewise, performance can have a reciprocal relationship to the experience of unpleasant symptoms. For example, the experience of severe pain can restrict an arthritis patient's physical activity, and inactivity may reciprocally increase the intensity of the pain.

The symptom experience can serve as a mediating or moderating variable between influencing factors and performance. A mediating relationship might be exemplified by the finding that Cesarean delivery is associated with higher levels of fatigue than vaginal delivery, and that, in turn, mothers with higher levels of fatigue interact less frequently with their infants than do those who are less fatigued. Fatigue is the mediator that helps explain the link between type of delivery and maternal parenting behavior (Milligan, Parks, & Lenz, 1996; Parks, Lenz, Milligan, & Han, 1999). A scenario in which pain is a moderator would be the relationship of age to the ability to climb stairs following knee replacement surgery. In situations where pain is low and all else being equal, the older the patient, the more limited the ability to climb stairs; however, where pain is high, age might well be unrelated to climbing performance.

The most recent version of the TOUS also asserts that performance can have a feedback effect on the physiologic, psychologic, and situational factors. A breast cancer patient's severe pain (symptom), for example, can impair her desire to interact with others, hence decrease or increase the frequency of her social interaction (performance). Decreased interaction with others in the social network can result not only in decreased network size as others withdraw from the network, but also in a reduction in the social support received from her network (situational influencing factors).

The three categories of influencing factors are hypothesized to influence one another and to interact with one another in their relation to the symptom experience. That is, physiologic complications of surgery can interact with a patient's anxiety or depression to create more severe pain than would be experienced had the psychologic factors not been operating as strongly. The positive impact of social support in mitigating the negative impact of physical illness or stress on the severity of symptoms exemplifies the interaction of situational factors with physiologic and psychologic factors.

The TOUS also hypothesizes that when patients experience more than one symptom, the symptom experiences are related to one another. The relationship can be an interactive one, even multiplicative. That is, the experience of a given unpleasant symptom, such as pain, is exacerbated or fundamentally changed in other ways when it occurs simultaneously with another symptom, such as nausea. Nipple pain and fatigue, two common symptoms in breastfeeding women during the first postpartum month, can be multiplicative and lead to premature weaning (an unwanted performance outcome). The management of one symptom at a time is clearly easier for the new mother. When she is bombarded with several symptoms, the effect is great. It is likely that the cumulative effect of multiple symptoms on function is greater than the sum of the individual symptoms; however, this conjecture has not been subjected to empirical testing.

USE OF THE THEORY IN NURSING RESEARCH

The research that has been generated to test the TOUS, or has used the TOUS as a middle range theory to highlight aspects of a phenomenon that need to be examined, is just beginning to be reported in the professional literature. The authors have received multiple inquiries from master's and doctoral students who have found the theory to be extremely relevant to the phenomena they are interested in examining. Several doctoral students plan to use the TOUS as the theoretical framework to guide their dissertation research. These works are still in progress.

Several of the research projects stimulated by the TOUS have been carried out by the theory's developers. For example, Pugh and Milligan (Milligan, Flenniken, & Pugh, 1996; Pugh & Milligan, 1995, 1998) conducted several experimental studies to test a positioning intervention to minimize fatigue in nursing mothers. Fatigue was found to be a major barrier to breastfeeding success. The multifaceted intervention was based on the TOUS. The most complex intervention (Pugh & Milligan, 1998), which was delivered in two home visits at 3 to 4 days postpartum and 12 days postpartum, included discussions of diet and exercise, the need for sleep and rest, ways to build the mothers' self esteem, use of social support, comfort measures such as warm compresses, and use of side-lying position while breastfeeding to conserve energy. The intervention, therefore, addressed all three TOUS categories of influential factors. It was found to be effective in that the experimental group of mothers had lower fatigue at 14 days postpartum and sustained breastfeeding for an average of 6 weeks longer than the control group mothers. In several current studies similar results were found (Pugh, Milligan, & Brown, 2001; Pugh, Milligan, Frick, Spatz, & Bronner, 2002).

Gift (1991) and Gift and McCrone (1993) examined the interplay between physical and psychologic factors in impacting the experience of dyspnea and found both types of influential factors to be important. A more recent study of dyspnea in a different clinical population (heart failure patients) by Parshall and colleagues (2001) was guided by the TOUS. The focus of this study of 57 heart failure patients who presented at the emergency department of an urban hospital was to describe their experience of dyspnea and to examine the influence of its duration, distress level, and intensity on the decision to seek emergency care. Dyspnea was the most distressing symptom experienced by 80% of the patients, and they reported high levels of distress and intensity at the point of deciding to go to the ED. The symptom experience for nearly half of the sample was characterized by several expressions of distress such as "smothering," "couldn't breathe," or "couldn't get air." Open-ended questions elicited a variety of descriptors of the negativity of the experience and also revealed an affective component. This study confirmed the salience, measurability, and interconnectedness of three of the dimensions of dyspnea (duration, intensity, quality) identified in the TOUS model. It also supported the hypothetical reciprocal relationship between the symptom experience and psychologic (i.e., emotional and affective) factors. A major consideration in the decision of 23% of the patients was that dyspnea interfered with their functional ability to walk and perform other normal activities, and that these limitations helped prompt the decision to seek care. This finding revealed the impact of the symptom experience on both proximal (functional status) and distal (care-seeking) outcomes.

On the other hand, in a secondary analysis of data from 273 cancer patients undergoing chemotherapy, Redeker, Lev, and Ruggiero (2000) found that psychologic factors and the symptoms of fatigue and insomnia were related but not in the predicted fashion. "Instead of amplifying the effect of the symptoms on performance outcomes as the [TOUS] suggests, the salience of fatigue and insomnia to quality of life decreased in the presence of the psychological factors, largely due to redundancy among these variables in relation to quality of life" (p. 284). This finding led the authors to question the centrality of the symptom experience in predicting quality of life, and, by inference, to question its role as an important mediating variable in the relationship between psychologic factors and the quality of life outcome. In this correlational study it was impossible to track the temporal sequence of the variables. The authors raised important questions about how changes in the relationships among influencing factors, symptoms, and outcomes (in this case quality of life) change over time and over the course of an illness. In responding to the Redeker, Lev, and Ruggiero study, Pugh, Milligan, and Lenz (2000) questioned the identification of insomnia as a symptom, rather than as a situational influencing factor, and also acknowledged that a limitation of the TOUS is that quality of life is not included as an outcome variable. Its status as a possible outcome has been suggested by several investigators who have applied the TOUS in research, and undoubtedly needs to be taken into account in further development of the theory.

The complex interplay of physical and psychologic factors in impacting symptoms and performance was revealed in a recent study of 50 lung and heart-lung transplant patients by Dabbs and colleagues (2000). The TOUS provided the theoretical framework for the study. Interviews and medical record reviews revealed surprisingly high levels of physical symptoms (9–28 physical symptoms reported, with a mean of 16.1) and psychological distress (27% reported elevated depressive symptoms and 35% reported elevated anxiety symptoms) 2.5–17 months post-transplant. Levels of symptoms were higher in lung transplant patients than in patients who received both heart and lungs. These investigators identified the type of surgery and medical complications as physiologic factors, and the presence of elevated anxiety and/or depressive symptoms as the psychologic factor impacting physical symptoms (the symptom experience) and physical impairment (the performance outcome). Elevated psychological distress was associated with increased physical symptoms and physical impairment, independent of the contribution of medical complications to the symptom experience and functional outcomes. The findings underscored the importance of psychological vulnerability and of developing strategies to reduce its impact.

The original version of the TOUS was used as the theoretical framework for a study of fatigue in 39 adult end-stage renal failure patients receiving hemodialysis (McCann & Boore, 2000). Based on the results of the study, the authors suggested a revision for the model that was, in fact, very similar to that proposed by Lenz and colleagues (1997). The findings suggested that physiologic factors (age, gender, physical health status, sleep, and biochemical measures of dialysis adequacy, hemoglobin, hematocrit, ferritin, urea, creatinine, albumin, phosphate, and calcium) and psychologic factors (anxiety and depression) act together and reciprocally to influence the intensity of fatigue. However, situational factors (role function, marital status, employment status and length of time on hemodialysis) were not related to fatigue. They concluded that "fatigue is influenced by and influences physiological and psychological factors, which in turn have reciprocal relationships with one another" (McCann & Boore, p. 1140). Fatigue did impact performance, as indicated by physical role, activity level, and motivation.

Hutchinson and Wilson (1998) conducted a secondary analysis of qualitative participant observation data to examine the fit of the TOUS for Alzheimer's Disease clients in order to determine its utility for planning nursing interventions. Their approach was to begin with the clinical population and to identify evidence of symptoms. However, much of their focus tended to be on objectively observable signs of the disease, rather than on subjectively experienced symptoms. In part, the relative lack of emphasis on subjective symptoms is attributable to the clinical population studied and difficulty in eliciting valid self-reported data. Subjective experiences are the focal subject matter of the TOUS. Hutchinson and Wilson's research supported several assertions of the TOUS, for example that several symptoms can occur simultaneously, and that the situational context, which includes caregiving and social interaction, is extremely important with Alzheimer's patients. However, they found the boundaries of the three influencing factor categories and symptom consequences/performance outcomes to be blurred and sometimes overlapping. For example, the psychologic factor component of the model (anxiety, memory loss, depression) was difficult to differentiate from the symptoms themselves. They concluded that the components of the TOUS are not necessarily mutually exclusive when applied to Alzheimer's Disease patients, but are better conceptualized as fluid and possibly interchangeable depending on the context in which they occur.

Their findings also were important in pointing out that symptoms can have impact on other symptoms, and may consequently be conceptualized as primary and secondary symptoms. They also noted that symptoms can have both primary and secondary outcomes, the latter reflecting outcomes for family members, caregivers, and others in the patient's environment. Their study raised a number of important issues and questions that are currently being considered by the TOUS authors.

USE OF THE THEORY IN NURSING PRACTICE

To date there is little published evidence of the application of the TOUS in clinical practice except in clinical intervention studies. Several of the studies described above have direct application in practice, thus indicating that the TOUS has definite clinical relevance. For example, Parshall and colleagues' (2001) findings suggest the basis for a multifaceted assessment of dyspnea in heart failure patients, both in ambulatory care settings where these patients are managed on an ongoing basis, and in emergency room settings when they seek care for dyspnea that has become particularly distressing. Such assessment can be used to identify ambulatory patients who are at risk for hospital admission, and ultimately to guide the design of interventions to decrease dyspnea and decrease hospitalization rates. Virtually all of the above studies emphasize the importance of assessing the occurrence of multiple symptoms simultaneously, since the pattern of symptom synergy was common across symptoms and clinical populations.

Similarly, the TOUS was the basis for the intervention tested by Pugh and Milligan (1998) to address physiologic, psychologic, and situational factors that operate to increase fatigue and thereby to discourage or truncate breastfeeding behavior. The multifaceted intervention proved to be effective in prolonging breastfeeding, even in a low-income population. This work is an outstanding example of a theory-based intervention.

O'Brien (personal communication, March 8, 2000) indicated that she had conducted qualitative and quantitative studies regarding nausea and vomiting in pregnancy. Qualitative interviews with 20 women on 24 occasions and a focus group revealed that the women experienced multiple symptoms and that the three categories of influencing factors in the TOUS provided a framework for organizing the findings. She suggests that instead of the relatively ineffective longstanding approach of applying individual interventions to the problem of nausea and vomiting during pregnancy, "a far more useful nursing approach would be to address influencing factors and their interaction with multiple symptoms when planning interventions that might provide symptom relief."

Symptom management is one of the most important problems addressed in today's clinical practice. It represents a domain that is squarely within—and perhaps even central to—nursing's practice domain. More specific models at lower levels of abstraction, such as the middle range theory of acute pain management (Good, 1998), or the middle range theory of chronotherapeutic intervention for postsurgical pain management (Auvil-Novak, 1997), can, and in fact should, be applied in managing individual symptoms such as pain (see Brown, 1996). However, the more generic TOUS is particularly valuable as a middle range theory that helps highlight certain aspects of the symptom experience and potential strategies for symptom management that are not addressed by more symptom-specific models. For example, the TOUS stresses the importance of a multivariate assessment of the symptom experience itself and of possible influencing factors, and provides a rationale and framework for applying a biopsychosocial approach. It suggests that multiple management strategies may need to be applied simultaneously, given the multivariate nature of the factors influencing symptoms. It also emphasizes the importance of considering the effect of several symptoms, occurring together, on the patient's functioning, and encourages assessment of functional patient outcomes. In response to criticism questioning its clinical utility (Brown, 1996), the TOUS authors (Lenz, Suppe, Gift, Pugh, & Milligan, 1996) asserted that

> In keeping with nursing's holistic focus, clinical practice with ill patients almost always involves attending to more than one symptom at a time. The [TOUS] is clinically applicable because it goes beyond symptom-specific concepts and theories to stimulate thinking about common factors that may influence more than one symptom, the ways in which multiple symptoms interact with one another and affect performance, and interventions that would mitigate multiple symptoms. [p. vi]

According to Cooley (2000), the TOUS is valuable, because it "proposes a way to integrate information about the complexity and interactive nature of the symptom experience" (p. 146). Hutchinson and Wilson (1998) also stress the importance of the model in encouraging nurses to design interventions in a way that takes into account the interactive nature of symptoms, influencing factors, and consequences, thereby making them client-specific. In its most recent version, the TOUS emphasizes the interplay among influential factors, symptoms, and performance outcomes; thus, it encourages creative thinking about new and different approaches to symptom management. Several clinicians have described it as having intuitive appeal because it is relatively straightforward, easy to understand and apply, and focused on relevant concerns.

CONCLUSIONS

Following a recent systematic review of studies examining symptoms in adults with lung cancer, Cooley (2000) concluded that there was a decided lack of explicit theoretical frameworks used to guide research. The Theory of Unpleasant Symptoms, which was grounded in clinical research and practice, is a midrange theory that holds considerable promise as a basis for additional research and as a guide to nursing practice. Although it is one of the few recent mid-range theories that have undergone revision based on empirical findings (Liehr & Smith, 1999), the TOUS remains a work in progress. The updated version addressed several of the weaknesses of the original; however, we recognize that selected aspects of the theory remain underdeveloped. Subsequent development has been relatively piecemeal, undertaken in response to specific published critiques or applications of the theory. The authors are committed to continued development and publication of updates.

The changes that were made to the theory in the revision added to the complexity of the model but also made it more consistent with the complex reality that constitutes the symptom experience. They have largely received empirical validation in several ill (heart failure, cancer, COPD, end-stage renal failure) and well (breastfeeding mothers, pregnant women) samples. Thus far, the symptoms that have been described in these studies have included pain, dyspnea, nausea and vomiting, and fatigue. Clearly, more research is needed in additional clinical populations and with additional symptoms. The current research suggests that the symptom dimensions identified in the TOUS are both relevant and measurable.

Additional conceptual/theoretical work is needed as well to address several of the issues that have been pointed out by investigators who have used the theory. For example, Hutchinson and Wilson (1998) used it to investigate both signs and symptoms. The TOUS has been framed thus far to focus on the subjective symptom experience, rather than on objective indicators of illness. The extent to which it can be extended to include signs, in addition to symptoms, needs to be examined. Likewise, its potential applicability to subjects or patients who have perceptual deficits, or are unable to describe the symptom experience (e.g., infants or unconscious patients) has been assumed, but has not yet been fully explored.

The complex relationships among the three categories of influencing factors and between these factors and the symptom experience need much fuller elaboration, and the categories themselves need continuing clarification. Although the potential relevance of all three types of factors has been quite well supported, there are some inconsistencies that need to be examined. For example, while one study did not find situational factors to be related to symptom intensity (McCann & Boore, 2000), another found them to be of paramount importance in Alzheimer's patients (Hutchinson & Wilson, 1998). The most influential factors need to be identified and the nature of their complex relationships to the symptom experience explicated. Psychologic influential factors have been found repeatedly to play a key role in exacerbating or mitigating symptoms; however, there is potential for conceptual and empirical overlap between psychological states (anxiety and depression in particular) and the affective or distress component of the symptom experience. The interplay between these two model components needs to be examined.

Finally, the performance component of the model needs additional development. Several of the investigations have revealed it to be more complex than originally thought. The notions of primary and secondary outcomes and temporally proximal and distal outcomes need to be incorporated in the model. Although the functional, pragmatic focus of the performance outcome was chosen purposefully, it does deemphasize other, more inclusive outcomes that may be important consequences of the symptom experience. Quality of life is a prime example. Functioning is generally a component of quality of life, but the latter is more inclusive. Its possible place within the TOUS is a topic that needs to be explored conceptually and empirically.

As was pointed out in the original description of the process that was used to develop the TOUS, it has been and continues to be the product of an exciting group interaction. Multiple, practice-grounded observations, contemplations, and lively discussions have led to its continued development. Its richness can only increase as the developers continue to address the input of others who have used the theory in research and practice.

REFERENCES

Auvil-Novak, S. E. (1997). A middle-range theory of chronotherapeutic intervention for postsurgical pain. *Nursing Research, 46,* 66–71.

Brown, S. J. (1996). Letter to the editor. *Advances in Nursing Science, 18*(4), vi.

Cooley, M. (2000). Symptoms in adults with lung cancer: A systematic research review. *Journal of Pain and Symptom Management, 19,* 137–153.

Dabbs, A. D., Dew, M. A., Stilley, C. S., Manzetti, J., Zullo, T., Kormos, R. L., & Iacono, A. (2000, March). *Psychosocial vulnerability, physical symptoms and physical impairment after lung and heart-lung transplantation.* Paper presented at Eastern Nursing Research Society annual meeting, State College, PA.

Dodd, M., Janson, S., Facione, N., Fawcett, J., Froelicher, E. S., Humphreys, J., Lee, K., Miaskowski, C., Puntillo, K., Rankin, S., & Taylor, D. (2001). Advancing the science of symptom management. *Journal of Advanced Nursing, 33,* 668–676.

Gift, A. G. (1990). Dyspnea. *Nursing Clinics of North America, 25,* 955–965.

Gift, A. G. (1991). Psychological and physiological aspects of acute dyspnea in asthmatics. *Nursing Research, 40,* 196–199.

Gift, A. G., & Cahill, C. (1990). Psychophysiologic aspects of dyspnea in chronic obstructive pulmonary disease: A pilot study. *Heart & Lung, 19,* 252–257.

Gift, A. G., & McCrone, S. H. (1993). Depression in patients with C.O.P.D. *Heart & Lung, 22*(4), 289–297.

Gift, A. G., & Pugh, L. C. (1993). Dyspnea and fatigue. *Nursing Clinics of North America, 28,* 373–384.

Good, M. (1998). A middle-range theory of acute pain management: use in research. *Nursing Outlook, 436,* 120–124.

Hutchinson, S. A., & Wilson, H. S. (1998). The theory of unpleasant symptoms and Alzheimer's disease. *Scholarly Inquiry for Nursing Practice, 22,* 143–158.

Larson, P. J., Carrieri-Kohlman, V., Dodd, M. J., Douglas, M., Fawcett, J., Froelicher, E., Gortner, S., Halliburton, P., Janson, S., Lee, K. A., Miaskowski, C., Savedra, M., Stotts, N., Taylor, D., & Underwood, P. (1994). A model for symptom management. *Image: Journal of Nursing Scholarship, 26,* 272–276.

Lenz, E. R., Pugh, L. C., Milligan, R., Gift, A., & Suppe, F. (1997). The middle-range theory of unpleasant symptoms: An update. *Advances in Nursing Science, 19*(3) 14–27.

Lenz, E. R., Suppe, F., Gift, A. G., Pugh, L. C., & Milligan, R. A. (1995). Collaborative development of middle-range nursing theories: Toward a theory of unpleasant symptoms. *Advances in Nursing Science, 17*(3) 1–13.

Lenz, E. R., Suppe, I., Gift, A. G., Pugh, L. C., & Milligan, R. A. (1996). Letter to the editor: Response to Brown. *Advances in Nursing Science, 18*(4), vi–vii.

Liehr, P., & Smith, M. J. (1999). Middle range theory: Spinning research and practice to create knowledge for the new millennium. *Advances in Nursing Science, 21*(4) 81–91.

McCann, K., & Boore, J. R. P. (2000). Fatigue in persons with renal failure who require maintenance haemodialysis. *Journal of Advanced Nursing, 32,* 1132–1142.

Milligan, R. A. (1989). Maternal fatigue during the first three months of the postpartum period. *Dissertation Abstracts International, 50,* 07B.

Milligan, R. A., Flenniken, P., & Pugh, L. C. (1996). Positioning intervention to minimize fatigue in breastfeeding women. *Applied Nursing Research, 9,* 67–70.

Milligan, R. A., Lenz, E. R., Parks, P. L., Pugh, L. C., & Kitzman, H. (1996). Postpartum fatigue: Clarifying a concept. *Scholarly Inquiry for Nursing Practice, 10,* 279–291.

Milligan, R. A., Parks, P. L., & Lenz, E. R. (1996, June). *Testing the theory of unpleasant symptoms.* Paper presented at the American Nurses' Association Council for Nursing Research Scientific Session, Washington, DC.

Parks, P. L., Lenz, E. R., Milligan, R. A., & Han, H. R. (1999). What happens when fatigue lingers for 18 months after delivery? *Journal of Obstetric, Gynecologic, and Neonatal Nursing, 28*(1), 87–93.

Parshall, M. B., Welsh, J. D., Brockopp, D. Y., Heiser, R. M., Schooler, M. P., & Cassidy, K. B. (2001). Dyspnea duration, distress, and intensity in emergency department visits for heart failure. *Heart & Lung, 30,* 47–56.

Pugh, L. C. (1990). Psychophysiologic correlates of fatigue during childbearing. *Dissertation Abstracts International, 51,* 01B.

Pugh, L. C., & Milligan, R. A. (1993). A framework for the study of childbearing fatigue. *Advances in Nursing Science, 15*(4), 60–70.

Pugh, L. C., & Milligan, R. A. (1995). Patterns of fatigue during pregnancy. *Applied Nursing Research, 8,* 140–143.

Pugh, L. C., & Milligan, R. A. (1998). Nursing intervention to increase the duration of breastfeeding. *Applied Nursing Research, 11,* 190–194.

Pugh, L. C., Milligan, R. A., & Brown, L. P. (2001). The breastfeeding support team for low-income predominantly minority women: A pilot intervention study. *Health Care for Women International, 22,* 501–515.

Pugh, L. C., Milligan, R. A., Frick, K. D., Spatz, D., & Bronner, Y. (2002). Breastfeeding duration and cost effectiveness of a support program for low-income breastfeeding women. *Birth, 29*(2), 95–100.

Pugh, L. C., Milligan, R. A., & Lenz, E. R. (2000). Response to "Insomnia, Fatigue, Anxiety, Depression, and Quality of Life of Cancer Patients Undergoing Chemotherapy." *Scholarly Inquiry for Nursing Practice, 14,* 291–294.

Redeker, N. S., Lev, E. L., & Ruggiero, J. (2000). Insomnia, fatigue, anxiety, depression, and quality of life of cancer patients. *Scholarly Inquiry for Nursing Practice, 14,* 275–290.

Rhodes, V., & Watson, P. (1987). Symptom distress—the concept past and present. *Seminars in Oncology Nursing, 3*(4), 242–247.

5

The Theory of Family Stress and Adaptation

Geri LoBiondo-Wood

efining family for the purpose of nursing research and practice is as complex as the range of families seen in society today. Attempts to visualize and identify what family is gives rise to many pictures, all with their own nuances and character. Yet, it is important to ground the conceptualization of a family to enable study. In the last half of the twentieth century, nurse family researchers have endeavored to explain through theory and research how some families, even amid misfortune, chaos, and tragedies, seemingly are able to cope and in some cases flourish. Explanation of family dynamics and what allows a family to grow and function across developmental levels and through normal and situational crises has led to the growth and the complexity of family theories and associated research.

A major area of work in family research has become known as family stress theory. The purpose of this chapter is to review a family stress framework known as the Double ABCX Model of Family Adaptation (McCubbin & Patterson, 1982, 1983a, 1983b). This middle range theory's purpose, major concepts and their relationship, and use in practice and research will be described.

PURPOSE OF THE THEORY AND HOW IT WAS DEVELOPED

To understand the Double ABCX Model, it is important to understand family stress theory. Family stress theory was originally developed by

Hill (1949, 1958), who, after World War II, studied families' responses to war, war separation, and eventual reunion. Hill's original ABCX family crisis model detailed three components, which produced a crisis, a stressor event, family's existing resources, and the family's perception of the stressor. How these three factors interacted indicated the crisis-proneness of the family. An important point to be understood as one reads the history of family stress theory is that the original work was based on the traditional nuclear family of mother, father, and children.

The Double ABCX Model (Figure 5.1) conceptualized by McCubbin and Patterson (1982, 1983a, 1983b) is an expansion of Hill's original model, which has its roots in sociology. To Hill's original model, postcrisis variables were added that predict family adaptation over time. The Double ABCX model has been used extensively to study family stressors such as chronic illness in children, cancer, and elder care. In order to emphasize adaptation as the key outcome of the Double ABCX Model, the extended model was renamed the Family Adjustment and Adaptation Response (FAAR) Model (Patterson, 1988, 1989).

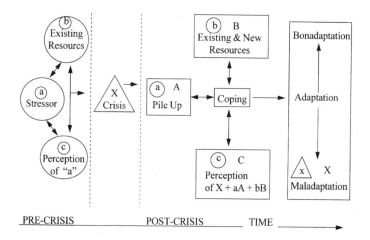

FIGURE 5.1   Double ABC-X Model of family adaptation.

Note: Reprinted with permission from: McCubbin, H. I., & Patterson, J. M. (1983). The family stress process: The double ABCX model of adjustment and adaptation. *Marriage and Family Review,* 6(7), 7–37.

As the body of family stress research grew and the variability of families was recognized, additional extensions were added to the model that focused on the key role that family types, strengths, and capabilities played in the understanding of family behavior. The extensions led to the development of another version of the family stress model called the T-Double ABCX Model of Family Adjustment and Adaptation. This model underscored the importance of family patterns of functioning for adjustment and adaptation (McCubbin & McCubbin, 1987).

The most recent conceptualization of the model was put forth to emphasize resiliency and includes Hill's ABCX Model, the Double ABCX Model and the FAAR model (McCubbin & McCubbin, 1988, 1993, 1996). All of these conceptualizations add important pieces to the puzzle of what the family is and how it functions and adapts in periods of tranquility as well as upheaval. The process of adaptation is active and includes the family's immediate environment and community relationships. McCubbin and McCubbin (1996) have outlined five overarching assumptions that underpin the middle range theory. These assumptions are:

1. Families over the course of life face hardships and changes as a natural and predictable aspect of family life.
2. Families develop basic competencies, patterns of functioning and capabilities to foster the growth and development of family members and the family unit, and to protect the family from major disruptions in the face of transitions and changes.
3. Families develop basic and unique competencies, patterns of functioning, and capabilities designed to protect the family from unexpected or non-normative stressors and strains and to foster the family's recovery following a family crisis or major transition or change.
4. Families draw from and contribute to the network of relationships and resources in the community, including its ethnicity and cultural heritage, particularly during periods of family stress and crises.
5. Families faced with crisis situations demanding changes in the family's functioning work to restore order, harmony and balance even in the midst of change. [p. 14]

The focus of this chapter will be on the Double ABCX Model of Family Adaptation (McCubbin & McCubbin, 1996). As noted in the description of historical roots, this middle range theory was the first expansion of Hill's original work. The use of the Double ABCX Model alone versus the use of its extensions is a source of discussion (McCubbin & McCubbin, 1996). The original Double ABCX Model is straight-forward in the definition of its variables and has many tested measures for research and clinical purposes, but it is possible to argue that ignoring the extensions may well be ignoring the highly complex and diverse processes and types of families seen in practice. An important consideration when choosing among the models and the model's extensions for research purposes is to follow the rule, as always, of carefully thinking through the problem that the research intends to explore and selecting a framework consistent with the problem being investigated. After careful consideration of the question within the area of family stress theory, one can choose from this rich theoretical base.

For me, the choice was made after I had spent time with children who had received a transplant or who were waiting for a transplant. I was especially aware of the transplant experience as it affected the families of these children. I found there was little literature on the family impact of having a child receive a transplant. Therefore, interventions and caring strategies that could be used to educate and support families throughout this long-term process were lacking. In order to systematically develop this area I began to think about designing a research program. The first step was to explore the short- and long-term family impact of having a child who received a transplant so that later work could include development of research-based interventions for children and their families.

Research not only needs a clear question but it also needs a clear theory base that is consistent with the problem. This need took me to the literature about family theories and their roots. There were certain elements that I was searching for: (1) the theory had to fit or complement nursing, (2) it had to address the individual in the family as well as the family unit, (3) it had to conceptualize the family as a unit of interacting individuals, (4) it had to be multifactorial in nature, (5) it had to address strengths as well as weaknesses, and (6) it had to address the adaptability of families. In my practice I saw the continued adaptability of families who were confronted with seeking a transplant for their child. I narrowed my search to a family stress and coping approach, and within this area I found the McCubbin Double ABCX Model. This framework was well developed, had been tested in instances both of health and illness, took into account family strengths and weaknesses, and both individual (mother and father) and family adaptability could be assessed. Multiple-tested instruments were available that were consistent with the model. The Double ABCX model met the criteria I had established and offered a testable structure to guide my research.

CONCEPTS OF THE THEORY

The key concepts of the Double ABCX Model are depicted in Figure 5.1. Each of the concepts contributes either positively or negatively to the family's ability to adjust and adapt. Each of the concepts is presented and discussed from the perspective of the theory.

Stressor (A)

The stressor was originally defined by Hill (1958) as a stressor event and later extended by McCubbin and Patterson (1983a, 1983b) as the "life event" or transition impacting the family unit that produces, or has the potential of producing, change in the family social system" (McCubbin & Patterson, 1983b, p. 8). The change can occur in any aspect of the family's life, for example in its roles, functions, or goals. Though not depicted in the model, discussion of stressors is often accompanied by discussion of hardships, which are the demands placed on the family that must be met as a result of the stressor event.

Existing Resources (B)

All families have some level of resources. The concept of existing resources is the family's use of community as well as intrafamilial coping resources. For instance, the parents' level of education and socioeconomic status serve as major resources in their efforts to maintain balance. Within the framework the stressor is viewed as interacting with the family's use of resources, which act as a buffer for resisting crisis. The resources in the family may be adequate or inadequate, depending on the nature of the stressor event or the family's level of functioning.

Perception of the Stressor (C)

The perception of the stressor is defined by Hill (1958) and McCubbin and Patterson (1983a, 1983b) as the meaning the family assigns to the crisis event and the total circumstances that lead to the crisis. How well a family is able to clarify the problem, grasp its parts, and understand the situation's tasks as controllable, contributes to the family's problem-solving ability. There are objective cultural views of a stressor's significance, but what matters within the family is the family's subjective interpretation of the event's effect. The variable of perception focuses on whether the family views the stressor as a manageable challenge or if they view it as unmanageable, with the potential for initiating family disintegration. Within the model, stress is distinct from a stressor. Whereas a stressor is an event, stress is a state of demand that arises from an actual or perceived demand–capability imbalance in the family's functioning (McCubbin & Patterson, 1983a, 1983b). Stress varies and can affect the family both psychologically and physiologically.

Crisis (X)

The crisis is the demand for change. It is a continuous variable that reflects the sum of the family's disorganization, turmoil, and disruption triggered by an event (Burr, 1973). Within the model the crisis is regarded as the family's inability to maintain stability due to the continuous struggle of the situation. The stressor (a), interacting with the resources (b) and the family perception of the stressor or how the family defines the stressor (c), produces the crisis (x) (Hill, 1949, 1958). If a family has the ability to meet the demands of a stressor event then a crisis may be averted.

Pile-up (aA Factor)

Pile-up is the effect of managing changes, strains, and stressors over time. The stressors families deal with change and accumulate, affecting each member. This concept was added in the extension of Hill's model to the Double ABCX Model. The idea of pile-up was based on longitudinal research in families where a father/husband was held prisoner or was missing in action during the Vietnam War (McCubbin & Patterson, 1983a, 1983b). The findings of this research suggested that families facing a stressor event experience phases of adjustment and adaptation exemplified by a range of processes in which the variables or factors of the model interact. The Double ABCX Model of Adaptation and Adjustment was conceptualized from the perspective that families rarely are managing a single event or stressor, but, in fact, manage a pile-up of stressors and strains over time. The demands may arise as a result of an individual in the family, the family system, and/or from the community in which the family resides. The demands are a result of the initial stressor and the resultant pressures of the stressor. McCubbin and Patterson (1983a, 1983b) suggest that five types of stressors contribute to a pile-up:

1. The initial crisis with its resultant need for role change, new adjustments and hardships, and realignment of family functions.
2. Normative transitions that occur concomitantly with the stressor event such as usual family developmental milestones, parenthood, adolescence, and dual career issues.
3. Prior strains or earlier strains that a family may not have fully resolved may emerge at the time of a new crisis. The prior strains may not necessarily be a one-time event but the result of long-developed patterns that come to the forefront disruptively in the time of crisis.
4. As the family or a family member tries to cope with the crisis others in the family may disapprove of the behavior change, adding to the strain of the situation.
5. Within a stressor there is ambiguity. It can be either intrafamily and lead to concern about the structure, roles, and functions of the family within, or it can be social and related to how the family is viewed in society at large.

Existing and New Resources (bB)

Existing and new and expanded resources allow the family to adapt and meet demands and needs. Usual mechanisms of support are the existing resources. A family in the face of a crisis will call on existing resources in order to prevent an event from creating further crisis. Expanded family resources are new resources strengthened or developed in response to the crisis or as a result of the pile-up of stressors. In a longitudinal study of families with children with cerebral palsy, McCubbin and Patterson (1982) identified four types of resources that strengthened or developed in response to the crisis situation. These included:

1. Self-reliance—personal resources of individual family members, such as self-esteem
2. Family integration—internal workings of the family that assist members, such as communication patterns
3. Social support—family members' knowledge that they are cared for, loved, valued, and belong to a network of mutual understanding and responsibility. Social support is considered the most important resource.
4. Collective group support (including group action)—networks of family, friends, and community beyond the immediate family group, who provide support.

Family Perception of the Stressor (cC)

The family's view, definition, and significance given to the stressor and its resultant hardships, the pile-up of stressors, and the meaning the family attaches to the total situation define the family's perception of the stressor. A family that aims at comprehending the meaning of the situation, can minimize the psychological toll related to the crisis, and can assist its members in managing the crisis is more able to cope, use and develop resources, and adapt. The family's perception of the crisis is a key element and becomes a central factor of family coping.

Coping

Coping is an active process encompassing the use of existing and new resources that help to strengthen the family unit, reduce the impact of the stressors, and enhance the family's perception of the crisis and its resultant behavioral responses. In the Double ABCX Framework coping with the crisis is related to adaptation. Coping has both behavioral and cognitive elements. Parents' coping strategies are an important management resource during a family crisis. Coping allows the family to eliminate, reduce, or avoid stressors and strain, manage the situation, and implement changes where necessary in order to maintain the family system. Coping then becomes a bridging concept in which the family's efforts are directed at managing situation stressors and facilitating family movement toward adaptation and adjustment.

Adaptation (xX)

Adaptation, the outcome variable in this middle range theory, means that the family has accommodated, compromised, and, through its inner workings, regulated and given meaning to a crisis. Family adaptation is considered at the individual family member level, the family system level, and the family as part of the community level. Each of these levels has demands and capabilities. Adaptation is realized when there is a balance between one of the levels with another. Family coherence, which is the ability of the family to balance the elements depicted in the model of the theory, is a core component of adaptation.

Adaptation exists as a continuum from bonadaptation to maladaptation. Bonadaptation is positive and occurs when the family has achieved a balance and has minimized the discrepancy between its resources and demands and has used coping strategies to accept and understand the meaning of the crisis within the family's system. This balance gives the family a sense of coherence. Maladaptation is the negative end of the continuum and is typified by family imbalance. The family that presents as maladaptive exhibits physical or psychological ill health, and deterioration in family integrity and family functioning.

RELATIONSHIPS AMONG THE CONCEPTS: THE MODEL

The process that the theory's model depicts is viewed as an interactive process of system-environment fit over time (see Figure 5.1). Based on research (McCubbin, Dahl, Lester, & Ross, 1977; McCubbin, Hunter, & Metres, 1974), the recognition that the family is not stagnant, and that crises have long-term implications, the Double ABCX Model was extended to include three stages of adaptation. These stages are resistance, restructuring, and consolidation. They were used to reconceptualize and extend the Double ABCX Model into the Family Adjustment and Adaptation Response (FAAR) Model. The processes in the model emphasize the importance of the element of time for the family and suggests that families do not move in a linear manner from crisis to adaptation. For an extensive discussion of the FAAR model and other additions to the Double ABCX Model, the reader is referred to the many works that have been published by the Center for Excellence in Family Studies at the University of Wisconsin—Madison and the publication *Resiliency in Families* (McCubbin, Thompson, & McCubbin, 1996).

Double ABCX Model—Strengths and Limitations

The Double ABCX Model has multiple strengths and limitations. Among the model's strengths are the fact that it is a tested middle range theory that focuses on the family as a whole and allows for measurement of multiple family variables. These variables are linked by conceptual definitions. All variables have been operationally defined with instruments that have been tested widely for their psychometric properties, and all have more than one measure that can be used to test each concept.

On the negative side, it has been noted that the model has a large number of concepts and that with all its extensions, the variables are sometimes not distinguished well from each other. For example, it has been noted that family resources overlap with family problem solving and coping (Rungreangkulkij & Gilliss, 2000). Earlier, Walker (1985), while emphasizing the importance of the framework, pointed out that individual resources are interchangeable with family resources even though they are conceptually distinct; she further suggested that an event-specific stressor may not be an adequate conceptualization because it is too narrowly focused. The crisis event, if viewed more broadly as a situation, allows for a more expanded view of the concept of crisis. McCubbin and McCubbin (1996) have stated that the crisis is not necessarily event specific but an imbalance that can be the result of a normative or developmental situation or of a traumatic situation that called the family members into action. Therefore, if one views the family and the work of the family as a process, one cannot say that it is one event that leads to a crisis but rather several components of a situation and how a family adjusts. In the later iterations of the model the crisis event has been minimized and the picture of the family and its resiliency in response to a situation has become a stronger focus.

Because of the number of variables in the model's extension and because of the overlapping of some of the concepts, it is important for researchers to clearly identify and define the variables being tested, the parts of the model that are being tested or which iteration of the model is being tested, and if the total model is being studied.

The clarity of these components will indicate which of the many measures for testing is the most appropriate and what type of analysis will be required. As more model variables are added to a study, the complexity of analysis increases, and the ability to be conceptually clear promises more meaningful research. Rungreangkulkij and Gilliss (2000) alert researchers to the challenge of multicolinearity and the use of complex statistical analysis when using the model to guide research.

USE OF THE THEORY IN NURSING RESEARCH

The Double ABCX Model has sometimes been used as a theoretical framework as a whole. For instance, McCubbin (1988) used the model to study family stress, resources and family types in families with chronically ill children; and later compared single-parent and two-parent families with handicapped children using the Typology Model, an expansion of the Double ABCX Model. McCubbin (1988) found no significant differences between single parent and two parent families in the accumulation of stressors and demands, resource strains, family types, family cohesion, family resources of esteem/communication, mastery/health, extended social support, and child health indices of physical health status. Single-parent families had significantly lower financial cooperation and situational optimism. This study matched families on the child's handicap severity and the parent's age and gender.

More often than not studies select and study specific variables from the model rather than the whole model. Van Riper (2000) used the resiliency extension of the model to guide her examination of the relationships among family demands, family resources, family problem-solving communication, coping, and sibling well-being in families of children with Down's syndrome. The instruments used, except for the measure of sibling well-being, were specifically developed for use when studying variables in the model. The results indicated that the siblings of Down's children had favorable self-concepts. Mothers reported that the siblings were socially competent and had a low level of behavioral problems. The family variables of demands, resources, problem solving, and coping were significantly related with at least one of the indicators of sibling well-being.

In another example of research using a limited set of the theory's variables, Suddaby, Flattery, and Luna (1997) used the Double ABCX Model but focused on measuring stress and coping among families awaiting their child's cardiac transplant. This study found parents' use of coping mechanisms decreased over a 3-month pretransplant period, yet overall stress remained at a moderate level and did not change significantly.

The Research of LoBiondo-Wood and Colleagues

The specific example of several studies from one research program that focused on children undergoing liver transplantation and their families will be described as framed within the Double ABCX Model. When an individual requires solid organ transplantation the processes involved in obtaining and maintaining the recipient's new organ affect the family as a whole. The stages before and after the transplant require adjustment and adaptation. Each stage of the process, for both the recipient and the family, has costs in terms of physical and psychological factors, time, money, and stress. LoBiondo-Wood and Williams conducted a study that used the Double ABCX Model (McCubbin & Patterson, 1983a, 1983b) as its guiding framework. In the study, only the postcrisis variables were measured in both the pretransplantation and posttransplantation periods. Data documenting these postcrisis findings will be reported, and the precrisis variables noted in the model will be discussed as related to the research (Figure 5.1).

Stressors (A)

By the time the parents of a child who needs a liver transplant make the decision with their care providers to seek a transplant evaluation and pursue transplantation, the child often has experienced multiple bouts of illness and/or surgery. The parents have had varying amounts of time to adjust to the idea that their child has a chronic and potentially fatal disease.

Existing Resources (B)

The existing resources for the family include use of community resources, parents' education level, and socioeconomic status. Availability of support from the extended family for a family entering the transplantation process is important.

Perception of the Stressor (C)

The meaning that the family gives to the child's illness and the help received from caregivers contribute to the family's definition of the stressor as easy or difficult.

Crisis (X)

The time until transplant and the impending needs and challenges that the family faces when seeking a transplant on behalf of their child constitutes the crisis.

Pile-up (aA)

For the family with a child with end-stage liver disease, the parents awaiting a transplant, and the parents who have a child who has received a transplant, stressors can be found at any point. The first type of stressor is inherent to the diagnosis and medical care needed in the face of recurring illnesses that accompany liver disease. Parents are told of long waiting lists and of the necessity of keeping the child as well as possible before the transplant; yet the parents also know that the sicker child receives a transplant first. Parents whose child is in the pretransplantation period may feel abandoned and forgotten. Other stressors include the family life changes and events that occur irrespective of the central stressor, such as child and parental developmental needs and job-related stressors. Stressors also pile up related to financial burdens, the feelings of loss of control, and the potential need to involve the public with fund raising. Long-term stressors include the uncertainty of the child's long-term prognosis and the painful affect that burdens parents of chronically ill children (Benning & Smith, 1994; Uzark, 1992).

Family Existing and New Resources (cC)

For families seeking and obtaining a transplant for their child, the network of resources and social support may vary over time. Potential support sources are family, friends, and community. Because of the long-term nature of the situation, the family, in order to adapt and adjust, must assimilate new resources and supports that will help them and the child before and after transplantation. During hospitalization, a strong network among the families and the health care team persists and can either serve as a source of support or reinforce stressors, such as would occur if one of the recipients in the network dies or needs retransplantation. Once the child is discharged and returns home old networks as well as newer ones must be maintained.

Perception of the Stressor (cC)

The process of seeking transplantation places multiple new stressors on an already stressed system; consequently, reframing and redefining the situation can occur over time. A family might perceive the diagnosis of a chronic and possibly fatal disease as a relief because it provides a label for the problem and a potential solution. The diagnosis also may be a threat because of the implications that the label brings with it. After transplantation parents voice concerns about whether their child will live and lead a normal life in light of the reality that liver transplantation does not cure the child's liver disease but rather trades the original disease for a new liver that requires lifelong care and has specific health needs (LoBiondo-Wood, Bernier-Henn, & Williams, 1992).

Coping

Coping requires the family to actively manage a variety of factors and situations at each stage of the transplant process. Coping is viewed as an active process of engaging management strategies, which may be psychological or behavioral. The movement to adjustment and adaptation is predicated on the assumption that the family has developed adaptive coping strategies.

Adaptation (xX)

The view of adaptation is based on McCubbin and Patterson's (1983a, 1983b) belief that adaptation is the continuum of outcomes toward which the family's efforts are directed. The process of adaptation is interactive over time. Though not using the Double ABCX Model, Mishel and Murdaugh (1987) found in a study of family adjustment one year following adult heart transplantation that family members initially thought that the patient would return to "normal" after the transplant. However, they found that adjustments were continually being made and the family member's belief of a return to normal was gradually eroded. In the process of reconceptualization and adjustment, the families became aware of the need to redefine the term *normal*.

In the LoBiondo-Wood, Williams, Kouzekanani, and McGhee (2000) study it was conceptualized that families seeking transplantation for their child live through an experience congruent with that depicted in the Double ABCX Model. Adaptation was not viewed as ending but as continuing over time. Before the transplant and after a successful transplant, the child and the parents have to cope, use resources, and deal with the stressors of the long-term situation. The pile-up of stressors at each stage of the process may lead to bonadaptation or maladaptation, depending on the family's ability to use new and old strategies.

In this study, after the variables were defined, instruments were chosen to measure them based on the conceptualization. The concepts of the ABCX Model, the variables, and the measurement instruments are outlined in Table 5.1. In the pretransplantation period the study found that higher family stressors, fewer coping skills, and higher perceptions of stress were related to more unhealthy family adaptation.

USE OF THE THEORY IN NURSING PRACTICE

Although technology has improved health care for individuals and families, the number of families with chronically ill members has increased. The variables of the Double ABCX Model focus on specific aspects of the illness trajectory that families experience. Therefore, the model can be useful in planning and implementing practice interventions. Before posing suggestions of how the model can be used in intervention it is necessary to mention some overall assumptions:

1. Stress in families is present, variable, and predictable in the situation of chronic illness.

TABLE 5.1 Instruments to Measure the Concepts of the Double ABCX Model

Concept	Measure	Number of items	Reliability*
aA Pile-up	Family Inventory of Life Events & Changes (FILE)	71	.78
bB Existing and New Resources	Family Inventory of Resource Management (FIRM)	69	.80
Coping	Coping Health Inventory for Parents (CHIP)	45	.89
cC Perception of the Stressor	Family Coping Coherence Index (FCCI)	4	.66
xX Adaptation	Family Adaptation Device (FAD)	60	.87

Source: LoBiondo-Wood, G., Williams, L., Kouzekanani, K., & McGhee, C. (2000). Family adaptation to a child's transplantation: Pretransplant phase. *Progress in Transplantation*, 10, 81–17.

2. All families have coping mechanisms that can mediate the processes of situations either positively or negatively.
3. Families' perception of the meaning of the chronic illness can affect their adaptation to the family member's illness.
4. Usual support systems must be supplemented with new support systems.
5. Family adaptation is not a stagnant outcome in the experience of chronic illness; each new phase of the illness requires the family to meet the challenges in order to maintain adaptation.
6. The family affects the individual and the individual affects the family in the processes of adaptation to chronic illness.

For nursing, these assumptions help to guide a practice that recognizes family needs beyond a one-time event or interaction. The model calls upon nurses not only to be able to understand the processes and stages of the illness, but also how families respond to the illness trajectory. Development of a short- and long-term plan for the individual and family, which includes physical and psychological illness parameters as well as attention to individual and family dynamics and health, is essential for a nurse guided by this middle range theory. As a plan is developed it is important to assess what aspects of the disease and the family dynamics present the most stress.

Each family member has unique strengths and vulnerabilities. Factoring each of these into a nursing practice plan is essential. The plan should incorporate strategies to enable family members to learn from each other, capitalize on each other's strengths, and be assistive when times of new illness-related crises arise. Coping has been referred to as a bridging concept; therefore assessing and planning for coping strategies is inherent to the plan. The practitioner caring for the individual and family experiencing a chronic illness is required to establish a long-term relationship built upon knowing the individual and the family. The long-term relationship rests on a foundation of trust ensuing as the nurse, the individual, and the family get to know each other over time.

CONCLUSIONS

The Double ABCX model and its multiple extensions has provided a wealth of instruments for testing family response to chronic illness. The model, extensions, and conceptual distinctions may seem cumbersome, but when the model is broken down and the elements that are consistent with a problem are delineated, the measurement and testing of hypotheses can be accomplished. The aim of using any model is to move its inherent ideas from testing to practice. To accomplish this end, prediction models need to be tested to determine which variables of the model and in what order best explain family adaptation.

Although a vast amount of theoretical and empirical work has been done since Hill introduced the model, there is still room for questions and development. The fit of ethnicity and culture needs further attention when testing the Double ABCX Model. Intervention studies that foster adaptation and adjustment are still necessary. How the instruments are analyzed in constructing a family picture with the vast variety of family types needs to be assessed. Instrument reliability and validity reports generally describe mothers' and fathers' scores separately rather than conceptualizing family scores or considering unique qualities of current family structures. In actuality, parents may be a male and a female, two individuals of the same gender, or two individuals from different generations within the family who coparent a child. This reality must be considered. Complex family structures require nurse researchers to clearly demonstrate how the family constellation is defined, how it can be addressed with the theory, and how the data will be interpreted. The realities of family research should not lead one to avoid the area but to embrace its multiple challenges and dynamic approaches.

REFERENCES

Benning, C. R., & Smith, A. (1994). Psychological needs of family members of liver transplant patients. *Clinical Nurse Specialist, 8,* 280–288.

Burr, W. F. (1973). *Theory construction and the sociology of the family.* New York: Wiley.

Hill, R. (1949). *Families under stress: Adjustment to the crises of war, separation, and reunion.* New York: Harper.

Hill, R. (1958). Generic features of families under stress. *Social Casework, 49,* 139–150.

LoBiondo-Wood, G., Bernier-Henn, M., & Williams, L. (1992). Impact of the child's liver transplant on the family: Maternal perspective. *Pediatric Nursing, 18,* 461–466.

LoBiondo-Wood, G., Williams, L., Kouzekanani, K., & McGhee, C. (2000). Family adaptation to a child's transplantation: Pretransplant phase. *Progress in Transplantation, 10,* 81–87.

McCubbin, H. I., Dahl, B. B., Lester, G., & Ross, B. (1977). The returned prisoner of war and his children: Evidence for the origin of second generational effects of captivity. *International Journal of Sociology of the Family, 7,* 25–36.

McCubbin, H. I., Hunter, E., & Metres, P. (1974). The adjustment of families of service men missing in action and prisoners of war: An overview. In: *Proceedings of the Army Current Trends Behavioral Science Conference.* Washington, DC: Department of the Army.

McCubbin, H. I., & McCubbin, M. A. (1987). Family stress theory and assessment: The T-Double ABCX Model of family adjustment and adaptation. In H. I. McCubbin & A. I. Thompson (Eds.), *Family assessment for research and practice* (pp. 3–34). Madison: University of Wisconsin—Madison.

McCubbin, H. I., & McCubbin, M. A. (1988). Typologies of resilient families: Emerging roles of social class and ethnicity. *Family Relations, 37,* 247–254.

McCubbin, H. I., & Patterson, J. M. (1982). Family adaptation to crises. In H. I. McCubbin, A. Cauble, & J. Patterson (Eds.), *Family stress, coping and social support* (pp. 26–47). Springfield, IL: Charles C Thomas.

McCubbin, H. I., & Patterson, J. M. (1983a). Family stress and adaptation to crises: A double ABCX model of family behavior. In D. Olson & B. Miller (Eds.), *Family studies review yearbook* (Vol. 1, pp. 87–106). Beverly Hills, CA: Sage.

McCubbin, H. I., & Patterson, J. M. (1983b). The family stress process: The double ABCX model of adjustment and adaptation. *Marriage and Family Review*, 6, 7–37.

McCubbin, H. I., Thompson, A. I., & McCubbin, M. A. (1996). *Family assessment: Resiliency, coping and adaptation.* Madison: University of Wisconsin Press.

McCubbin, M. A. (1988). Family stress, resources, and family types: Chronic illness in children. *Family Relations*, 37, 367–377.

McCubbin, M. A., & McCubbin, H. I. (1993). Family coping with health crises: The Resiliency Model of Family Stress and Adaptation. In C. Danielson, B. Hamel-Bissell, & P. Winstead-Fry (Eds.), *Families, health and illness* (pp. 21–63). New York: Mosby.

McCubbin, M. A., & McCubbin, H. I. (1996). Resiliency in families: A conceptual model of family adjustment and adaptation in response to stress and crises. In *Family assessment: Resiliency, coping and adaptation* (pp. 1–64). Madison: University of Wisconsin Press.

Mishel, M. H., & Murdaugh, C. L. (1987). Family adjustment to heart transplantation: Redesigning the dream. *Nursing Research*, 36(6), 332–338.

Patterson, J. M. (1988). Families experiencing stress. The family adjustment and adaptation response model. *Family System Medicine*, 6(2), 202–237.

Patterson, J. M. (1989). Illness beliefs as a factor in patient-spouse adaptation to coronary artery disease. *Family Systems Medicine*, 7(4), 428–442.

Rungreangkulkij, S., & Gilliss, C. L. (2000). Conceptual approaches to studying family caregiving for persons with severe mental illness. *Journal of Family Nursing*, 6, 341–366.

Suddaby, E. C., Flattery, M. P., & Luna, M. (1997). Stress and coping among parents of children awaiting cardiac transplantation. *Journal of Transplant Coordination*, 7, 36–40.

Uzark, K. C. (1992). Caring for families of pediatric transplant recipients: Psychosocial implications. *Critical Care Clinics of North America*, 4, 255–261.

Van Riper, M. (2000). Family variables associated with well-being in siblings of children with Down's Syndrome. *Journal of Family Nursing*, 6, 267–286.

Walker, A. (1985). Reconceptualizing family stress. *Journal of Marriage & Family*, 47(4), 827–837.

6

The Theory of Community Empowerment

Cynthia Armstrong Persily and Eugenie Hildebrandt

The community empowerment theory was developed to give direction to improving health in communities. The first conceptualization of the theory came out of participatory action research using an exploratory design. The middle range theory is a merging of empowerment and community development theory for promoting health by building relationships both at individual and community levels (Hildebrandt, 1994, 1996).

PURPOSE OF THE THEORY AND HOW IT WAS CREATED

The community empowerment middle range theory seeks to provide a framework for research and practice through development of effective interventions at individual and community levels. As such, it explicates for nursing the direct transfer of knowledge and expertise from nurse professionals to lay people to promote health. The theory was designed to structure a community involvement approach that enables community people to increase their knowledge and health care decision-making capabilities.

Persily has been involved for the past 20 years in the area of women's health and childbearing as a practitioner, educator, and researcher.

111

Her research has emphasized nursing care with high-risk pregnancy. Her previous research experience has been critical to the development of this middle range theory. Beginning in 1987, Persily participated as a research clinical nurse specialist at the University of Pennsylvania School of Nursing in the project entitled "Early Discharge and Nurse Specialist Transitional Care of Women with Diabetes in Pregnancy," funded by the National Center for Nursing Research. In this randomized clinical trial of early discharge, she provided the early discharge and follow-up intervention that was being tested as the independent variable. Her dissertation research came directly from the study and examined the relationship among women's perceptions of the impact of the diagnosis and treatment of high risk pregnancy and treatment adherence, help seeking from professionals, and outcomes. It was found that women who perceived a high life impact from their pregnancy were more likely to seek help from care providers regarding social, psychological, and economic issues than to seek help about how to care for themselves. This finding led to the idea that it may not be necessary for nurses to provide all interventions with an at-risk group of pregnant women; rather, a combination of professionals and other providers may be more appropriate (Persily, 1995). Persily built on her dissertation research, and began to design a study in which lay providers worked with health care professionals to offer services to pregnant women in rural communities. After a pilot study, it was determined that there was a need for broader community involvement, and thus began her search for a model to guide that involvement. In searching the literature relative to community involvement in health promotion, Persily discovered Hildebrandt's newly published work on a model and exemplar for community participation (Hildebrandt, 1996). Persily made contact with Hildebrandt, who had tested the model in a postapartheid city of 100,000 people in South Africa. The published model was used to guide research in four community-based interventions. Through a series of discussions, Persily and Hildebrandt agreed that adaptation of the Hildebrandt model could provide useful guidance if developed as a middle range theory of community empowerment.

MAJOR CONCEPTS OF THE THEORY

The middle range theory of community empowerment has three major concepts: involvement, lay workers, and reciprocal health. Community empowerment is the involvement of lay workers in the promotion of reciprocal health. Communities are multidimensional and complex, and tools that help people generalize experiences from one complex situation to another are especially valuable in these multifaceted settings. The middle range theory of community empowerment is a structure created to support this generalization of experiences. The authors firmly believe the words of Lewin (1951): "there is nothing more practical than a good theory" (p. 169). The community is the entity from which the nature and scope of a public health problem, as well as the capacity to respond to that problem, emerges (American Public Health Association, 1991). That is, the answers to health problems and the potential for improved health lie in the community. This premise is made clear in the *Healthy People 2010* goals, which charge individuals, organizations, and communities to take responsibility for determining how they will work singularly and collectively to achieve goals by the year 2010 (U.S. Department of Health and Human Services, 2000).

Involvement is linking a group of community people to identify their common ground of needs, resources, and barriers, and to build support or coalitions to mount a response to a problem through planning, carrying out, and maintaining interventions. Health care professionals facilitate involvement when they share information and control with community residents by teaching and supporting consumers in identifying and participating in the management of health problems for self, family, and community.

Lay workers are trained persons who share backgrounds with the families they visit. Unlike health care workers, lay workers are indigenous to the communities in which they work and are from similar cultural backgrounds. Their knowledge of community resources and values and their firsthand life experiences enable them to reach out to families not easily accessible to outsiders. Lay workers are a vital link to community programs for families at risk. They assist with access to health and social services, offer guidance, provide counseling, and share learned life skills with families. The use of lay workers to promote community health has been formalized through lay visiting programs. Home visiting, using a variety of providers including lay workers, increases the use of preventive services and encourages healthy behaviors (Blondel & Breart, 1995; Olds et al., 1997; Rogers, Peoples-Sheps, & Suchindran, 1996; Zotti & Zahner, 1995). Lay visiting programs are one means of meeting individual and community health care needs (Julnes, Konefal, Pindur, & Kim, 1994; LaPierre, Perrault, & Goulet, 1995; Mahon, McFarlane, & Golden, 1991; McFarlane & Wriist, 1997; Rogers, Peoples-Sheps, & Sorenson, 1995).

Reciprocal health is defined as the actualization of inherent and acquired human potential (Pender, Murdaugh, & Parsons, 2002) and is a desired outcome of community empowerment where the community and professionals engage to promote proactive healthy behaviors. Reciprocal health emerges when professionals and community residents work together, respecting and sharing what each has to offer, and thereby magnifying the potential for participants to manage their own health (World Health Organization, 1991a, 1991b). In contrast to reactive approaches that derive from an illness model, the concept of reciprocal health is positive and proactive, with communities participating to attain their highest potential (Israel, Checkoway, Schulz, & Zimmerman, 1994).

FOUNDATIONAL LITERATURE

Community development literature proposes that individuals and groups grow through community participant interaction and achievement of identified goals. The practice of community development is guided by models that advocate the support of people and communities to develop their strength and confidence while working on problems they have identified as important (Facet, Paine-Andrews, Francisco, & Schultz, 1995; Fiske, Hill, Krouskos, Legged, & Seagull, 1989). Community development models have been tested with varying results. Farley (1993) worked with an impoverished community in Alabama in a multigenerational project. Her qualitative intervention explored strategies of inclusion that fostered professional–citizen partnership. She focused on the problems that mattered most to community people. Farley's results indicated that traditional power structures and stakeholder desire to maintain the status quo were barriers to health promotion. She proposed that these results support the need for empowering community people so that sustainability of care delivery systems is built into the traditional power structure so that when outside care delivery personnel leave the community, new services will be maintained.

Several authors have proposed community interventions that promise enhanced health through enhanced empowerment. Swider and

McElmurry and colleagues (1995) developed a community empowerment intervention for use in two densely populated urban settings. Community health workers were trained to help mobilize community residents to improve health. The Community Health Worker curriculum included problem solving, exercises in group dynamics, skill development for working within political systems, and strategies to build self-reliance in order to facilitate change and empower participants. Building on this original empowerment intervention, McElmurry, Tyska, Gugenheim, Misner, and Poslusny (1995) used a leadership development approach where low to middle level agency staff people were educated to deliver the intervention and facilitate change. Findings in both studies indicated that traditional power structures in communities made change difficult to sustain.

Flynn and colleagues (Flynn, Ray, & Rider, 1994; Flynn, Rider, & Bailey, 1992) tested a community development model using action research. The assumptions underlying their model were:

1. the empowerment process can be learned
2. experiencing the process best accomplishes learning it
3. broad-based leadership from the community is more likely to be successful than localized–restrictive leadership

Flynn emphasized community leadership development, addressing the weaknesses described in previous studies of community development.

Zakus (1998) gathered data from 40 health centers to evaluate the community participation strategy that had been adopted by the Mexican government, which used volunteers to staff town-based centers and health outposts. Here, too, the power structure and status quo were barriers. The findings suggest that the communities were not encouraged to organize themselves, but instead the national Ministry of Health co-opted the resources of the communities to meet their objectives for expanding health services. The process increased rather than decreased community dependence on the Ministry of Health, thereby decreasing empowerment of the people.

Empowerment has been defined in a number of ways in the professional and lay literature. It is defined in the *Oxford English Dictionary* as "to invest, legally or formally, with power and authority, to impart or bestow power or authority, to impart or bestow power to an end or for a purpose, to enable, permit, to gain or assume power over" (1989, p. 192). Empowerment is the process of developing problem-solving capacity and self-competence by which people gain mastery over their lives. It is applicable at individual, family, and community levels. Empowerment is consistently emphasized by the World Health Organization (WHO, 1978) and widely advocated in primary health care as a critical component for improving the general health of vulnerable populations worldwide.

In the nursing literature, individual empowerment has been defined relative to the nurse–client dyad and as related to changes in health behaviors. Ellis-Stoll and Popkess-Vawter (1998) define individual empowerment as a "participative process through a nurse client dyad designed to assist in changing unhealthy behaviors" (p. 64). They further add that this process is designed to assist the client to develop proactive, healthy behaviors. Clifford (1992) believes empowerment is a process closely linked to caring and that caring for clients is intrinsic to the profession and important for the process to be successful. Rafael (1995) also links empowerment to the process of participation, defining it as "a process in which clients participate with nurse facilitators, with the desired outcome client control toward authentic self determination" (p. 25).

Because the concepts of empowerment and health are closely linked, an empowering partnership between health care providers and communities is vital for effective community health. When considering the concept of empowerment, it is important to recognize different views. Some sources distinguish between the process of empowering and that of becoming empowered. Others consider these processes as one and the same, and still others consider them as a type of cause and effect relationship. For example, the World Health Organization notes that community empowerment is thought to occur when professionals share information and control (empowering) with community residents in ways that result in neighborhoods and communities where people are effective participants in managing their own health care (empowered) (WHO, 1991a, 1991b). This is a cause–effect view, suggesting that becoming empowered is a result of empowering. Israel and colleagues (1994), on the other hand, do not distinguish between the two processes, when they define community empowerment as "the ability of people to gain understanding and control over personal, social, economic and political forces in order to take action to improve their life situations" (p. 152).

RELATIONSHIPS AMONG THE CONCEPTS: THE MODEL

The concepts, when considered together, demonstrate the potential for empowerment of community people through the involvement of lay workers in promoting reciprocal health (see Figure 6.1). Within any community, lay workers serve as resources that are used in addition to the traditional health care providers, thereby increasing access and extending opportunities for health promotion. In some rural communities and in developing countries, the lay worker is the only health care resource within the community. Lay workers and the health promotion opportunities they provide unite health care providers and the community to facilitate community involvement and attain reciprocal health.

USE OF THE THEORY IN NURSING RESEARCH

In Hildebrandt's (1994) participatory action studies in South Africa, she used an exploratory descriptive design to develop strategies to meet the health needs of black South Africans in a township setting. Representative cluster sampling was used to determine the needs and capacities of the South African elders and their families. Data were gathered through interviews by trained, paid persons who were indige-

FIGURE 6.1   Middle range theory of community empowerment.

nous to the community. The use of indigenous workers helped to diminish barriers engendered by distrust, race, and language. While the original intent of the study was to gather information about the growing elderly population and develop strategies directed at that group, the strategy directed by the research involved the multigenerational families of the elderly. The research intent changed to designing strategies for the elderly as a part of the community, and not as an isolated group. A process model of strategies based on the assumption that trust can be built on shared information, interaction, and partnership was developed. The steps of the model include:

1. Seek information
2. Seek support
3. Establish a work group to determine a plan and goals
4. Determine tasks, deadlines, and person responsible
5. Determine interim and start-up dates
6. Nurture the new program
7. Measure goals accomplished
8. Keep community informed of progress

Needs identified in the study clustered around health and nutrition, roles and status, economic resources, and community amenities. Once the needs were identified, the community prioritized them and chose the programs in partnership with the researcher. Four programs were developed and implemented. They included a health education and screening program to provide diabetes and hypertension screening and health education to the elderly community members; a literacy program, which initiated a library story hour to promote literacy among the young and demonstrate new roles for the elderly through intergenerational helping behaviors; a food gardening program to address the move away from traditional eating patterns experienced by the urban poor when they left their rural settings; and a nutrition education program to give community homemakers needed information about nutritionally sound, low cost foods. It was found that lay workers and health care personnel could effectively respond to basic human needs of all age groups in the community, there was a considerable investment of time and resources to introduce community involvement, and it was appropriate to empower lay people in the promotion of community health.

The authors are in the process of developing a randomized clinical trial entitled Rural Community Empowerment: Perinatal Outcomes and Costs. The study is based on the community empowerment theory. Its purpose is to compare maternal and infant outcomes and cost of care between two groups of rural women. The control group will receive routine prenatal care and the intervention group will receive care based on the community empowerment middle range theory. The intervention will be introduced in two stages. In the first stage (years 1–2$^1/_2$), Resource Mothers will serve as lay workers providing services to pregnant women. In the second stage (years 2$^1/_2$–4$^1/_2$), a Community Mentoring Board will be added to the Resource Mother intervention. Both the control and the intervention groups in both stages will be composed of rural pregnant women who seek care at one of the four participating rural health sites. The control group will receive prenatal care services that are routine for all women in the site. In the intervention group, women will be assigned to a Resource Mother at the time of their positive pregnancy test. Resource Mothers will visit women in their homes monthly throughout pregnancy and the first six months of the infant's life. In the second stage of implementation, Resource Mother services will be guided by a Community Mentoring Board who will partner with health care providers to assure that individual and community needs are met. Strategies will be shared across sites through quarterly meetings so that lay workers can learn from each other. Process evaluation will analyze the type of services provided by Resource Mothers in the first stage, and analyze the level of involvement of the community in the program in the second stage. It is proposed that involvement of lay workers (Resource Mothers) will lead to reciprocal health (maternal and infant outcomes, strengthened Resource Mothers and Community Mentoring Board), thus leading to community empowerment.

The specific questions to be answered in each stage of this study include:

1. What are the effects of an intervention guided by community empowerment theory on:
   A. *Maternal Outcomes:* Adequacy of prenatal care (month of prenatal care registration, gestational age, and number of prenatal care visits), changes in risk behaviors (smoking), nutritional status, incidence of preterm delivery, attendance at follow-up postpartum/family planning visits, maternal affect (anxiety, hostility and depression), satisfaction with prenatal care, repeat pregnancies at six months after delivery

B. *Infant Outcomes:* Gestational age, infant birth weight, well child checkups, immunization status, health status at six months of age
C. *Cost of Care:* Hospitalization (maternal and infant), prenatal/postnatal and infant care services, Resource Mothers program costs (intervention group)?
2. What are the major issues addressed during Resource Mothers' contacts with pregnant women?
3. What is the level of community and health professional involvement and responsibility in the Resource Mothers program over time?
4. Does the perceived level of empowerment among Resource Mothers and Community Mentoring Board members change over time?

The Community Mentoring Board (introduced in stage two of the intervention) guides the transfer of knowledge and information from health care professionals to lay women workers from the community (Resource Mothers), who, in turn, teach and support pregnant women who are at risk for reasons that include education deficits, poverty, race, gender or social bias, or living in deprived environments. Health professionals work with the Community Mentoring Board and the Resource Mothers to implement interventions for improving individual and community health outcomes. Resource Mothers involve the entire family in the interventions through home visiting, and are viewed as providers at the intersection of traditional health care and individual/community forces. As a critical interface between health promoting forces, Resource Mothers offer the possibility for managing barriers uncovered in early research. Interventions carried out by the Resource Mothers are targeted to individual problems with the intention of effecting intermediate and long-term health outcomes guided by the Community Mentoring Board and health care providers. It is anticipated, as the program develops, that this shift in power from the formal health care system to the community will lead to the outcome of empowered individuals and an empowered community. Study outcomes will provide important data about lay worker effects on perinatal outcomes and cost, major issues addressed, and interventions used by lay workers. Progression of the study will enable evaluation of the effects of the addition of a community mentoring board on perinatal outcomes and cost, the amount of involvement and responsibility assumed by rural communities, and the effects of the use of this theory on empowerment.

USE OF THE THEORY IN NURSING PRACTICE

There are many opportunities for use of the middle range theory of community empowerment in promoting reciprocal health in advanced practice nursing. For example, a rural family having no access for travel to prenatal or postnatal and infant care appointments would benefit from a lay worker who can identify a local church volunteer program to provide transportation and follow-up with the family. This interaction at the individual level offers to improve health for one family. If taken to the community level, recognition of a high incidence of missed prenatal, postnatal, and infant care appointments due to lack of transportation could launch a community intervention. Lay workers at the interface with health care providers and community could engage community members to identify the need for rural transportation, work with community agencies to generate funding proposals for a transportation program, work with local transportation services to evaluate routes and schedules, and access funding to accomplish improved transportation opportunities. Actualizing this opportunity means increased community competence. The community would be empowered to move on at a new level of accomplishment.

CONCLUSIONS

The community empowerment middle range theory highlights the link among theory, practice, and research to develop more effective nursing interventions. It is adapted from Hildebrandt's Community Involvement in Health Empowerment model that was designed and successfully pilot tested in primary health care research with a vulnerable Black population in South Africa and is the basis for research with vulnerable populations in the United States (Hildebrandt, 1994). Both the original conceptual model and the middle range theory incorporate the components of community empowerment and citizen participation that are central to Flynn's Healthy Cities work (Flynn et al., 1992, 1994). The community empowerment theory structures community participation with lay workers to promote reciprocal health. The potential of the theory lies in its dual approach of reducing the effect of limited access and limited health care resources in caring for vulnerable populations; and using unique, nontraditional ways to promote health.

The theory is presented here as a beginning foundation for future development through use in practice and research. Application of the theory in practice provides opportunities to maximize the potential of a community through achievements of outcomes related to the health of individuals and groups. Research questions derived from the theory will structure studies to examine relationships among the concepts that will lead to refinement of the theory.

REFERENCES

American Public Health Association. (1991). *Healthy communities 2000: Model standards for community attainment of the year 2000 national health objectives.* Washington, DC: Author.

Blondel, B., & Breart, G. (1995). Home visits during pregnancy: Consequences on pregnancy outcome, use of health services and women's situations. *Seminars in Gerontology, 19,* 263–271.

Clifford, P. (1992). The myth of empowerment. *Nursing Administration Quarterly, 16,* 1–5.

Ellis-Stoll, C., & Popkess-Vawter, S. (1998). A concept analysis on the process of empowerment. *Advances in Nursing Science, 21,* 62–68.

Facet, S., Paine-Andrews, A., Francisco, V., & Schultz, J. (1995). Using empowerment theory in collaborative partnerships for community health and development. *American Journal of Community Psychology, 23,* 677.

Farley, S. (1993). The community as partner in primary health care. *Nursing and Health Care, 14,* 244–249.

Fiske, G., Hill, A., Krouskos, D., Legged, D., & Seagull, O. (1989). The community development in health project. *Community Health Studies, 8,* 93–99.

Flynn, B., Ray, D., & Rider, M. (1994). Empowering communities: Action research through healthy cities. *Health Education Quarterly, 21,* 395–405.

Flynn, B., Rider, M., & Bailey, W. (1992). Developing community leadership in healthy cities: The Indiana model. *Nursing Outlook, 40,* 121–126.

Hildebrandt, E. (1994). A model for community involvement in health (CIH) program development. *Social Science Medicine, 39,* 247–254.

Hildebrandt, E. (1996). Building community participation in health care: A model and example from South Africa. *Image, 28,* 155–159.

Israel, B., Checkoway, B., Schulz, A., & Zimmerman, M. (1994). Health education and community empowerment: Conceptualizing and measuring perceptions of individual, organizational and community control. *Health Education Quarterly, 2,* 149–170.

Julnes, G., Konefal, M., Pindur, W., & Kim, P. (1994). Community based perinatal care for disadvantaged adolescents: Evaluation of the resource mothers program. *Journal of Community Health, 19,* 41–53.

LaPierre, J., Perreault, M., & Goulet, C. (1995). Prenatal peer counseling: An answer to the persistent difficulties with prenatal care for low income women. *Public Health Nursing, 12,* 53–60.

Lewin, K. (1951). *Field theory in social science: Selected theoretical papers*. New York: Harper.

Mahon, J., McFarlane, J., & Golden, K. (1991). De madres a madres: A community partnership for health. *Public Health Nursing, 8*, 15–19.

McElmurry, B. J., Tyska, C., Gugenheim, A. M., Misner, S., & Poslusny, S. (1995). Leadership for primary health care. *Nursing and Health Care: Perspectives on Community, 16*, 229–233.

McFarlane, J., & Wriist, W. (1997). Preventing abuse to pregnant women: Implementation of a mentor mother advocacy model. *Journal of Community Health Nursing, 14*, 237–249.

Olds, D., Eckenrode, J., Henderson, C., Kitzman, H., Powers, J., Cole, R., Sidora, K., Morris, P., Pettitt, L., & Luckey, D. (1997). Long term effects of home visitation on maternal life course and child abuse and neglect. *Journal of the American Medical Association, 278*, 637–643.

Oxford English dictionary (2nd ed.). (1989). Oxford, England: Oxford University Press.

Pender, N. J., Murdaugh, C. L., & Parsons, M. A. (2002). *Health promotion in nursing practice*. Upper Saddle River, NJ: Prentice Hall.

Persily, C. (1995). Helpseeking in high risk pregnancy: The role of the CNS. *CNS: The Journal of Advanced Practice, 9*, 207–220.

Rafael, A. (1995). Advocacy and empowerment: Dichotomous or synchronous concepts? *Advances in Nursing Science, 18*, 25–32.

Rogers, M., Peoples-Sheps, M., & Sorenson, J. (1995). Translating research into MCH service: Comparison of a pilot project and a large-scale resource mothers program. *Public Health Reports, 110*, 563–569.

Rogers, M., Peoples-Sheps, M., & Suchindran, C. (1996). Impact of a social support program on teenage prenatal care use and pregnancy outcomes. *Journal of Adolescent Health, 19*, 132–140.

Swider, M., & McElmurry, B. (1990). A women's health perspective in primary health care: A nursing and community health worker demonstration project in urban America. *Family and Community Health, 13*, 1–17.

U.S. Department of Health and Human Services. (2000). *Healthy people 2010* (conference edition, in two volumes). Washington, DC: Author.

United States General Accounting Office. (1990, July). *Home visiting: Promising early intervention strategy for at risk families*. (GAO/HRD-90-83). Washington, DC: U.S. Government Printing Office.

World Health Organization. (1978). Declaration of Alma-Ata. *World Health, 28*–29.

World Health Organization. (1991a). *Environmental health in urban development*. Technical Report Series, No. 807. Geneva: Author.

World Health Organization. (1991b). *Community involvement in health development: Challenging health services*. Technical Report Series, No. 809. Geneva: Author.

Zakus, J. (1998). Resource dependency and community participation in primary health care. *Social Science & Medicine, 46*, 475–494.

Zotti, M., & Zahner, S. (1995). Evaluation of public health nursing home visits to pregnant women on WIC. *Public Health Nursing, 12*, 294–304.

7

The Theory of Meaning

Patricia L. Starck

A theory of meaning based on the work of Viktor E. Frankl was developed primarily to treat individuals with psychiatric or psychological disorders. It has been expanded to assist the average human being to cope with everyday stresses of life and catastrophic, life-changing events. It has also evolved past the individual level for use with groups, and applies to the level of community/society.

PURPOSE OF THE THEORY AND HOW IT WAS CREATED

In Europe during Frankl's professional era, a precise set of assumptions and philosophy was called a school of thought rather than a theory. Thus, Frankl, as a Viennese psychiatrist and neurologist, studied in the First School of Viennese Psychiatry, known as the Will to Pleasure, espoused by Freud. Later, the Second School, or the Will to Power, developed by Adler, came into vogue. Frankl (1978) acknowledged the worth of Freud and Adler, as well as behaviorists who followed, but believed that

> Man can no longer be seen as a being whose basic concern is to satisfy drives and gratify instincts or, for that matter, to reconcile id, ego and superego; nor can the human reality be understood merely as the outcome of conditioning processes or conditioned reflexes. Here man is revealed as a being in search of meaning—a search whose futility seems to account for many of the ills of our age. [p. 17]

Frankl called his theory the Will to Meaning, and it became known as the Third School of Viennese Psychiatry. He postulated that human beings are motivated to seek answers to such questions as "Why am I here?," and went on to develop treatment, which he termed *logotherapy*, the practice of helping people find meaning and purpose in life, no matter what their life circumstances.

There is a common misperception that Frankl's theory emerged as a result of his internment in German concentration camps during World War II. This misperception was a source of irritation to Frankl as he clarified that in actuality, he formulated his ideas about meaning in life when he was a young child, with his first clear understanding at age 5. After his medical education he planned to write a book about the theory. However, the plan was interrupted when he was seized by the Nazis in Germany and imprisoned (Fabry, 1991). During the concentration camp experience, he validated the theory. He found that in spite of great suffering, survival behaviors were more evident in those who had a strong reason to live than in those who did not. Frankl preserved the theory by recreating a manuscript he had lost when he was imprisoned. During his internment at four different concentration camps over a $2^1/_2$ year period, he wrote on scraps of paper to keep his mind focused on his reason to survive. After his release at the end of World War II, he published the book that was later titled *Man's Search for Meaning*, under the title *From Death Camp to Existentialism*. In the book he described his experience in prison, detailing the unimaginable sufferings of the imprisoned. He began to develop his concept of human suffering by defining suffering as a challenge. In the experience of suffering, the challenge to the individual is to decide how to respond to unavoidable, deplorable life circumstances. It is an opportunity to show courage and to behave decently in spite of circumstances. He coined the term *logotherapy* from the Greek word, *logos*, denoting meaning. Logotherapy is the practice of the theory, intended to assist individuals to find purpose in life regardless of circumstances.

Frankl's work has been examined in light of Kerlinger's (1973) criteria for a theory that describes, explains, and predicts human behavior (Starck, 1985a). The postulates are the central core of the theory and are generalized statements of truth that serve as essential underpinnings for this body of knowledge. The postulates follow:

A person's search for meaning is the primary motivation of life. This meaning is unique and specific in that it must and can be fulfilled by the person alone. [Frankl, 1984, p. 121]

A person is free to be responsible, and is responsible for the realization of the meaning of life, the *logos* of existence. [Frankl, 1961, p. 9]

A person may find meaning in life even when confronted with a hopeless situation, when facing a fate that cannot be changed. [Frankl, 1984, p. 135]

A person's life offers meaning in every moment and in every situation. [Fabry, 1991, p. 130]

The Theory of Meaning is a framework that lends itself to interdisciplinary endeavors. Frankl's work has been used as the basis for research and practice in many fields, including medicine, psychology, counseling, education, ministry, and nursing. Travelbee (1966, 1969, 1972) was the first nurse to use Frankl's work in practice. She used parables and other stories to help psychiatric patients realize that human suffering comes to all, and that we have the means to combat these problems, no matter the circumstances.

I had the great privilege of knowing Viktor E. Frankl, MD, PhD, over a twenty-year period, beginning when I was a doctoral student seeking ways to promote rehabilitation of spinal cord injured patients. I came upon Frankl's work and wrote to him. He responded and encouraged me, saying I would be the first to apply his theory and practice to physically disabled individuals. I met him in 1979 when I presented my dissertation, including the logotherapeutic nursing intervention I had designed, to the first World Congress of Logotherapy. I was deeply honored when he quoted my work in his publications and presentations.

I later received further training in Logotherapy from his protegee, Elizabeth Lukas, PhD, a logotherapist from Munich, Germany. I visited with Dr. and Mrs. Frankl in their home in Vienna, and received several treasured mementos—a photograph of him and me together, his sketches of our two profiles, and a reprint of one of his early publications.

I was pleased to invite him to come to the University of Texas Health Science Center at Houston in 1985, where he gave a 90-minute lecture to a packed auditorium. We made a videotape of this lecture, and another tape in which I interviewed him about human suffering. In this latter tape, we were joined by Jerry Long, a quadriplegic who became a doctorally prepared logotherapist after his injury at age 17. I saw Dr. Frankl at several more World Congresses until his health prevented his travel. Their only child, a daughter, became a logotherapist and carries on his work in Vienna. His two grandchildren have also developed their careers in ways to enhance his work.

Dr. Frankl died in 1996, the same week that Princess Diana of England and Mother Theresa of India died. His work goes on as educators, practitioners, and researchers from various disciplines continue to broaden and enrich his theory.

CONCEPTS OF THE THEORY

Three major concepts from Frankl's work, which are the building blocks of the theory, are life purpose, freedom to choose, and human suffering. These concepts are supported by three human dimensions: the physical or soma, the mental or psyche, and the spiritual or noos (Frankl, 1969). The physical and the mental dimensions can become ill and the spiritual dimension can become blocked or frustrated. To explain this three-dimensional assumption, Frankl (1969) described laws of dimensional ontology. He sought to illustrate the simultaneous ontological differences and the anthropological unity of these three dimensions by using geometrical structures as an analogy, to show qualitative differences while not destroying the unity of the structure. Dimensional ontology rests on two laws:

1. "One and the same phenomenon projected out of its own dimension into different dimensions lower than its own is depicted in such a way that the individual pictures contradict one another" (p. 23). For example, a cylinder when projected vertically would be perceived as a rectangle from the vertical view (from the side), but as a circle when projected as a horizontal view (from above). The meaning ascribed to the shape is relative to one's view. Therefore, this law articulates the complexity of dimensions emerging from a single phenomenon.
2. "Different phenomena projected out of their own dimension into one dimension lower than their own are depicted in such a manner that the pictures are ambiguous" (p. 23). This second law articulates the quality of potential sameness occurring when multiple distinct phenomena are viewed in relation to each other. For example, a cylinder, a cone, and a sphere all cast shadows as a circle when projected above onto a horizontal plane. It would be possible to ascribe the same meaning to each of these distinct shapes given a particular perspective.

Frankl's point is that while we have these three dimensions of soma, psyche, and noos, we can be both parts and a whole, and that from different points of view, different impressions and, therefore, different meanings, reveal themselves. He called attention to the fact that a problem in one dimension may show up as a symptom in another. For example, spiritual emptiness may manifest in a physiological symptom such as intense headaches. An important understanding when considering dimensional ontology is Frankl's emphasis on the human spirit, the noos, and the "defiant" power of the noos. Fabry (1991) interpreted this conceptualization as, "You *have* a body and a psyche, but you *are* your noos (spirit)" (p. 127). The human spirit can defy the odds and rise above the other dimensions. Examples of the power of the noos will be provided throughout this chapter as vignettes are shared and stories are told about people who excelled beyond expectations to accomplish extraordinary feats. The noos is essential to the pursuit of life purpose.

Life Purpose

Life purpose is the central concept of the theory of meaning. It is the summary of reasons for one's existence, answering the questions "Who am I?" and "Why am I here?" A sense of life purpose brings satisfaction with one's place in the world. Life purpose is that to which one may feel called and to which one is dedicated. There is a theme to one's life purpose—making a contribution, leaving the world a better place. The major premise of Frankl's theory is that the search for meaning in one's life is an overriding search for purpose. Life purpose flows from the "uniqueness of the person and the singularity of the situation" (Frankl, 1973, p. 63). Every person is "indispensable and irreplaceable" (Frankl, 1973, p. 117).

Fabry (1991) explained "meaning" from various existential viewpoints. The French existentialists, Sartre and Camus, believed that life itself had no meaning other than the meaning that humans gave to it. In contrast, the German existentialists, including Frankl, maintained that meaning exists and that the task is to discover it, and in discovering meaning one also discovers life purpose. Fabry emphasized that our human spirits are the instruments for finding a purpose in life through tapping the spiritual treasure in each of us. Frankl asserts that each person must discover his or her own meaning. It cannot be prescribed by another. A professional caregiver working with a person who has recently suffered a loss cannot tell the person how to look for meaning in another dimension of life, but can help to guide the person to find new avenues of meaning through shifting views of soma, psyche, and noos. "And meaning is something to be found rather than to be given, discovered rather than invented" (Frankl, 1969, p. 62).

Frankl (1984) postulated that meaning in life always changes but never ceases to be. He specified three different ways to find meaning on the path to uncovering life purpose: (1) by creating a work or doing a deed that moves beyond self, (2) by experiencing something or encountering someone, and (3) by the attitude we take toward our own fate. In the first way, a strong sense of purpose or meaning in life may be seen when a terminally ill person hangs on tenaciously to the achievement of some goal such as a child graduating from college. This will to meaning is a strong life force that can defy the odds given by the most expert clinician. Frankl (1984) also emphasized that our past achievements are monuments of meaning in our lives. "All we have done, whatever great thoughts we may have had, and all we have suffered, all this is not lost, though it is past; we have brought it into being. Having been is also a kind of being, and perhaps the surest kind" (p. 104). Fabry (1980) distinguished between "meaning of the moment" in everyday choices we make and "universal meaning," or the bigger picture that we may not completely understand at this time. Meaning of the moment is the everyday situation where one has a chance to act in a meaningful way through action, experiences, and the stand one takes. Ultimate meaning is the trust that there is order in the universe and that humans are part of that order; it is the opposite of seeing the world as chaotic and humans as the victims of whim.

Self-transcendence (Frankl, 1969) is related to life purpose. It is described as getting outside the self for a cause greater than the self. It is creating a work or doing a deed that reaches beyond one's egocentricity toward others, even though it may be difficult to do when life has been cruel (Fabry, 1991). Self-transcendence is contrasted with self-awareness. In self-awareness, the focus is internal such as guilt, past traumas, or other feelings. By contrast, self-transcendence is distancing from oneself. In the distancing, a different view of the situation comes to light along with a changed meaning of the situation. For example, parents who have lost a child to violence may put energy toward getting new legislation passed that will protect children and prevent the type of loss they have suffered from happening to others. The hardship is deliberately endured so that others may benefit. Self transcendence should not be confused with self-actualization as defined by Maslow (1968). Frankl (1975) stated that "what is called 'self-actualization' is ultimately an effect, the unintentional by-product of self-transcendence" (p. 78).

A second way to find meaning and enable life purpose is through experiences like loving or encountering another human being. Frankl believed that love goes beyond an individual and is long lasting. "Love is so little directed toward the body of the beloved that it can easily outlast the other's death, can exist in the lover's heart until his own death" (Frankl, 1973, p. 138).

The third way to find meaning on the path of life purpose is choosing one's own attitude to whatever life presents. Choosing to remain positive, brave, or optimistic in spite of difficult circumstances illustrates this way of finding meaning. Purpose in life can come when a choice is made to deliberately change one's attitude and so view the situation in a different way.

Frankl identified two states that describe a lack of meaning: existential frustration and existential vacuum. Existential frustration is a searching for meaning in which there is a state of being unsettled, of wanting more from life (Frankl, 1969). Existential vacuum is a sense of utter despair, of hopelessness, that life has no meaning and all is of no use (Frankl, 1969). This is an inner emptiness where one feels trapped in unhappiness. Times of transition may lead to an existential vacuum, such as when a person is dissatisfied with work and yet afraid of risking change. Existential vacuum may also occur during times of loss, such as the sudden, unexpected death of a child, when one does not trust values that have formerly been a guide. Fabry (1980) believes that lack of meaning is a major problem in society because people repress their natural desire to find meaning, causing them to feel that life has no purpose, no challenges, and no obligations. This problem is experienced as a crisis among the rich and the poor, the old and the young, the successful and those who have failed. Fabry (1980) identified unhealthy ways that people cope, including drugs, workaholism, thrill-seeking, and overeating. This crisis experience may also serve as a stimulus to find a more meaningful existence.

A poignant example of finding meaning and accomplishing life purpose, even at the end of life, is a story that will live in history as one in which individuals transcended self for the good of others. On September 11, 2001, passengers on United Airlines flight #93 found that fate had placed them on a plane hijacked by terrorists intent on a suicide mission to destroy innocent lives and symbols of American democracy. With the aid of cell phone technology, some passengers learned there had already been terrorist attacks by other flights that morning and there was no doubt what their fate was to be. Many talked to family members about the things that gave meaning to their lives—the love they had, the expressed wish for the family to go on to complete meaningful lives. Yet, in the face of their own deaths, they had freedom of choice. They had a chance to transcend their own fears, one last chance to do something good for humanity. In the last moments of their lives they could and did perform a selfless act—they make sure the plane did not reach its intended target, but rather crashed in a nonpopulated area in Pennsylvania. In accomplishing this unexpected life purpose, they gave meaning to their lives and left a legacy of heroism, not only for their loved ones, but for every American citizen. Even if among this group there was one whose life had been meaningless, when that one exercised his freedom to act and to transcend his own needs, by this one act in the final moments, his life was flooded with meaning and purpose.

Freedom to Choose

Freedom to choose is the second concept of the theory of meaning. It is the process of selecting among options over which one has control. In enduring the most intense imaginable hardship, that of the Holocaust, Frankl (1973) pointed out that there is value to be found in a person's attitude toward the limiting factors of life. Being confronted by an unalterable destiny where one can act only by acceptance provides a unique opportunity to choose one's attitude. "The way in which he accepts, the way in which he bears his cross, what courage he manifests in suffering, what dignity he displays in doom and disaster, is the measure of his human fulfillment" (Frankl, 1973, p. 44). One can be subjected to torture, humiliation, and worse, and yet retain the attitude to face one's fate with courage. It is the attitude of the sufferer that drives the behavior, not the actions of the persecutor. The right to choose one's own attitude may be thought of as spiritual freedom or independence of mind.

We who lived in concentration camps can remember the men who walked through the huts comforting others, giving away their last piece of bread. They may have been few in number, but they offer sufficient proof that everything can be taken from a man but one thing: the last of the human freedoms—to choose one's attitude in any given set of circumstances, to choose one's own way. [Frankl, 1984, p. 86]

Freedom to be self-determining within the limits of endowment and environment was validated during Frankl's experiences in the concentration camps.

. . . in this living laboratory and on this testing ground, we watched and witnessed some of our comrades behave like swine while others behaved like saints. Man has both potentialities within himself; which one is actualized depends on decisions but not on conditions. [Frankl, 1984, p. 157]

Fabry (1991) offered practical guidelines for modifying attitudes by considering that something positive can be found in all situations. Some sample questions to stimulate one's attitude change are "What am I still able to do that would benefit someone? Whom do I love and wish to protect in this situation?" (p. 43). By asking these questions, one shifts the attention away from what has been lost and from self to others. Fabry (1991) suggested that one's attitude can begin to change by "acting as if" one has the attribute. For example if a person wanted to be courageous, then to act "as if" would beget a change in attitude.

Lukas (1984, 1986) introduced several ideas important to Frankl's work. She expanded understanding of one's freedom to choose by indicating that life events can be classified as either fate or freedom. Fate is when we cannot change the situation; freedom includes what one can do, including choosing what attitude to adopt. When confronting a problem, the person should ask, "Where are my areas of freedom? Which possible choices do I have, and which one do I want to actualize?"

Human Suffering

Human suffering is the third concept of the theory of meaning. It is a subjective experience that is unique to an individual and varies from simple transitory discomfort to extreme anguish and despair (Starck &

McGovern, 1992). Frankl did not define suffering, but rather described it as a subjective, all-consuming human experience. He believed that "the meaning of suffering . . . is the deepest possible meaning" (Frankl, 1969, p. 75), and that the ultimate meaning of life or of human suffering can never be found. He used the following comparison:

> If I point to something with my finger, the dog does not look in the direction in which I point, it looks at my finger and sometimes snaps at it. And what about man? Is not he, too, unable to understand the meaning of something, say the meaning of suffering, and does not he, too, quarrel with his fate and snap at its finger? [Frankl, 1969, p. 145]

Frankl was clear that there is no meaning *in* suffering. For example, there is no meaning in cancer. However, one can find meaning *in spite of* having cancer. Suffering is a part of the human experience. Things happen to us that are undeserved, unexplainable, and unavoidable. We do not need to look for meaning in these events; rather, meaning comes from stances we take toward the suffering, for example, the courageous way a person chooses to live with the cancer. Frankl (1975) described the worst kind of suffering as "despair, suffering without meaning" (p. 137).

RELATIONSHIPS AMONG THE CONCEPTS: THE MODEL

Figure 7.1 depicts the relationships among the concepts of the theory. It suggests that meaning is a journey toward life purpose with the freedom to choose one's path in spite of inevitable suffering.

USE OF THE THEORY IN NURSING RESEARCH

Instruments

A number of instruments have been developed by protégés of Frankl. These tools have been used in both research and clinical practice. All are available from the Viktor E. Frankl International Institute for Logotherapy in Abilene, Texas. Instruments that quantify meaning and instruments that can serve as a clinical guide to planning interven-

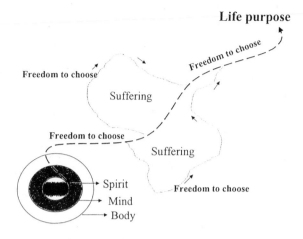

FIGURE 7.1   Theory of meaning.

tions include the Purpose in Life (PIL) test (Crumbaugh, 1968; Crumbaugh & Maholick, 1976), the Seeking of Noetic Goals (SONG) test (Crumbaugh, 1977), and the Meaning in Suffering Test (MIST) (Starck, 1985b). Another useful instrument is the List of Values created by Crumbaugh (1980). This is a list of 20 values. The person is directed to choose his or her top five values in life. There are various other instruments available, including the Logotest developed by Elizabeth Lukas, PhD, in Munich for use in the practice of logotherapy, and the Life Purpose Questionnaire developed by R. R. Hutzell. Table 7.1 compares the most frequently used instruments, distinguishing the purpose of each instrument and providing psychometric information. The reader may contact the Institute for more information.

Nursing Research

Several nursing researchers who have referenced Frankl's work have made significant contributions in the area of suffering and the search for meaning with a variety of groups. Using qualitative research, Kahn and Steeves (1986, 1994, 1995) and Steeves and Kahn (1987) have described the concept of suffering as an individual's experience of threat to self and as meaning given to events such as pain or loss.

TABLE 7.1 Instruments Used to Measure Meaning and Purpose

Instruments	Purpose (What the instrument captures)	Samples (General)	Reliability	Validity	Example citation
PIL	Degree of existential vacuum	Adults	.85 Pearson correlation, Spearman-Brown corrected to .92	Construct and criterion	Crumbaugh (1968)
SONG	Degree of strength/ motivation to find life meaning	Adults	.71 Pearson correlation, Spearman-Brown corrected to .83	Construct	Crumbaugh (1977)
MIST	Degree of meaning found in unavoidable suffering	Adults	.82 split-half; .81 Cronbach's Alpha	Logical construct	Kuuppelomaki & Lauri (1998)
Life Purpose Questionnaire	Degree of life meaning	Adults	.90	Construct and criterion	Hutzell & Peterson (1986)

They cited the ability of hospice patients and families to find meaning in spite of suffering through discrete experiences during which they were affected by something greater than themselves (Steeves & Kahn, 1987). They identified the goal of nursing care in such situations as helping to establish and maintain the conditions necessary for and helpful to experience meaning. They identified eight aphorisms of suffering (Kahn & Steeves, 1995) that characterize the experience. The aphorisms note the individual encompassing nature of suffering, the recognition of suffering through its expression rather than the experience itself, and the influence of a caring environment on the suffering process (Kahn & Steeves, 1995).

Steeves, Kahn, and Benoliel (1990) investigated how nurses experience and react to a person's suffering, with themes progressing from understanding suffering from the perspective of the patient's medical condition and ending with nurses personalizing the suffering as their own. With bone marrow transplant patients, Steeves (1992) investigated the process of "meaning making" and "life interpretation." A change in the social position of the patient was influenced by protective isolation and communication problems. Patients described searching for understanding with examples of experiences of meaningfulness. Steeves (1996) illustrated the use of storytelling in helping individuals and families find meaning in loss and grief.

Coward (1991, 1994, 1995, 1996, 1998; Coward & Lewis, 1993; Coward & Reed, 1996), a nurse researcher concerned with breast cancer patients and persons with HIV/AIDS, has studied meaning and purpose in life as well as the phenomenon of self-transcendence. The approach she has used combines the work of several authors, including Frankl, in defining self-transcendence.

Starck (1979) was the first person to apply Frankl's theory and practices to a physically disabled population with a permanent spinal cord injury (SCI). Starck conducted a study, the purpose of which was to determine whether a logotherapeutic nursing intervention could favorably influence the perception of meaning and purpose in life for persons disabled with SCI. A model using Frankl's theory, Travelbee's (1969) approaches to interpersonal communication, and Maslow's (1968) hierarchy of needs was developed and applied with the subjects. Both the PIL and the SONG were used as pre- and posttests to measure the effectiveness of the intervention. The patients $(N = 25)$ were referred from a regional spinal cord injury center, and home visits were conducted for both the control and the experimental groups. The nursing intervention involved use of written parables or provocative thoughts to stimulate reflective thinking and application to the patient's life. For example, one parable described two frogs who fell into a churn of milk. One gave up and drowned; the other fought his fate and splashed around. Soon the milk had turned to butter and he was afloat on top. In relation to this parable, study participants discussed how they might rally the human spirit to cope with permanent paralysis.

Although there was evidence that some clients increased their sense of meaning and purpose in life, there was no support for the effectiveness of the nursing intervention at a statistically significant level. However, there were several findings of clinical importance that were not heretofore found in the literature. These findings included the following: (1) these patients could not stand on scales to monitor weight, and insidious weight gain complicated health problems inherent to their limited mobility; (2) fear in the environment thwarted seeking fuller meaning in life; (3) having lost the mobility and thus the ability to flee from danger, safety was of great concern; and (4) the telephone was viewed as a means of physical protection as well as emotional comfort. One of the clients objected to having a wheelchair ramp on the house for fear that it would alert burglars that a handicapped person might be alone in the house. These findings suggest that there were many factors that could interfere with attainment of goals for a meaningful life.

Many SCI patients had found meaning in spite of severe physical limitations. For example, a girl seriously injured in a random shooting read the newspaper every day to find stories of misfortune. She then typed letters with her mouthstick to offer words of encouragement and motivation. Another quadriplegic, who was the first in his family to graduate from high school, took on the role of tutoring younger relatives.

Starck (1992) studied suffering in a nursing home environment and found that suffering was operationally defined as loss. Although there were physical, social/emotional, and economic losses, the greatest losses were in the spiritual domain. These were loss of autonomy, loss of freedom of choice, and a loss of a sense of purpose in life. Furthermore, it was found that the nursing home staff responded to those who complained about the suffering inherent in their condition with negative sanctions, and to those who were quiet and passive sufferers with a caring response.

USE OF THE THEORY IN NURSING PRACTICE

Fabry (1980) has described logotherapy as "guiding people toward understanding themselves as they are and *could be* and their place in the totality of living (p. xiii). When contrasted with traditional psychotherapy, it is less retrospective and introspective (Frankl, 1984). Other comparisons between psychotherapy and logotherapy are found in Table 7.2. The goal of logotherapy is to help persons separate themselves from their symptoms, to tap into the resources of their nooetic dimension, and to arouse the dynamic power of the human spirit. Helping another to find meaning may be described as promoting an unfolding of what is already there. It is helping the other to discover his or her own values, and facilitating awareness of subconscious beliefs and commitments.

Frankl does not advocate techniques in a routine procedural sense but rather encourages creativity based on the situation at hand. Frankl (1969) has described three logotherapeutic approaches. These approaches are dereflection, paradoxical intention, and Socratic dialogue. Both dereflection and paradoxical intention "rest on two essential qualities of human existence, namely, man's capacities of self-transcendence and self-detachment" (Frankl, 1969, p. 99).

Dereflection

Dereflection is the act of deemphasizing or ceasing to focus on a troublesome phenomenon, issue, or problem; it is putting this issue aside. Dereflection strengthens the capacity for self-transcendence.

TABLE 7.2   Contrasts Between Psychotherapy and Logotherapy

Psychotherapy	Logotherapy
Depth psychology	Height psychology
Sees life in terms of problems	Sees life in terms of solutions
Focuses on obstacles	Focuses on goals
Is reductionistic	Is holistic
Emphasis on uncovering	Emphasis on discovering
Analytical style	Uniqueness and improvisation style
Psychiatrist listens	Logotherapist talks

Obsessions are recognized as hyperreflection or excess attention, described as the "compulsion to self-observation" (Frankl, 1973, p. 253). The urge for better sexual performance is an example. "Sexual performance or experience is strangled to the extent to which it is made either an object of attention or an objective of intention" (Frankl, 1969, p. 101).

Complaining is an example of hyperreflection, as an excessive amount of attention is given to the self. Dereflection helps the person to stop fighting an anxiety, a neurosis, or a psychosis, and spares the person the reinforcement of additional suffering. If a person is depressed, dereflection can help to achieve distance between the person and the depression, "to see himself—not as a person who is depressed but—as a full human being who has depressions with the capacity to find meaning despite the depressions" (Fabry, 1991, p. 136).

Paradoxical Intention

Paradoxical intention is intentionally acting the opposite to one's desired ends, thereby confronting one's fears and anxieties. Paradoxical intention strengthens the capacity for self-distancing. By distancing from the triggers of problems, these triggers become ineffective. Paradoxical intention is helpful in dealing with the problem of anticipatory anxiety. The object of the person's fear is fear itself. The underlying dynamic is apprehension about the potential effects of the anxiety attacks. And, of course, the fear of the fear increases the fear, producing precisely what the person is afraid of. The person is caught in a restricting cycle. The aim of therapy is to break the cycle, to interfere with the feedback mechanism. In logotherapy, one is asked to replace fear with a paradoxical wish, to wish for the very thing one fears. By this treatment, Frankl said, "the wind is taken out of the sails of the anxiety" (1984, p. 147). This approach makes use of the specifically human capacity for self-detachment. For example, in sleep disturbances when a person worries that he or she will not be able to get to sleep and focuses on trying to go to sleep, sleep will not come. The fear of sleeplessness results in the hyperintention to fall asleep, which inevitably leads to sleeplessness. Paradoxical intention is used to advise the person not to try to sleep, but rather to try to do just the opposite, to stay awake as long as possible. The person who has been trying to stay awake wakes up to find that he or she has been asleep.

Paradoxical intention can be used to change unwanted behavior patterns. This does not depend upon understanding how and why the behavior started. It simply breaks the cycle of fear.

Socratic Dialogue

Socratic dialogue is a conversation of questions and answers, probing deeply into existential issues such as one's values. It is rhetorical debate to trigger a change in attitude, behavior, or both. Socratic dialogue is self-discovery discourse and seeks to get rid of masks that have been put on to please or to be accepted. The therapist poses questions so that patients become aware of their unconscious decisions, their repressed hopes, and their unadmitted self-knowledge. In Socratic dialogue, experiences of the past are explored as well as fantasies for the future in order to modulate attitude (Fabry, 1980). Socratic dialogue requires improvisation and intuition and asks probing questions like the following:

Was there a time when life had meaning?

Who do you know that leads a meaningful life? What keeps you from living like this person?

Who are the people who need you?

Tell me about an experience that made you see things differently.

Tell me something you said you couldn't do but you did it.

As an example, Lukas (1984), working with a patient who had strong values in physical ability and who had undergone a leg amputation, asked the question, "Does the value of human existence depend on the use of two legs?" (p. 47).

Fabry (1991) proposed five guideposts to probe areas of meaning. These are self-discovery, choice, uniqueness, responsibility, and self-transcendence. He also identified a number of creative methods and exercises to illustrate choice where family members act out the role of others in the way they wish the others had responded. The flashlight technique can be useful in self-discovery and in aggressive discussion. The facilitator shines the flashlight on the partner who says something offensive to the other, indicating that the person must rephrase what has been said without hostility or sarcasm, thus helping to reshape attitudes and behaviors. Fabry (1991) also has guidelines for groups, wherein the Socratic dialogue becomes a multilogue.

CONCLUSIONS

The Theory of Meaning can be a useful guide to helping people cope with unexpected life events that threaten their purpose in relation to their unique circumstances. Both nurse researchers and practitioners can draw from this approach in order to understand ordinary stress of life as well as life-changing events, including human suffering, and to be therapeutic in their responses to it.

For more information about continuing work being done with Viktor Frankl's ideas contact: The Viktor E. Frankl International Institute for Logotherapy, Box 15211, Abilene, TX 79698-5211.

REFERENCES

Coward, D. D. (1991). Self-transcendence and emotional well-being in women with advanced breast cancer. *Oncology Nursing Forum, 18*, 857–863.

Coward, D. D. (1994). Meaning and purpose in the lives of persons with AIDS. *Public Health Nursing, 11*, 331–336.

Coward, D. D. (1995). The lived experience of self-transcendence in women with AIDS. *Journal of Obstetric, Gynecologic and Neonatal Nursing, 24*, 314–318.

Coward, D. D. (1996). Self-transcendence and correlates in a health population. *Nursing Research, 45*(2), 116–121.

Coward, D. D. (1998). Facilitation of self-transcendence in a breast cancer support group. *Oncology Nursing Forum, 25*(1), 75–84.

Coward, D. D., & Lewis, F. M. (1993). The lived experience of self-transcendence in gay men with AIDS. *Oncology Nursing Forum, 20*, 1363–1368.

Coward, D. D., & Reed, P. G. (1996). Self-transcendence: A resource for healing at the end of life. *Issues in Mental Health Nursing, 17*, 275–288.

Crumbaugh, J. C. (1968). Cross-validation of purpose in life test based on Frankl's concepts. *Journal of Individual Psychology, 24*, 74–81.

Crumbaugh, J. C. (1977). The seeking of noetic goals test (SONG): A complementary scale to the purpose in life test (PIL). *Journal of Clinical Psychology, 33*, 900–907.

Crumbaugh, J. C. (1980). *Logotherapy—new help for problem drinkers*. Chicago: Nelson-Hall.

Crumbaugh, J. C., & Maholick, L. T. (1976). *Purpose in Life test*. Abilene, TX: Viktor Frankl Institute for Logotherapy.

Fabry, J. B. (1980). *The pursuit of meaning*. New York: Harper & Row.

Fabry, J. B. (1991). *Guideposts to meaning: Discovering what really matters*. Oakland, CA: New Harbinger.

Frankl, V. E. (1961). Dynamics, existence, and values. *Journal of Existential Psychiatry, II*(5), 5–16.

Frankl, V. E. (1969). *The will to meaning*. New York: New American Library.

Frankl, V. E. (1973). *The doctor and the soul*. New York: Vintage.

Frankl, V. E. (1975). *The unconscious God*. New York: Simon & Schuster.

Frankl, V. E. (1978). *The unheard cry for meaning*. New York: Simon & Schuster.

Frankl, V. E. (1984). *Man's search for meaning: An introduction to Logotherapy*. Boston: Beacon.

Hutzell, R. R. (n.d.). *Life Purpose Questionnaire*. Abilene, TX: Viktor Frankl Institute of Logotherapy.

Hutzell, R. R., & Peterson, T. J. (1986). Use of the Life Purpose Questionnaire with an alcoholic population. *International Journal of Addiction, 22*, 51–57.

Kahn, D. L., & Steeves, R. H. (1986). The experience of suffering: Conceptual clarification and theoretical definition. *Journal of Advanced Nursing, 11*, 623–631.

Kahn, D. L., & Steeves, R. H. (1994). Witnesses to suffering: Nursing knowledge, voice, and vision. *Nursing Outlook, 42*, 260–264.

Kahn, D. L., & Steeves, R. H. (1995). The significance of suffering in cancer care. *Seminars in Oncology Nursing, 11*(1), 9–16.

Kerlinger, F. H. (1973). *Foundations of research* (2nd ed.). New York: Holt, Rinehart, and Winston.

Kuuppelomaki, M., & Lauri, S. (1998). Cancer patients' reported experiences of suffering. *Cancer Nursing, 21*, 364–369.

Lukas, E. (1984). *Meaningful living: A logotherapeutic guide to health*. Cambridge, MA: Schenkman.

Lukas, E. (1986). *Meaning in suffering: Comfort in crisis through logotherapy*. Berkeley, CA: Institute of Logotherapy Press.

Maslow, A. (1968). *Toward a psychology of being*. New York: Van Nostrand.

Starck, P. L. (1979). Spinal cord injured clients' perception of meaning and purpose in life, measurement before and after nursing intervention. *Dissertation Abstracts International, 40*(10), 4741. (UMI No. 8007891)

Starck, P. L. (1985a). Logotherapy comes of age: Birth of a theory. *The International Forum of Logotherapy: Journal of Search for Meaning, 8*(2), 71–75.

Starck, P. L. (1985b). *The Meaning in Suffering Test*. Berkeley, CA: Institute of Logotherapy Press.

Starck, P. L. (1992). Suffering in a nursing home: Losses of the human spirit. *The International Forum of Logotherapy: Journal of Search for Meaning, 15*(2), 76–79.

Starck, P. L., & McGovern, J. P. (1992). The meaning in suffering. In P. L. Starck & J. P. McGovern (Eds.), *The hidden dimension of illness: Human suffering* (pp. 25–42). New York: National League for Nursing Press.

Steeves, R. H. (1992). Patients who have undergone bone marrow transplantation: Their quest for meaning. *Oncology Nursing Forum, 19*, 899–905.

Steeves, R. H. (1996). Loss, grief, and the search for meaning. *Oncology Nursing Society, 23,* 897–903.

Steeves, R. H., & Kahn, D. L. (1987). Experience of meaning in suffering. *Journal of Nursing Scholarship, 19*(3), 114–116.

Steeves, R. H., Kahn, D. L., & Benoliel, J. Q. (1990). Nurses' interpretation of the suffering of their patients. *Western Journal of Nursing Research, 12*(6), 715–731.

Travelbee, J. (1966). *Interpersonal aspects of nursing.* Philadelphia: F. A. Davis.

Travelbee, J. (1969). *Intervention in psychiatric nursing: Process in the one-to-one relationship.* Philadelphia: F. A. Davis.

Travelbee, J. (1972). To find meaning in illness. *Nursing, 72*(2), 6–7.

8

The Theory of
Self-Transcendence

Pamela G. Reed

The theory of self-transcendence is an empirical theory of nursing. It was created from a belief in the developmental nature of human beings and the relevance of developmental phenomena for well-being. Nursing is not only a human science but a developmental science as well. The theory was initially created out of an interest in acknowledging the developmental nature of older adults as integral to mental health and well-being. Although the role of development had been an accepted perspective in work with children and adolescents, little attention was given to its significance among adults and especially among older adults.

PURPOSE OF THE THEORY AND HOW IT WAS DEVELOPED

The purpose of the theory of self-transcendence is to enhance understanding about well-being in later adulthood. The theory is also applicable to any person whose life situation increases awareness of vulnerability and personal mortality. It is consistent with life-span development, which posits that development is influenced less by chronological age and the passage of time and more by normative and nonnormative life events and the accruement of life experiences.

The idea for a theory of self-transcendence was influenced by three major events. First, the life span movement of the 1970s, in developmental psychology, provided philosophic awareness and empirical evidence that development did indeed continue on beyond adolescence, into adulthood, and throughout processes of aging and dying (Reed, 1983). Second, Martha Rogers' (1970) early postulations about the nature of change in human beings provided further inspiration for development of the theory (Reed, 1997b). Third, the theory of self-transcendence was encouraged by clinical experiences in applying developmental theories in child and adolescent psychiatric-mental health care. A nursing approach to fostering mental health and well-being required an understanding of developmental processes inherent in human beings. Self-transcendence facilitates integration of complex and conflicting elements of living, aging, and dying.

Health events in particular confront people with increased complexity in terms of new people in their lives, new information, and new feelings and concerns. For example, the diagnosis of a chronic illness necessitates relationships with new people (health care providers) and community resources. It introduces strange, new information and terminology about the illness itself, medications, and other treatments and self-care activities. Chronic illness also initiates, if not intensifies, concerns about one's future and that of one's family, and raises fears about pain and mortality. Self-transcendence can help the person organize these challenges into some meaningful system to sustain well-being and a sense of wholeness across the trajectory of the illness.

ASSUMPTIONS AND MAJOR CONCEPTS

The theory of self-transcendence rests on two major assumptions. First, it is assumed that human beings are integral with their environments, as postulated in Rogers' science of unitary human beings. Human beings are "pandimensional" (Rogers, 1980, 1994), coextensive with their environment, and capable of an awareness that extends beyond physical and temporal dimensions (Reed, 1997a). This awareness may be experienced through altered states of consciousness but more often, and more the focus of this theory of self-transcendence, is an awareness found in everyday practices in reaching deeper within the self and reaching out to others and to one's God. Self-transcendence embodies experiences that connect rather than separate a person from self, others, and the environment. It is a concept that enables description and study of the nature of human pandimensionality within everyday contexts of living.

The second assumption is that self-transcendence is a developmental imperative, meaning that it is an innate human characteristic that demands expression, much like other developmental processes such as walking among toddlers, reasoning among adolescents, and grieving in those who have suffered a loss. These resources are a part of being human and realizing one's full potential. Similarly, self-transcendence is not something one chooses or declines from using; it chooses the person. As such, the person's participation in it is integral to well-being, and nursing should have a role in facilitating this process.

Self-Transcendence

Self-transcendence is the major concept of the theory. It is the capacity to expand self-boundaries intrapersonally (toward greater awareness of one's philosophy, values, and dreams), interpersonally (to relate to others and one's environment), temporally (to integrate one's past and future in a way that has meaning for the present), and transpersonally (to connect with dimensions beyond the typically discernible world). Self-transcendence is a characteristic of developmental maturity wherein there is enhanced awareness of the environment and an orientation toward broadened perspectives about life.

Neo-Piagetian theories about development in adulthood and later life were foundational in formulating the concept of self-transcendence. Beginning in the 1970s, life span development researchers discovered patterns of thinking in older adults that extended beyond Piaget's formal operations, once thought to be the final stage of cognitive development. Life span developmental theories on social-cognitive development extended Piaget's original theory on reasoning, which had identified formal operations (abstract and symbolic reasoning) in youth and young adulthood as the apex of cognitive development. Researchers identified abilities in older adults indicating that cognitive development continued well into later life beyond the phase of formal operations. Arlin's (1975) problem finding stage, Riegel's (1976) and Basseches' (1984) dialectic operations, and Koplowitz's (1984) unitary stage are examples of these patterns. Theorists described these abilities as postformal thinking.

It is now widely recognized that older adults use postformal patterns of thought in reasoning about their world. In contrast to patterns used by young adults, postformal thought is more contextual, more pragmatic, more spiritual, and more tolerant of ambiguity and the paradoxes inherent in living and dying (Commons, Demick, & Goldberg, 1996; Sinnott, 1998). Postformal reasoning incorporates personal experience as well as scientific evidence and an awareness of the larger social and temporal contexts that extend beyond the self and immediate situation. The adult who uses postformal thinking does not seek absolute answers to questions in life but rather seeks meaning of life events as integrated within a moral, social, and historical context. The person has an appreciation of the greater environment and things unseen, as well as an inner knowledge of self. There is a perspective of relativism balanced by the ability to make a commitment to one's beliefs.

Self-transcendence was conceptualized as an indicator of postformal thinking. Older adults and others facing end-of-life issues acquire an expanded awareness of self and environment. With this matured approach to life and death, people reflect strivings more in line with generativity and ego integrity than with the more self-focused strivings for identity and intimacy from earlier developmental phases (Sheldon & Kasser, 2001). Self-transcendence is expressed through various behaviors and perspectives such as sharing wisdom with others, integrating the physical changes of aging, accepting death as a part of life, and finding spiritual meaning in life.

Well-Being

A second major concept of the theory is well-being. Well-being is a sense of feeling whole and healthy, in accord with one's own criteria for wholeness and health. It is theorized that self-transcendence, as a basic human pattern of development, is logically linked with positive, health-promoting experiences and is therefore a correlate if not a predictor and resource for well-being. Well-being may be defined in many ways, depending upon the individual or patient population. Indicators of well-being are as diverse as are human perceptions of health and wellness. Examples of indicators of well-being include life satisfaction, positive self-concept, hopefulness, and meaning in life. Well-being is a correlate and an outcome of self-transcendence.

Vulnerability

Another key concept in the theory is vulnerability. Vulnerability is awareness of personal mortality. It is theorized that self-transcendence, as a developmental capacity, emerges naturally in health experiences that confront a person with issues of mortality and immortality. Life events that heighten one's sense of mortality, inadequacy, or vulnerability can—if they do not crush the individual's inner self—trigger developmental progress toward a renewed sense of identity and expanded self-boundaries (Corless, Germino, & Pittman, 1994; Erikson, 1986; Frankl, 1963; Marshall, 1980). Examples of these life events include serious or chronic illness, disability, aging, parenting, childbirth, bereavement, career-related and other life crises. Self-transcendence is evoked through such experiences and may enhance well-being by transforming these significant life experiences into healing (Reed, 1996).

RELATIONSHIPS AMONG THE CONCEPTS: THE MODEL

The model of the theory of self-transcendence is presented in Figure 8.1. Three basic sets of relationships exist among the concepts in the theory. First, it is expected that there is a relationship between the experience of vulnerability and self-transcendence such that increased levels of vulnerability, as brought on by health events for example, influence increased levels of self-transcendence. However, this may hold only within certain levels of experienced vulnerability. The relationship between vulnerability and self-transcendence is best characterized as a nonlinear relationship in that very low and very high levels of vulnerability are not expected to relate to increased levels of self-transcendence.

A second relationship exists between self-transcendence and well-being. This relationship is posited to be direct and positive when the indicator of well-being is a positive one. For example, self-transcendence relates positively to sense of well-being and morale, but relates negatively to level of depression as an indicator of well-being.

Third, there is a diversity of personal and contextual factors that may moderate these two central relationships. A wide variety of per-

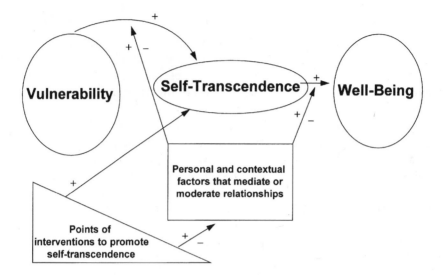

FIGURE 8.1   Model of theory of self-transcendence.

sonal and contextual factors and their interactions influence the process of self-transcendence as it relates to well-being. Examples of these factors are age, gender, cognitive ability, health status, past significant life events, and the sociopolitical environment. As moderators, these factors either enhance or diminish the strength of the relationships. For example, having previously suffered a significant loss may diminish the positive relationship between an experience of vulnerability and self-transcendence. Advanced age or education may potentiate the relationship between self-transcendence and well-being. Continued research into other personal and contextual factors is needed to better understand the potential role of these variables in the theory and their interrelationships.

Other concepts and relationships can be identified to extend the theory of self-transcendence. The theory was initially constructed to better understand the role of self-transcendence at the end of life. Since then, researchers' findings have extended the boundaries of theory beyond later life and end-of-life illness experiences to include other experiences of vulnerability. For example, end-of-life health experiences were found to be significant correlates of self-transcendence among younger adults. In another study, middle-aged adults were studied, using the variables of parenting and self-acceptance as indicators of self-transcendence.

Because of my nursing commitment toward gaining better understanding of the inherent resources that foster human well-being, I have approached the study of self-transcendence as an independent variable, a contributor to well-being and possible predictor of well-being outcomes, rather than as the dependent or outcome variable. Nursing interventions that support the person's inner resource for self-transcendence may focus directly on facilitating self-transcendence. Interventions may also focus on influencing some of the personal and contextual factors that mediate or moderate the relationships between vulnerability and self-transcendence, and between self-transcendence and well-being (see Figure 8.1).

In contrast to self-transcendence as an independent variable, some scholars have conceptualized it as an outcome (or dependent) variable of interest (Coward, 1998; Haase, Britt, Coward, Leidy, & Penn, 1992). In these cases, self-transcendence is regarded more as an indicator of well-being rather than as a correlate or facilitator of well-being. In addition, other antecedents of self-transcendence may be identified. For example, in Haase and colleagues' (1992) concept analysis, spiritual perspective was identified as an "antecedent" of self-transcendence. This is congruent with Reed's model in that spirituality may represent the person's pandimensional nature, which facilitates emergence of self-transcendence. Others may not view spirituality and self-transcendence as two separate concepts. More research on the model is needed to identify empirical support for the various relational statements that have been proposed.

Self-transcendence is a concept relevant to the discipline of nursing. Themes of self-transcendence are evident in foundational nursing theories (Reed, 1996). In Watson's (1999) theory of human caring, as written and revised since 1985, transcendence is integral to understanding the essence of patients and nurses and their inner strivings toward greater self-awareness and inner healing.

In Parse's (1992) theory of human becoming, cotranscending is a major theme underlying the philosophical assumptions of her theory. Cotranscending involves a relational process of developing new ways of living and transforming the self that incorporate yet reach beyond the old ways. Mobilizing transcendence is an exemplary nursing practice within Parse's paradigm.

Newman's (1994) theory of health postulates a transcendence of time and space as one reaches beyond illness to develop an awareness of one's patterns, self-identity, and a higher level of consciousness. Through this process, there is health and well-being in even the most difficult of illness experiences. Although all of these theorists present unique views of transcendence, theorists generally share the idea of expanding awareness beyond the immediate or constricted views of oneself and the world to transform life experiences into healing (Reed, 1996).

Self-transcendence is also congruent with Newman's (1992) unitary transformative paradigm, which presents human beings as embedded in an ongoing developmental process of changing complexity and organization, a process integrally related to well-being. According to Reed's (1997a) redefinition of nursing, self-transcendence is a "nursing process"—a self-organizing process inherent among human systems and related to well-being. It is a nonlinear process by which one's conceptual boundaries undergo change in concert with the dynamic context in which one lives.

Other disciplines, particularly transpersonal psychology and psychiatry, have addressed the concept of self-transcendence. Cloninger and his colleagues (Cloninger, Svrakic, & Svrakic, 1997) conceptualized self-transcendence as a factor in the organization of the personality and in development of psychopathology. Cloninger measured self-transcendence as one of three dimensions in his instrument, the Temperament and Character Inventory (TCI). Psychologists Frankl (1963) and Maslow (1969) are frequently cited for their emphasis on the self-transcendent capacity of human beings.

USE OF THE THEORY IN NURSING RESEARCH

Reed's (1991b) Self-Transcendence Scale (STS) has been used in much of the research that most directly relates to the theory. The STS is a 15-item unidimensional scale. It originated from a 36-item instrument, the Developmental Resources of Later Adulthood (DRLA) scale (Reed, 1986, 1989), which measured the level of developmentally based psychosocial resources in a person. The DRLA was constructed from an extensive review of theoretical and empirical literature on adult development and aging, selected nursing conceptual models and life span theories, and clinical encounters with older adults. A "self-transcendence" factor, which explained nearly half of the variance in the instrument and had good internal consistency, was identified within the scale. The STS was developed around this empirically based factor. The STS was subsequently used in research to measure intrapersonal, interpersonal, temporal, and transpersonal experiences that reflect expanded boundaries of the self in developmentally mature adults. The STS, a brief scale, has demonstrated reliability and construct validity, and is easy to administer as a questionnaire or in an interview format. Many researchers and graduate students have since used the instrument in studying self-transcendence as related to various health experiences.

Initial Research

The initial research that was used to build the theory of self-transcendence focused on well elders and elders who were hospitalized for psychiatric treatment of depression (Reed, 1986, 1989). Elders were selected as a group potentially facing end-of-life issues. Correlational and longitudinal studies were designed to examine the nature and significance of the relationship between self-transcendence and mental health outcomes. It was found consistently that self-transcendence was a correlate and predictor of mental health in these elders. Correlations were significant and of moderate magnitude. Reed's (1986) longitudinal study provided empirical evidence for a link between self-transcendence and subsequent occurrence of depression among mentally healthy adults; this link was not significant, although the correlation was in the expected direction among clinically depressed adults.

Self-transcendence was next examined for its relevance to mental health among the oldest-old, adults 80 to 100 years of age (Reed, 1991a). Quantitative and qualitative data generated further support for the theory. Significant inverse correlations of moderate magnitude were found between self-transcendence and both depression and overall mental health symptomatology. In addition, four conceptual clusters representing different aspects of self-transcendence were generated from a content analysis: generativity, introjectivity, temporal integration, and body transcendence. Elders who scored high on depression reflected weak patterns in these four areas, particularly in body-transcendence, inner-directed activities, and positive integration of present and future. These qualitative findings provided further support for the theory.

Research by Coward

Coward, who as a doctoral student studied with Reed, continued research into self-transcendence with a focus on middle-aged adults confronting their mortality through serious illness, advanced cancer, and AIDS. Coward (1990, 1995) initially studied the lived experience of self-transcendence in women with advanced breast cancer. Results from her phenomenological study were consistent with findings from quantitative studies. Self-transcendent perspectives were salient in this group, which had a heightened awareness of personal mortality; self-transcendence was expressed in terms of reaching out beyond self to help others, to permit others to help them, and to accept the present, unchangeable events in time. This research validated Reed's (1989) quantitative measure of self-transcendence. In subsequent phenomenological research, Coward and Lewis (1993) explored self-transcendence in women and men with AIDS. Despite increased fear and sadness at the prospect of death, all participants indicated self-transcendent perspectives, which in turn helped them find meaning and achieve emotional well-being.

Findings from a study in which structural equation modeling was used to analyze responses in a sample of women with advanced breast cancer indicated that self-transcendence led to decreased illness distress through the mediating effect of emotional well-being. Self-transcendence had a significant and direct positive effect on emotional well-being (Coward, 1991).

Coward (1996) also studied healthy adults, who ranged in age from 19 to 85 years. She was interested in extending the theory of self-transcendence by examining its salience in a group of adults who were not as actively confronted with end-of-life issues as were other seriously ill populations. Self-transcendence was again found to be a significant and strong correlate of well-being indicators, namely coherence, self-esteem, hope, and other variables assessing emotional well-being. Coward concluded that while her research supported the hypothesized relationship between self-transcendence and mental health variables, the findings, as generated from a sample of healthy adults, did not necessarily support the theoretical link between awareness of end-of-life issues and self-transcendence. Coward cited Frankl (1969) in proposing that self-transcendence is an essential human characteristic that may surface at any time in the life span.

Although Coward's interpretation of the results may expand the boundaries of the theory in terms of populations where self-transcendence may be salient, her results do not necessarily dispute the idea that some awareness of human mortality is integral to self-transcendence. Awareness of mortality is a basic characteristic of the human condition among both healthy and ill adults. This awareness may emerge slowly from the accumulation of life experiences as well as with a suddenness brought on by a health crisis event. How life experiences increase awareness of personal vulnerability and subsequently influence self-transcendence needs continued study.

In summary, Coward's program of research has provided empirical evidence to support and possibly extend the theory of self-transcendence. Her findings from various studies have consistently indicated that self-transcendence is significantly related to indicators of well-being, as found in adults facing the end of life through women's health experiences of advanced breast cancer and AIDS, and men's experience with AIDS. Her research with a healthy population provided further support for the theory of self-transcendence while raising new questions about the significance of awareness of personal mortality in the emergence of self-transcendence.

Other Research

Other research conducted within the recent past has provided support for the theory of self-transcendence. In 1991, Walton and colleagues explored self-transcendence as measured by a 58-item scale based upon Peck's (1968) developmental stages of old age. They identified a significant inverse relationship between self-transcendence and loneliness among 107 healthy older adults.

In research into suicide by Buchanan, Farran, and Clark (1995), the findings supported the hypothesis that self-transcendence was integral to older adults coping with the changes in later life. Other important factors in coping were loss of spouse and friends, loss of work, and state of finances. In studying 35 elders hospitalized for depression, the researchers found that desire for death and self-transcendence were significantly and inversely related at $r = -.55$, $p < .001$. All other relationships between self-transcendence and suicide ideation were in the expected direction but were not significant, likely due to the small sample size.

In a phenomenological study of eight women who had completed breast cancer therapy, Pelusi (1997) found that the journey of surviving breast cancer very much involved self-transcendence. In this population, self-transcendence was expressed as setting life priorities, finding meaning in life, and looking within self.

Self-transcendence and quality of life were studied in 46 HIV-positive adults by Mellors, Riley, and Erlen (1997). Data analysis revealed a significant moderate positive relationship between self-transcendence and quality of life for the group, particularly for those who were the most seriously ill. The dimensions of quality of life that related most significantly to self-transcendence were health and functioning, and psychological/spiritual dimensions.

Chin-A-Loy and Fernsler (1998) examined self-transcendence among 24 men, aged 61 to 84, attending a prostate cancer support group. The participants scored fairly high on the STS, averaging a score of 50 out of a possible 15 to 60. The high level of self-transcendence in this group indicated that they had developed ways to expand beyond the limitations posed by their cancer, despite or perhaps because of aging and living with prostate cancer.

Klaas (1998) studied self-transcendence and depression in 77 depressed and nondepressed elders. Her results in both groups supported the theory of self-transcendence. Significant negative correlations were found between depression and self-transcendence. In addition, self-transcendence was significantly and positively correlated with meaning in life in this group. Last, the depressed group of elders scored significantly lower on the STS as well as on Meaning in Life. Scores on the STS and the Purpose in Life test were significantly and positively related, supporting the construct validity of the STS.

A significant positive relationship was found between self-transcendence and activities of daily living among 88 chronically ill elders in research by Upchurch (1999). She proposed a theoretical model in which self-transcendence, as a developmental strength and part of human essence, may partly explain why some elders continued to remain independent while others did not, regardless of health status.

More recently, in an attempt to explore this concept in a group that was healthy as well as younger than the elders typically studied, Ellermann and Reed (2001) reported on their study of self-transcendence in middle-aged adults. Theorizing as Coward did several years earlier that self-transcendence was a life span phenomenon and not confined to later life, they sought evidence that extended applications of the theory of self-transcendence. They identified parenting, self-acceptance, and spirituality as expressions of self-transcendence in middle-aged adults in particular, and related these experiences to mental health. The results indicated a strong inverse relationship between self-transcendence and level of depression in this group, particularly among women.

In comparing their findings to those from other studies, Ellermann and Reed (2001) found that self-transcendence was higher among groups of older participants, although still salient among the middle-aged participants. Gender differences were identified, including the finding that self-transcendence was more predominant among women than men. Their research not only supported the theory of self-transcendence but also introduced questions about the role of human experiences such as parenting and spirituality in the theory; that is, do they function as indicators, correlates, or antecedents of self-transcendence?

Unpublished Research

Unpublished research into self-transcendence has been reported in master's theses and dissertations. A recent example is Walker (2000), who conducted his dissertation research based upon his model of "transformative aging." Self-transcendence was conceptualized as a process of transforming among middle aged adults from the baby boomer generation. Walker studied self-transcendence as an outcome variable, indicative of well-being. This approach was of interest in view of the fact that the majority of studies, my work included, conceptualized self-transcendence more as an independent variable, predictive of well-being. Among his significant findings was that the variable "mastery of stress" predicted self-transcendence, and the variable "aging readiness" predicted both mastery of stress and self-transcendence. His findings have implications for engaging the resource of self-transcendence to assist middle-aged and older adults in mastering the stress and existential anxiety triggered by the growing awareness of mortality that occurs in middle age.

Billard (2001) examined the role of self-transcendence in the well-being of aging Catholic sisters for her doctoral research. Specifically, she combined Reed's (1987) Spiritual Perspective Scale with Reed's (1991a) Self-Transcendence Scale to measure the concept of "spiritual transcendence" and its relationship to the variable of "emotional intelligence" in a sample of 377 elder Catholic sisters. She found that spiritual transcendence, along with selected personality and demographic factors, contributed significantly to explaining emotional intelligence. Fostering spiritual transcendence was recommended as a resource for helping aging sisters transform their own lives and the lives of others in positive ways.

Decker (1999) studied moral reasoning and self-transcendence within the context of several contextual and developmental factors to better understand end-of-life treatment preferences among 126 older adults. Self-transcendence was theorized to be a correlate of moral reasoning. Findings indicated that self-transcendence was significantly related to the level of integrated moral reasoning and may help explain why reasoning about end-of-life treatment options reflects a complex and integrated approach among some elders.

In her master's thesis research, Runquist (2001) examined self-transcendence along with the variables of spiritual perspective, fatigue, and health status to identify significant correlates of well-being in 61 homeless men and women. She theorized that self-transcendence, coupled with physical health factors, may serve as a resource for well-being in this population. Among the various findings, Runquist identified the existence of a strong positive relationship between self-transcendence and well-being. In addition, two variables, self-transcendence and health status, together explained a significant 60 percent of the variance in well-being, with self-transcendence having the greater correlation with well-being. These findings suggest that an effective clinical approach with homeless persons does not necessarily require extensive clinical applications to enhance well-being. Attention to the spiritual side of living, in addition to physical health, may be equally important in fostering well-being among homeless persons.

The dissertation and thesis studies of these and many other graduate students (e.g., Draur, 1997; Kamienski, 1997) have provided creative and consistent evidence to support the theory of self-transcendence. This is so regardless of whether Reed's Self-Transcendence Scale was used in the research. That other measures and indicators of self-transcendence were used and generated supportive findings is evidence of the stability of the theory.

USE OF THE THEORY IN NURSING PRACTICE

Research findings have shown that self-transcendence is integral to well-being across a diversity of health experiences that confront a person with end-of-life issues. Nursing practices that facilitate self-transcendence result in healing outcomes during these health events, as in, for example, diminished depression over time among clinically depressed elders, increased hopefulness and care of self among chronically ill elders, sense of well-being among persons with advanced breast cancer or with HIV/AIDS, and decreased suicidal ideation among hospitalized depressed elders. Although these particular health events have been the focus in self-transcendence research, many if not most health events confront a person with vulnerability and mortality, and therefore are potential contexts for promoting healing and well-being through self-transcendence.

Encouraged by these results, nurses have continued to identify other health experiences in which they can promote well-being by facilitating self-transcendence: for example, bereavement (Joffrion & Douglas, 1994), family caregivers of adults with dementia (Acton & Wright, 2000), and maintenance of sobriety and well-being (McGee, 2000).

With the rise of managed care, advanced practice nurses increasingly have to provide spiritual care to specialty populations; this care extends beyond that typically provided by primary care practitioners (McCormick, Holder, Wetsel, & Cawthon, 2001). This care includes an integrative approach to spiritual care that includes facilitating self-transcendence.

Strategies for Practice

Intrapersonal strategies help the person expand inward and make room to integrate loss in all its diverse experiences. Meditation, prayer, visualization, life review, and journaling are techniques of self-transcendence that nurses can guide and facilitate (Acton & Wright, 2000; McGee, 2000). These approaches assist a person to look inward to clarify and expand knowledge about the self and find or create meaning and purpose in the experience. Encouraging patients to keep a journal, for example, helps them become more aware of their process of transformation and transcendence. Recognition of the process and the pattern of their own healing is empowering for patients. The nurse may also encourage cognitive strategies that help patients integrate a health event into their lives. Acquiring information about the illness, using positive self-talk, and engaging in meaningful and challenging activities are all techniques that can help a person integrate and grow from the illness experience (Coward & Reed, 1996).

Interpersonal strategies for facilitating self-transcendence focus on connecting the person to others, through formal or informal means, including face-to-face, telephone, or through the Internet. Maintaining meaningful relationships and strengthening affiliations with civic groups and with a supporting faith community are also strategies that the nurse can facilitate (McCormick et al., 2001). Nurse visits, peer counseling, informal networks, and formal support groups are examples of interpersonal strategies that the nurse can help arrange for the person (Acton & Wright, 2000).

Support groups are often cited as an effective way of connecting people facing a difficult life situation. Groups that bring together people of similar health experiences can facilitate self-transcendence by connecting the person to others who can share the loss and exchange information and wisdom about coping with the experience, and by providing an opportunity to reach beyond the self to help another. Joffrion and Douglas (1994) reported that nurses can facilitate self-transcendence during bereavement by helping the person participate in church or civic groups, develop or resume a hobby, share personal experiences of grief with others, and support others who have experienced loss. Coward (1998) developed a series of support group sessions to facilitate self-transcendence. These sessions involved hearing each woman's cancer story, identifying problem-solving skills related to the health experience, expressing feelings about the situation, and listening to others' stories about the illness experience.

Altruistic activities facilitate self-transcendence. They provide a context for learning new things and expanding awareness about oneself and one's world (Coward & Reed, 1996). Altruism also enhances a person's inner sense of worth and purpose. McGee (2000) explained that practicing humility and providing service to others are tools of self-transcendence that can empower individuals to maintain a healthy lifestyle. Connections between people, whether to receive or provide support, are key strategies for enhancing self-transcendence.

Group psychotherapy is another intervention strategy for enhancing self-transcendence. Young and Reed (1995) found that this intervention approach was effective in generating a variety of outcomes for a group of elders: for example, intrapersonally in terms of achieving self-enrichment, self-esteem, and self-affirmation; interpersonally in terms of bonding with and helping others, enabling self-disclosure, and overcoming self-absorption; and temporally in terms of gaining acceptance of one's past and feeling empowered about the future.

Schumann (1999) found that self-transcendence enhanced well-being in ventilated patients. Spiritual connections enabled patients to use temporal perspectives of past and future to empower themselves; they synchronized their lives with the realities of being on a ventilator and anticipating extubation, and were then better able to manage this life-threatening health experience.

Transpersonal strategies are designed to help the person connect with a power or purpose greater than self. The nurse's role in this process is often one of creating an environment in which transpersonal exploration can occur. For example, to foster self-transcendence in family caregivers of adults with dementia, Acton and Wright (2000) identify the importance of helping arrange for in-home assistance or day care so the family members have the time and energy to engage in activities that promote transpersonal awareness. Religious activities and prayer in particular are frequently identified as significant to the well-being of persons facing life crises. McGee (2000) explains the need for the nurse to provide an environment in which patients can look beyond themselves toward a higher power for help, and be inspired to help others. In addition, several of the strategies that foster intrapersonal growth also can foster a sense of transpersonal connection, such as meditation, visualization, and journaling.

CONCLUSIONS

Professional nurses are defined in large part by their ability to engage the human capacities for healing and well-being. Self-transcendence was presented as an innate human capacity for well-being. It represents "both a human capacity and a human struggle that can be facilitated by nursing" (Reed, 1996, p. 3). A goal in developing the theory was to gain better understanding of the dynamics of self-transcendence as it relates to health and well-being. This knowledge, in addition to that acquired through personal knowing and practice experience, can be used by nurses to foster well-being through strategies of self-transcendence.

Rogerian and life span principles of development, external to the theory, influenced the theory's development. Philosophic views include the pandimensionality of human beings and the innate human potential for healing and well-being. Several nursing theories were also foundational to the theory of self-transcendence.

There is consistency among the elements internal to the theory—the concepts, their definitions, and proposed relationships. Positive relationships were identified between vulnerability and self-transcendence and between self-transcendence and well-being. However, new twists in the stated relationships may yet be discovered. For example, vulnerability may not always positively relate to self-transcendence; mediating variables may reverse that relationship. Experiences of vulnerability that are too intense may impede self-transcendence. The turn of the century and the terrorist attacks of September 11, 2001, mark a time of intense feelings of vulnerability as well as hope in humanity's ability to transcend difficulty. The theory is significant in that it is a theory for the present. Self-transcendence reflects a nursing perspective of human beings and proposes a mechanism by which human beings generate well-being in times of vulnerability. This process has been supported by research. Nursing, through its theories and practices that inspire human transcendence, can make a significant contribution to sustaining human beings within the context of their everyday experiences.

The theory now reaches beyond the initial focus on elders to include any adult who experiences vulnerability. Future research may further broaden the scope to include other normative life transitions and developmental events among youth and children, whose processes of self-transcendence have yet to be explored. The scholarship of advanced practice nurses, graduate students, and researchers can offer new insights into personal, contextual, and cultural factors that influence the process of self-transcendence.

Self-transcendence may very well be a developmental imperative for younger as well as older people, for those healthy and ill. If so, nursing must be there to generate the knowledge and provide the expert support that facilitates this cost-effective and holistic process of well-being.

REFERENCES

Acton, G. J., & Wright, K. B. (2000). Self-transcendence and family caregivers of adults with dementia. *Journal of Holistic Nursing, 18,* 143–158.

Arlin, P. K. (1975). Cognitive development in adulthood: A fifth stage? *Developmental Psychology, 11,* 602–606.

Basseches, M. (1984). *Dialectical thinking and adult development.* Norwood, NJ: Ablex.

Billard, A. (2001). *The impact of spiritual transcendence on the well-being of aging Catholic sisters.* Unpublished doctoral dissertation, Loyola College, Baltimore, MD.

Buchanan, D., Farran, C., & Clark, D. (1995). Suicidal thought and self-transcendence in older adults. *Journal of Psychosocial Nursing, 33*(10), 31–34.

Chin-A-Loy, S. S., & Fernsler, J. I. (1998). Self-transcendence in older men attending a prostate cancer support group. *Cancer Nursing, 21*, 358–363.

Cloninger, C. R., Svrakic, N. M., & Svrakic, D. M. (1997). Role of personality self-organization in development of mental order and disorder. *Development and Psychopathology, 9*, 881–906.

Commons, M., Demick, J., & Goldberg, C. (1996). *Clinical approaches to adult development.* Norwood, NJ: Ablex.

Corless, I. B., Germino, B. B., & Pittman, M. (1994). *Dying, death, and bereavement: Theoretical perspectives and other ways of knowing.* Boston: Jones and Bartlett.

Coward, D. (1990). The lived experience of self-transcendence in women with advanced breast cancer. *Nursing Science Quarterly, 3*, 162–169.

Coward, D. (1991). Self-transcendence and emotional well-being in women with advanced breast cancer. *Oncology Nursing Forum, 18*, 857–863.

Coward, D. (1995). Lived experience of self-transcendence in women with AIDS. *Journal of Obstetric, Gynecologic, and Neonatal Nursing, 24*, 314–318.

Coward, D. (1996). Self-transcendence and correlates in a healthy population. *Nursing Research, 45*, 116–122.

Coward, D. (1998). Facilitation of self-transcendence in a breast cancer support group. *Oncology Nursing Forum, 25*, 75–84.

Coward, D., & Lewis, F. (1993). The lived experience of self-transcendence in gay men with AIDS. *Oncology Nursing Forum, 20*, 1363–1369.

Coward, D., & Reed, P. G. (1996). Self-transcendence: A resource for healing at the end of life. *Issues in Mental Health Nursing, 17*, 275–288.

Decker, I. M. (1999). *Moral reasoning, self-transcendence, and end-of-life decisions in a group of community dwelling elders.* Unpublished doctoral dissertation, University of Arizona, Tucson.

Draur, G. A. (1997). *Intrinsic religious motivation, adverse life events, coping practices, and the development of self-transcendence in older women.* Unpublished doctoral dissertation, University of Nebraska, Lincoln.

Ellermann, C. R., & Reed, P. G. (2001). Self-transcendence and depression in middle-aged adults. *Western Journal of Nursing Research, 23*, 698–713.

Erikson, E. H. (1986). *Vital involvement in old age.* New York: Norton.

Frankl, V. E. (1963). *Man's search for meaning.* New York: Pocket Books.

Frankl, V. E. (1969). *The will to meaning.* New York: New American Library.

Haase, J. E., Britt, T., Coward, D. D., Leidy, N. K., & Penn, P. E. (1992). Simultaneous concept analysis of spiritual perspective, hope, acceptance and self-transcendence. *IMAGE: Journal of Nursing Scholarship, 24*, 141–147.

Joffrion, L. P., & Douglas, D. (1994). Grief resolution: Facilitating self-transcendence in the bereaved. *Journal of Psychosocial Nursing, 32*(3), 13–19.

Kamienski, M. C. (1997). *An investigation of the relationship among suffering, self-transcendence, and social support in women with breast cancer.* Unpublished doctoral dissertation, Rutgers, the State University of New Jersey, Newark.

Klaas, D. (1998). Testing two elements of spirituality in depressed and non-depressed elders. *The International Journal of Psychiatric Nursing Research, 4,* 452–462.

Koplowitz, H. (1984). A projection beyond Piaget's formal operational stage: A general systems stage and a unitary stage. In M. L. Commons, F. A. Richards, & C. Armon (Eds.), *Beyond formal operations: Late adolescence and adult cognitive development* (pp. 272–296). New York: Praeger.

Marshall, V. M. (1980). *Last chapter: A sociology of aging and dying.* Monterey, CA: Brooks-Cole.

Maslow, A. H. (1969). Various meanings of transcendence. *Journal of Transpersonal Psychology, 1,* 56–66.

McCormick, D. P., Holder, B., Wetsel, M. A., & Cawthon, T. W. (2001). Spirituality and HIV disease: An integrated perspective. *Journal of the Association of Nurses in AIDS Care, 12*(3), 58–65.

McGee, E. M. (2000). Alcoholics Anonymous and nursing. *Journal of Holistic Nursing, 18*(1), 11–26.

Mellors, M. P., Riley, T. A., & Erlen, J. A. (1997). HIV, self-transcendence, and quality of life. *Journal of the Association of Nurses in AIDS Care, 2,* 59–69.

Newman, M. (1992). Prevailing paradigms in nursing. *Nursing Outlook, 40,* 10–13.

Newman, M. (1994). *Health as expanding consciousness* (2nd ed.). New York: National League for Nursing.

Parse, R. (1992). Human becoming: Parse's theory of nursing. *Nursing Science Quarterly, 5,* 35–42.

Peck, R. C. (1968). Psychological development in the second half of life. In B. L. Neugarten (Ed.), *Middle age and aging* (pp. 88–92). Chicago: University of Chicago Press.

Pelusi, J. (1997). The lived experience of surviving breast cancer. *Oncology Nursing Forum, 24*(8), 1343–1353.

Reed, P. G. (1983). Implications of the life-span developmental framework for well-being in adulthood and aging. *Advances in Nursing Science, 6,* 18–25.

Reed, P. G. (1986). Developmental resources and depression in the elderly: A longitudinal study. *Nursing Research, 35,* 368–374.

Reed, P. G. (1987). Spirituality and well-being in terminally ill hospitalized adults. *Research in Nursing and Health, 10*(5), 335–344.

Reed, P. G. (1989). Mental health of older adults. *Western Journal of Nursing Research, 11*(2), 143–163.

Reed, P. G. (1991a). Self-transcendence and mental health in oldest-old adults. *Nursing Research, 40,* 7–11.

Reed, P. G. (1991b). Toward a theory of self-transcendence: Deductive reformulation using developmental theories. *Advances in Nursing Science, 13*(4), 64–77.

Reed, P. G. (1996). Transcendence: Formulating nursing perspectives. *Nursing Science Quarterly, 9*(1), 2–4.

Reed, P. G. (1997a). Nursing: The ontology of the discipline. *Nursing Science Quarterly, 10*(2), 76–79.

Reed, P. G. (1997b). The place of transcendence in nursing's science of unitary human beings: Theory and research. In M. Madrid (Ed.), *Patterns of Rogerian knowing* (pp. 187–196). New York: National League for Nursing.

Riegel, K. F. (1976). The dialectics of human development. *American Psychologist,* *31,* 631–647.

Rogers, M. E. (1970). *Introduction to the theoretical basis of nursing.* Philadelphia: F. A. Davis.

Rogers, M. E. (1980). A science of unitary man. In J. P. Riehl & C. Roy (Eds.), *Conceptual modes for nursing practice* (2nd ed., pp. 329–337). New York: Appleton-Century-Crofts.

Rogers, M. E. (1994). The science of unitary human beings: Current perspectives. *Nursing Science Quarterly, 7*(1), 33–35.

Runquist, J. J. (2001). *Spirituality, self-transcendence, fatigue, and health status as correlates of well-being in homeless persons.* Unpublished master's thesis, University of Arizona, Tucson.

Schumann, R. R. (1999). *Intensive care patients' perceptions of the experience of mechanical ventilation.* Unpublished doctoral dissertation, Texas Women's University, Denton.

Sheldon, K. M., & Kasser, T. (2001). Getting older, getting better? Personal strivings and psychological maturity across the life span. *Developmental Psychology, 37,* 491–501.

Sinnott, J. D. (1998). *The development of logic in adulthood: Postformal thought and its applications.* New York: Plenum.

Upchurch, S. (1999). Self-transcendence and activities of daily living: The woman with the pink slippers. *Journal of Holistic Nursing, 17,* 251–266.

Walker, C. A. (2000). *Aging among baby boomers.* Unpublished doctoral dissertation, Texas Women's University, Denton.

Walton, C. G., Shultz, C., Beck, C. M., & Walls, R. C. (1991). Psychological correlates of loneliness in the older adult. *Archives of Psychiatric Nursing, 5*(3), 165–170.

Watson, J. (1999). *Nursing: Human science and human care.* Sudbury, MA: Jones & Bartlett. (original work published 1985).

Young, C., & Reed, P. G. (1995). Elders' perceptions of the effectiveness of group psychotherapy in fostering self-transcendence. *Archives of Psychiatric Nursing, 9,* 338–347.

9

The Theory of Attentively Embracing Story

Mary Jane Smith and Patricia Liehr

Our belief in the healing potential of story sharing and our recognition of the importance of building theory at the intersection of practice and research were essential to the development of the middle range theory of attentively embracing story. An article on the theory of attentively embracing story was first published in 1999 (Smith & Liehr). In her response to the theory, Reed (1999) described its central ontology: "story is an inner human resource for making meaning," and its central epistemology: "middle-range theory bonds research and practice in a method of knowledge development" (p. 205).

PURPOSE OF THE THEORY AND HOW IT WAS RESHAPED

Stories are a fundamental dimension of the human experience. They bind humans to other humans and times to other times (Taylor, 1996). Stories express who people are, where they've been, and where they are going. The purpose of the theory of attentively embracing story is to describe and explain story as the context for a nurse–person health-promoting process. The theory was developed to provide a story-centered structure for guiding nursing practice and research. The core nursing process for practice and research is the nurse/person relationship. In this relationship the nurse gathers a story about a health situation that matters to the person.

The authors had a long-term relationship that started in an educational program and cultivated discussion of common values about nursing practice and research. Smith began studying rest in 1975 with her dissertation research (Smith, 1975). Later, she conceptualized rest as "easing with the flow of rhythmic change in the environment" (Smith, 1986, p. 23). Liehr's (1992) dissertation examined the blood pressure effects of talking about the usual day and listening to a story. These early works were harbingers of what was to come in collaboration.

Years passed and we both pursued our own work. A serendipitous meeting at a nursing conference led to discussion of the importance of story for promoting health and human development. In talking about our individual work, we were struck by the commonalities that surfaced when we gathered stories. It became clear that story was our context for guiding practice and research. This clarity demanded the articulation of a theory as a basis for further work. It was important that the theory be at the middle range level of abstraction to ensure applicability. The theory was developed in an enthusiastic discourse that fits the description by Belenky, Clinchy, Goldberger, and Tarule (1996) "as a place where people work at the very edges of their abilities, constantly pushing each other's thinking into new territory, giving names to things that have gone unnamed, dreaming of better ways, describing common ground and finding ways to realize shared dreams" (p. 13).

We began trying to name the theory to reflect our experience with patients and research participants. We had an image of the way story sharing mattered to people when we listened with full attention. It took time to engage in the creative process of naming the theory. After several months and many names, we had the name and we knew it. There was a click of coherence. Once the theory was named, each of us began to view practice and research situations through the lens of attentively embracing story. The concepts were forged in intense back-and-forth scrutiny, moving from the conceptual to the empirical and back again.

FOUNDATIONAL LITERATURE AND ASSUMPTIONS

Attentively embracing story is a middle range theory holding assumptions congruent with unitary and neomodernist perspectives (Parse,

1981; Reed, 1995; Rogers, 1994). In these nonreductionistic views, human beings are transforming and transcending in mutual process with their environment. The mutual, ever-changing motion of creating meaning is at the core of the unitary perspective. Developmental personal history and human potential for health and healing are at the core of the neomodernist perspective.

The human story is a health story in the broadest sense. It is a recounting of one's current life situation to clarify present meaning in relation to the past with an eye toward the future, all in the present moment. The idea of story is not new to nursing. Several extant nursing theories explicitly or implicitly incorporate dimensions of narrative (Newman, 1999; Parse, 1981; Peplau, 1991; Watson, 1997). The nursing literature frequently addresses the importance of the nurse's story (Benner, 1984; Chinn & Kramer, 1999; Ford & Turner, 2001) and less often considers the use of story as a nursing intervention. Sandelowski has evaluated both the research (1991) and practice (1994) merits of the human story. Burkhardt and Nagai-Jacobson (2002) call attention to the power of story: "In the process of telling and hearing stories, persons often come to new insights and deeper understandings of themselves because stories include not only events in our lives, but also the meanings and interpretations that define the significance of the events for particular lives" (p. 296). McAdams (1993) describes the processes occurring when interpreted meaning supports healing: "Stories help us organize our thoughts, providing a narrative for human intentions and interpersonal events that is readily remembered and told. In some instances, stories may also mend us when we are broken, heal us when we are sick" (p. 31).

The assumptions of the theory are that persons (1) change as they interrelate with their world in a vast array of flowing connected dimensions, (2) live an expanded present where past and future events are transformed in the here and now, and (3) experience meaning as a resonating awareness in the creative unfolding of human potential. The first assumption grounds a sensitivity to the complexity of entangled health-story dimensions to highlight persons moving with, through, and beyond their unfolding story. The second assumption invites a focus on the storyteller's present health experience with the listener's understanding that the storyteller's unique perspective incorporates the past and future in the here and now. The third assumption supports the human propensity to create meaning through awareness of thoughts, feelings, behavior, bodily experience, and other human expressions, all in the rhythm of the unfolding health-story.

MAJOR CONCEPTS

Attentively embracing story is composed of three interrelated concepts: (1) intentional dialogue as querying emergence in true presence, (2) connecting with self-in-relation as reflective awareness on personal history, and (3) creating ease as re-membering disjointed story moments with flow in the midst of anchoring. The central descriptor of this middle range theory is the human story composed through intentional dialogue, centered on a complicating health challenge.

Intentional dialogue is purposeful engagement with another to summon the story of a complicating health challenge. There is intention to engage in dialogue about the unique life experience of one's pain, confusion, joy, broken relationships, satisfaction, or suffering as a catalyst to seek a message and begin a process of change. Telling one's story happens in a trusting relationship with another where the nurse walks with the storyteller along a path, journeying a little further along to uncover what is happening, and paying attention to the unfolding movement of story, where both the storyteller and the nurse come to know better who they are (Campbell, 1988; Keen & Valley-Fox, 1989). Intentional dialogue energizes the experience of being alive by touching that which matters most of all to the storyteller. Throughout the flow of the story, the nurse holds fast to what has real meaning for the person who is recollecting what is past in the here and now, and accepting self as truly alive in the present moment of hopes, dreams, and expectations. In giving full attention to the other, the nurse "conveys to the speaker that his contribution is worth listening to, that as a person he is respected enough to receive the undivided attention of another" (Rogers, 1951, p. 34).

There are two processes of intentional dialogue: true presence and querying emergence. True presence is the nurse's nonjudgmental rhythmical focusing/refocusing of energy on the other, which is open to what was, is, and can be. It is "bringing one's humanness to the moment while simultaneously giving self over to the other who is exploring the meaning of the situation" (Liehr, 1989, p. 7). True presence is crucial to walking with the other who is attentively embracing story. It is the substance of the nurse's activity during story sharing. Attending to the emergence of the unfolding health story assumes true presence and focuses on seeking clarification of the patterns that connect the beginning, middle, and end of a story. The nurse lives true presence by staying in while staying out. There is an all-at-once staying close to the story rhythm from the perspective of the storyteller while simultaneously distancing to discern patterns of connectedness. If the story is told over many encounters, it helps the nurse to make notes about story progress, possible patterns, and hunches about meaning.

Querying the emergence of the health-story is clarification of vague story directions. Both the nurse and the storyteller attend to the story of the complicating health challenge. The nurse concentrates and tries to understand the story from the other's perspective. Nothing can be assumed about the story; only the storyteller knows the details. The story is never finished. There is always more to the story, including parts that the individual may not want to tell. The nurse in true presence stays with the longing to tell and the desire to tell only so much at a time.

Connecting with self-in-relation is the active process of recognizing self as related with others in a story-plot. Hall and Allan (1994) identified self-in-relation as a central concept in their model for nursing practice and focused on the meaning of the concept for nurse–client interaction, noting that the "self is created in relation to others" (p. 112). Surrey (1991), who has developed a theory of self-in-relation, proposes it as the primary developmental process for women. The conceptualizations of Hall, Allan, and Surrey fit with our ideas in some places and misfit in others, but their ideas confirm a common ground of valuing self-in-relation as a dimension of human development and caring processes.

In the theory of attentively embracing story, connecting with self-in-relation is composed of personal history and reflective awareness. Personal history is the unique narrative uncovered when individuals reflect on where they have come from, where they are now, and where they are going in life. Venturing into the story is following the path of life as recollected. In the recollection, the nurse invites an awareness of self-in-relation to the complex context of a unique life. In following the story path, the nurse encourages reckoning with a personal history by traveling to the past to arrive at the story beginning, moving through the middle, and into the future all in the present, thus going into the depths of the story to find unique meanings that often lie hidden in the ambiguity of puzzling dilemmas. Self is affirmed in recognition and acceptance of nuances, faults and strengths, as well as understanding of how one has lived and how one envisions future hopes and dreams.

Reflective awareness, which is the opposite of taking life for granted, is being in touch with bodily experience, thoughts, and feelings. It relates to being in touch with one's view of and place in the world and, more concretely, in the moment (Kabat-Zinn, 1994). As the nurse guides reflective awareness on bodily experiences, thoughts, and feelings in a given moment of story, the storyteller becomes present to what is known and unknown, allowing unrecognized meaning to surface. Maslow (1967) describes the desire to know and the simultaneous fear of knowing. He states, "It is certainly demonstrable that we need the truth and we love to seek it. And yet it is just as easy to demonstrate that we are also simultaneously afraid to know the truth" (p. 167). Meaning changes when the unknown comes to light as known in an expanded present moment where there is coherence and integration. Reflective awareness on the personal history of story enlivens one's connection with self-in-relation to others and the world. It establishes an environment for creating ease.

Creating ease is an energizing release experienced as the story comes together in movement toward resolving. It happens in the context of a person's search for ease and the nurse's intention to enable ease. The two dimensions of creating ease are: re-membering disjointed story moments and flow in the midst of anchoring. Re-membering disjointed story moments is connecting events in time through the realization, acceptance, and understanding that come as health-story fragments sort and converge as a meaningful whole. Polanyi (1958) discusses understanding as "a grasping of disjointed parts into a comprehensive whole" (p. 28). In the nurse–person dialogue, there is a re-membering of disconnected moments as the nurse moves with the person through the story. Patterns surface as individuals shed a momentary light on the meaning of important experiences. Often, the nurse does not divert attention to the highlighted experiences when they are first introduced, but tucks them into the background while staying with the foreground story. With focused presence over time, the nurse enables the other to illuminate issues, values, ideas, and context, uncovering coherent patterns of meaning in the tapestry of life experience. Disjointed moments are woven together as the storyteller re-members the health story in the presence of a caring nurse.

Flow is an experience of dynamic harmony, and anchoring is an experience of comprehending meaning. As patterns are discerned, named, and made explicit, anchoring and flowing occur all at the same time. Meaning surfaces while anchoring in a moment of pattern clarity, allowing a sense of flow and calmness. "Flow is the way people describe their state of mind when consciousness is harmoniously ordered and they want to pursue whatever they are doing for its own sake" (Csikszentmihalyi, 1990, p. 6). Csikszentmihalyi describes the harmony that ensues when one anchors to meanings, which capture purposeful unity and focus on life direction. He provides descriptions of individuals who used changing health situations to achieve clarity of purpose, noting that "a person who knows how to find flow from life is able to enjoy even situations that seem only to allow despair" (Csikszentmihalyi, 1990, p. 193). Justice (1998), in describing pain, states that "when I keep mindful of the connections I have with a larger wholeness and order, I can often lift myself out of my pain or relieve it" (p. 108). He advocates paying attention to both sides of life to enable a sense of a larger wholeness or order. A whole story encompasses a life of gladness and melancholy, restriction and freedom, fear and security, and discrepancy and coherence. No story is one-sided. The person experiencing loss is also experiencing gain and the one who is lonely often has uplifting interactions with others. As the disjointed story moments come together as a whole, there is a simultaneous anchoring and flow through recognition of meaning, which energizes release from the confines of an untold story. This is ease. It is resonating energy, enabling vision even for only a moment—a powerful moment creating possibilities for human development.

RELATIONSHIPS AMONG THE CONCEPTS: THE MODEL

The theory comes to life in practice and research through the dimensions of story. Franklin (1994) asserts that stories are composed of complicating, developmental, and resolving processes. When gathering health-story data, the complicating process focuses on a health challenge that arises when there is a change in the person's life; the developmental process is composed of the story-plot that links to the health challenge and suffuses it with meaning; and the resolving process is a shift in view that enables progressing with new understanding.

The relationships among the concepts of the theory are depicted in Figure 9.1. This model is different from the first model of the theory (1999), which attempted to show the dynamic nature of the theory but failed to capture the all-at-once nature of intentional dialogue,

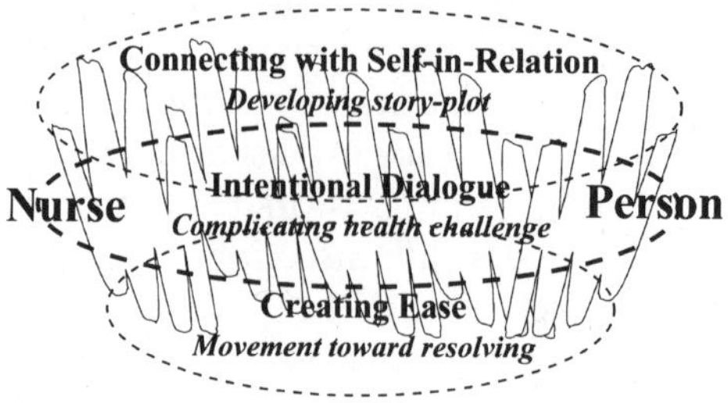

FIGURE 9.1   Attentively embracing story.

connecting with self-in-relation and creating ease. Further thinking and discussion led to the current model that attempts to depict a common flow of energy between nurse and person where story emerges. In this shared flux of energy all the concepts of story come together. The new model moves the theory more toward the middle of the body of middle range theory by articulating story processes (complicating health challenge, developing story-plot, movement toward resolving) that provide a base for gathering story in research and practice. Story-plot is the organizing theme that brings events of the story together in a meaningful whole (Polkinghorne, 1988). It is proposed that developing story-plot about a complicating health challenge facilitates movement toward resolving.

Attentively embracing story is connecting with self-in-relation through intentional dialogue to create ease. This description highlights the relationships among the concepts. Implicit in the description is the suggestion that story process begins with intentional dialogue to support connecting with oneself in relationship with others and with one's world with the possibility of experiencing ease. There is no doubt that the relationship among the concepts appears linear. However, the intent is that these concepts are in a dynamic interrelationship, a quality that is difficult to depict in a model. For example, moments of ease surface when the nurse first engages the person in a caring way to identify what really matters. Even a brief encounter with a caring nurse enables a connection before story parts come together as a whole. Needless to say, the complexity of human interaction defies linearity. As nurse scientists we are called to fit language to the relationships among the concepts as best we can, recognizing that the simplicity necessary for models conflicts with the complexity recognized in most nursing phenomena.

PRELUDE TO RESEARCH AND PRACTICE: GATHERING THE STORY

The theory proposes common processes for gathering a story, whether the nurse is doing research or practice. These common processes, complicating health challenge, developing story-plot, and movement toward resolving, will be generally discussed before providing examples of their use in practice and research.

Complicating Health Challenge

Generation of story begins when the nurse asks about a complicating health challenge. The issues of importance, that is "what matters" to the storyteller, arise from intentional dialogue and are shared in relation to the present moment. Attentive presence to "what matters" is a way of "being with," which places the storyteller in the center of attention. It carries the storyteller into the moment so that the present moment can be explored as mystery. Movement into the moment calls for connecting with the clear and centered intention to listen and hear the story-plot, with the storyteller leading the direction.

Developing Plot

Next, the nurse invites a reflection on the past, focusing on issues that have importance for the complicating health challenge in the present moment. These issues are the beginnings of the developing story-plot and are critical to understanding self-in-relation. Significant relationships and life circumstances cited by the storyteller are central to the present complicating health challenge as well as to future hopes and dreams. Sometimes, story-plot can best be uncovered by taking pen to paper and drawing relationship structures such as a family tree, which notes important relationships and serves as a base for understanding connecting with self-in-relation. The authors have described the use of a story path (Liehr & Smith, 2000) as a relationship structure that links present, past, and future of an unfolding story-plot. Csikszentmihalyi (1997) believes that "the only path to finding out what life is about is a patient, slow attempt to make sense of the realities of the past and the possibilities of the future as they can be understood in the present" (p. 4).

Movement Toward Resolving

Resolving happens in keeping the storyteller immersed in the "now" health experience. Finding a center of stillness and letting go of busyness and distractions energizes mindful attention to the story and propels movement toward resolving. Kunz (1985) contends that "centering quiets both the mind and emotions and thereby helps develop the power of focusing and intent" (p. 299). The experience of flow happens when the person is fully engaged in overcoming a challenge "that is just about manageable" (Csikszentmihalyi, 1997, p. 30). In a centered-present focus, one is free to take on the complicating health challenge and to view it in a manageable way. Oftentimes this shift to a manageable view energizes a sense of ease. It is an opportunity to change thinking and feeling and to move on differently.

USE OF THE THEORY IN NURSING PRACTICE

The question leading the story when the foremost intention is caring-healing is "what matters" to the client about the complicating health challenge. In eliciting the story, the nurse leads the client along, clarifying meaningful connections about what is happening in everyday living in the context of the client's complicating health challenge. Sharing the health challenge story brings developing story-plot and movement toward resolving to the surface. The resulting story about "what matters" to the client provides distinct information about how one person lived the presenting health challenge. The following story came from a single visit that occurred in an outpatient cardiac rehabilitation center. Stories like this contribute to interdisciplinary care, offer case studies for student learning, and inspire research.

Practice Health Story

Nicholas, who is 70 years old, met with the advanced practice nurse following angioplasty and stent placement. The purpose of the visit was to address challenges arising with lifestyle change. When the nurse asked Nicholas to focus on what matters to him now, he said "Did you know that my doctor hates me—he will allow me no alcohol?" Although he said it jokingly, he explained that each time he and his wife, Joni, sat down to dinner without their usual glass of wine, he was "just pushed over the edge to unbearable." Change in financial status was the next issue he introduced. It was unclear when he would be able to return to work, and there was some question as to whether he would return at all. Finances were tight, resulting in resignation from his country club membership. For the first time in his life, he had to consider social plans in light of available money. There was a pause in the story telling and the nurse asked whether the issues that mattered most at this time had been identified. He nodded. He was then asked to talk about past events that contributed to his experience of the present. He talked about his angioplasty and stent placement and recalled his surprise at this cardiac event. He had no history of heart disease and had begun contemplating retirement. However, the thought of retirement was frustrating because he could not enjoy hobbies he had cultivated over the years: assembling and painting model airplanes and reading historical novels. After mentioning these limits, he explained that he was legally blind as a result of eye surgery two years ago. He quickly shifted to a different issue and mentioned the death of his wife. Since he had already talked about his wife, Joni, the nurse was confused with the mention of his wife's death. When asked about his wife's death, he said, "Marie was my first wife. She was killed in an auto accident long before I married Joni." When asked about the time of Marie's death, he said he didn't know, but that he and Joni had been married twenty years. The nurse made no effort to press the issue of Marie's death, just like she hadn't pressed for information about the eye surgery. It seemed that Nicholas needed to keep these details hazy for now, and the nurse honored the duration and direction of the discussion he chose. Nicholas and Marie have six children who are healthy, married, and living across the United States. He described a strong relationship with his oldest daughter, who lives in the same city and visits during the week to have lunch with him.

Several related story-plot dimensions have surfaced: the death of his wife Marie in an auto accident, marriage to Joni, the experience of his cardiac event, relationships with children, and the loss of his sight. All are intricately related to Nicholas's transforming health challenge. Near the end of the session, Nicholas became visibly thoughtful and said, "You know what's hardest is the loss of energy. I am just so damned tired. I don't know how to live with it." With this comment he shifted the dialogue direction back to his present experience. He was asked to focus on the tiredness he was having every day, how he experienced it, and the uneasiness he felt living with it. He described his frequent need to take naps, his failed attempts to help his wife in attending to monthly bills, and his refusal to make weekend visits to his children even though he had been doing it for many years. The importance of integrating naps into the day and paying attention to early cues to rest were discussed, as well as the importance of reporting tiredness to his physician.

As Nicholas discussed his tiredness, it became clear that his view incorporated an expectation that this situation would not improve and might even get worse. He described his tiredness as a condition he would have to endure, expecting it would dictate his everyday choices for the rest of his life, just like his loss of sight. The nurse said, "I am wondering how those 'loss of sight' glasses you are wearing may be distorting your vision about your recovery." Nicholas paused as he processed his thoughts. He eased back into his chair and took a deep breath. It was a moment of movement toward resolving. The intensity of the story-sharing experience is most easily noticed in such a moment when there is a shift in perspective. One notices intensity as it is released and new patterns surface.

The reader will notice that the story of Nicholas is a reconstructed one shared through the lens of the nurse who gathered it. In this case, it is the nurse's view of what happened, and the story centers around the idea of recognizing a shifting vision. Other practice health stories reconstructed through application of the theory of attentively embracing story include a story of exploring a new territory of calmness (Smith & Liehr, 1999) and one about setting aside life burdens (Liehr & Smith, 2000). Summers (2002) used the theory as a foundation for mutual timing, a concept she believes is critical for effective health care encounters.

USE OF THE THEORY IN NURSING RESEARCH

Health-story gathered for the purpose of scholarly inquiry requires an analysis strategy based on a research question. Analyses appropriate for story data include both qualitative and quantitative approaches. The phenomenological research method is an example of an established way to analyze narrative data (Giorgi, 1985; Smith & Liehr, 1999; Van Manen, 1990). The use of a quantitative indicator may raise questions about the fit between the analysis strategy and the paradigmatic and theoretical underpinnings. A quantitative analysis, which captures story progression, offers congruence. Quantification is not intended to represent a measure of the story, but rather a chronicle of story moments over time. It may be used as a descriptive indicator over the course of a single story-sharing dialogue or an indicator of change as the story is told at several different times.

Examples of approaches for analysis of story-generated data will be presented with a phenomenological research question for qualitative analysis and a descriptive research question for quantitative analysis. In order to provide this example, data were collected with four participants who experienced a cardiac event within the past eight weeks. The dialogue focused on the complicating health challenge, and the stories reflected the inextricable link among the challenge, story-plot, and beginning of resolving. Each dialogue was recorded and took place in a five-minute time period. The scope of story information gathered in this limited amount of time highlights the participants' desire to tell their story to someone who was truly engaged in listening and hearing it. Participants' immersion in their health challenge enabled acquisition of meaningful stories in a short time.

Qualitative Analysis

The research question for the qualitative analysis was: What is the story of recovering from a cardiac event for persons in a cardiac rehabilitation program? Each of the four stories was read carefully and analyzed for story moments in the words of the participant. Story moments were distilled into themes. The story moments and themes for participant #1 can be found in Table 9.1. The themes of the other participants can be found in Table 9.2. Themes for the four participants were pulled together into a story of recovering from a cardiac event.

Research Health Story

The following story addresses recovering from a cardiac event for persons in a cardiac rehabilitation program:

TABLE 9.1   Qualitative Analysis for Participant #1

Story moments	Story themes
I got really tired during running but I blamed it on the running. I never really liked to run. I started to run when I hurt my arm and couldn't play racquetball. Racquetball is more fun and a better workout than running.	Tiredness when running was attributed to not really wanting to run.
When my wife started running, I would run with her. I would always end up a little short of breath and very tired. I should have recognized that as slow as she was running there was no reason, given the shape I was in, that I should not have been able to run for an extended period. Eventually, I started to guess that the tiredness and especially the breathlessness were not about running.	In retrospect, recognizes shortness of breath and fatigue he had when engaging in activity as symptoms.
When I became totally out of breath I knew something was wrong. I went to the hospital and had to have cardiac surgery.	Escalating symptoms were fully acknowledged when he became severely short of breath and requested medical treatment.
The heart condition is the most debilitating time I've had. I feel weak and unable to do some of the things I want to do.	Discord between what he wants to do and is able to do results from weakness.
It feels like a race against my age, and I've got to stay ahead of my age.	Racing against time to stay ahead of his age.
Actually I am better now than ever before and I should be able to play racquetball before the month is over.	Ups and downs of the past are recognized within the context of making strides in feeling better than ever and looking forward to resuming favorite activities.

TABLE 9.2   Story Themes for Three Participants*

Participant #2

- Yearns for the good old days when he was in his prime and really strong.
- Long periods of inactivity in his truck along with encroaching shortness of breath planted the thought that he was out of shape.
- Pervasive tiredness that was in opposition to the way he knows himself.
- Confronted with the sudden twist of experiencing a heart attack that threatened the ground of his being.
- Uncertain as he grapples with a desire to not return to driving a truck and to commit to lifestyle change and believes the passing of time will bring answers.

Participant #3

- Loss of usual mobility occurred as a complication of surgery, which was expected to be uncomplicated.
- Pain, shortness of breath, and fatigue were mislabeled and attributed to feelings associated with unexpected loss of mobility.
- Suddenly he was faced with severe pain and shortness of breath that led to hospitalization for heart attack.
- Increasing inertia in the shadow of back problems.
- Forward movement is clouded by loss of mobility and uncertainty about his ability to move beyond tiredness.

Participant #4

- Deep and intense pain broke his heart when his wife died of breast cancer and his daughter was killed in an accident.
- Feels limited by tiredness but not sick.
- Concern about his youngest son to whom he ascribes the cause for his heart attack.
- Bewildered by son's behavior when at times he is thoughtful and kind and at other times mean and angry.
- Overwhelmed by thought of keeping up with son who he fears may be stealing and taking drugs.
- Hopes for some change and plans to attempt greater vigilance with his son.

*Themes for Participant #1 are in Table 9.1.

Recovering from a cardiac event is struggling with the unexpected nature of the event, yet acknowledging subtle cues that the event was coming. Profound tiredness permeates activity changes and relationship evaluation as one recovers. The process of redefining self as someone who has had a cardiac event incorporates uncertainty and trust that life will move to a different normal.

Quantitative Analysis

This example offers analysis of story data using a quantitative approach with Linguistic Inquiry and Word Count (LIWC), a software program developed by Pennebaker, Francis, and Booth (2001). This quantitative language analysis allows acquisition of an indicator of what happened during the process of story sharing (Liehr et al., 2002). The four verbatim stories used for qualitative analysis were reanalyzed. The research question for the quantitative analysis was: What words are used to tell the story of recovering from a cardiac event for persons in a cardiac rehabilitation program? The story data will provide a descriptive indicator of the expanded moment of recovering shared in this single story-sharing dialogue. If the researcher was interested in changing word use over the period of recovery, a different question would be posed and data would be collected several more times during the months after the cardiac event. This example is provided to demonstrate the promise of linguistic analysis for analyzing health-story data.

The LIWC program is a word-based computerized text analysis software that discerns linguistic elements (word count and sentence punctuation); affective, cognitive, sensory, and social words; and words that reflect relativity and personal concerns. Seventy-two dimensions of language use comprise the LIWC structure for narrative evaluation. The structure has had psychometric testing, and reliability and validity estimates are reported by Pennebaker and King (1999).

Preparation of the nurse–client transcripts for analysis included deletion of the nurse's words, correction of spelling errors, and removal of utterances that did not constitute recognizable words. Each transcript was saved as a text file. Table 9.3 shows selected LIWC dimensions (personal concerns, human expressions, relativity) linked to the story processes (complicating health challenge, developing story-plot, movement toward resolving) of the middle range theory of attentively embracing story. The LIWC program computes the percentage of words used for each word dimension (number of words

TABLE 9.3   Word Dimensions Associated with Story Processes and Average Percentage of Recovery Story Words Used by Participants for Each Dimension

Story processes and word dimensions	Average percentage*
Process: Complicating health challenge	
Dimension: Personal concerns	
• Occupation	1.4
• Leisure activity	1.4
• Money and financial issues	.3
• Metaphysical issues	.3
• Bodily states and functions	3.9
Process: Developing story-plot	
Dimension: Human expressions	
• Affective	4.3
positive feelings, including optimism and energy	2.3
negative feelings, including anxiety, fear, anger, sadness	2.0
• Cognitive	6.8
• Sensory and perceptual	2.2
• Social	5.2
Process: Movement toward resolving	
Dimension: Relativity	
Present tense	11.4
Past tense	7.2
Future tense	1.0

*average percentage, calculated as the number of analyzed words tapping these selected dimensions relative to the total number of analyzed words in the transcripts; dimensions overlap and not all dimensions are represented.

used in a dimension relative to entire narrative passage for each participant). It meshes with the Statistical Package for the Social Sciences (SPSS) to enable statistical analysis. For the purposes of this example, descriptive statistics are reported.

Descriptive statistics indicate, for instance, that participants talked more about their bodily states (3.9%) than any other personal concerns. Also, 11.4% of participants' words were present tense, suggesting that the dialogue focused on the present moment more than the past (7.2%) or the future (1%). Cognitive words were used more frequently (6.8%) than affective words (4.3%), and the use of positive feeling words (2.3%) was comparable to negative feeling words (2.0%).

Pennebaker (1997) has found that better health outcomes are associated with a higher use of positive feeling words and a moderate number of negative feeling words. Both high and low use of negative feeling words was associated with poorer health outcomes. In studies of journaling about traumatic events, he found that persons who shift from low to high use of cognitive process words are more likely to have improved health and higher grades after journaling. Pennebaker (2000) offers an explanation of the shift to increasing use of cognitive process words: "In reading the essays of people who showed this pattern of language use, it became apparent that they were constructing a story over time. Building a narrative, then, seemed to be critical in reaching understanding" (p. 10). Although most of Pennebaker's research has used a writing intervention, he suggests that it is reasonable to expect similar results with writing and speaking, as long as participants are encouraged to reflectively explore what they are thinking and feeling.

The LIWC program provides an avenue for analyzing words over time. It is a measure of process that is congruent with the proposed inquiry. The question of a shift in story language could readily be analyzed with longitudinal story data. For instance, by using the baseline data (Table 9.3) and then adding story sessions at 6 and 12 months, examiners would see shifts in story surfacing. Given the previous findings by Pennebaker and colleagues (Pennebaker, 1997, 2000) one might expect an increase in cognitive words as participants create a coherent story, joining disjointed story moments into a comprehensible whole. "Translating personally upsetting experiences into language in a story format . . . may accomplish for us what oral storytelling accomplished for our ancestors—improvements . . . in health and closer social bonds" (Pennebaker, 2000, p. 15).

CONCLUSIONS

Collaborative work on the theory of attentively embracing story began in 1996 and the theory was first published in 1999. In the seven years since we first began thinking through the meaning of story-sharing for health, we have accomplished a great deal and still are at a beginning. Development and publication of the theory led to further consideration and description of use in practice (Liehr & Smith, 2000). Consideration also turned to research; we have spent the last several years refining the methodologic processes central to both practice and research. We believe that phenomenologic methods are appropriate for the qualitative analysis of story data, and linguistic analysis, using software programs such as LIWC, show promise for quantitative analysis. One direction that continues to draw our attention is presentation of a meaningful theory structure for advanced practice nurses. For instance, we think that health stories routinely gathered in practice settings are a potentially prolific research base, which if theory-guided and analyzed, could provide powerful direction for practice.

Both authors have research in some phase of completion. Smith has used the story gathering structure to guide data collection in a study of intervening in drinking-driving situations. Liehr has recently examined story-centered care in a group of persons with stage one hypertension. In addition, Summers (2002) used the theory to derive the concept of mutual timing. Burkhardt and Nagai-Jacobson (2002) cited the theory when discussing the strength of a theory base for gathering a health story.

Each time we share another dimension of our thinking with the nursing community, we learn more about the theory and formulate next directions. Middle range theory development is scholarship in progress with practice and research. As these thoughts are shared, new questions are realized, and so the story goes.

REFERENCES

Belenky, M. F., Clinchy, B. M., Goldberger, N., & Tarule, J. M. (1996). *Women's ways of knowing: The development of self, voice, and mind.* New York: Basic Books.

Benner, P. (1984). *From novice to expert.* Menlo Park, CA: Addison-Wesley.

Burkhardt, M. A., & Nagai-Jacobson, M. G. (2002). *Spirituality: Living our connectedness.* Albany, NY: Delmar.

Campbell, J. (1988). *The power of myth.* New York: Doubleday.

Chinn, P. L., & Kramer, M. K. (1999). *Theory and nursing integrated knowledge development.* New York: Mosby.

Csikszentmihalyi, M. (1990). *Flow: The psychology of optimal experience.* New York: Harper & Row.

Csikszentmihalyi, M. (1997). *Finding flow.* New York: Basic Books.

Ford, K., & Turner, D. (2001). Stories seldom told: Pediatric nurses' experiences of caring for hospitalized children with special needs and their families. *Journal of Advanced Nursing, 33,* 288–295.

Franklin, J. (1994). *Writing for story.* Middlesex, England: Penguin.

Giorgi, A. (1985). *Phenomenology and psychological research.* Pittsburgh, PA: Duquesne University Press.

Hall, B. A., & Allan, J. D. (1994). Self in relation: A prolegomenon for holistic nursing. *Nursing Outlook, 15,* 110–116.

Justice, B. (1998). *A different kind of health: Finding well-being despite illness.* Houston, TX: Peak.

Kabat-Zinn, J. (1994). *Wherever you go, there you are.* New York: Hyperion.

Keen, S., & Valley-Fox, A. (1989). *Your mythic journey.* Los Angeles: Jeremy P. Tarcher.

Kunz, D. (1985). Compassion, rootedness and detachment: Their role in healing. In D. Kunz (Ed.), *Spiritual aspects of the healing arts* (pp. 289–305). Wheaton, IL: The Theosophical Publishing House.

Liehr, P. (1989). A loving center: The core of true presence. *Nursing Science Quarterly, 2,* 7–8.

Liehr, P. (1992). Uncovering a hidden language: The effects of listening and talking on blood pressure and heart rate. *Archives of Psychiatric Nursing, 6,* 306–311.

Liehr, P., & Smith, M. J. (2000). Using story theory to guide nursing practice. *International Journal of Human Caring, 4,* 13–18.

Liehr, P., Takahashi, R., Nishimura, C., Frazier, L., Kuwajima, I., & Pennebaker, J. W. (2002). Expressing health experience through embodied language. *Journal of Nursing Scholarship, 34,* 25–30.

Maslow, A. H. (1967). Neurosis as a failure of personal growth. *Humanitas, 8,* 153–169.

McAdams, D. P. (1993). *The stories we live by.* New York: Guilford.

Newman, M. A. (1999). The rhythm of relating in a paradigm of wholeness. *Image: Journal of Nursing Scholarship, 31,* 227–230.

Parse, R. R. (1981). *Man-living-health: A theory of nursing.* New York: Wiley.

Pennebaker, J. W. (1997). *Opening up.* New York: Guilford.

Pennebaker, J. W. (2000). Telling stories: The health benefits of narrative. *Literature and Medicine, 19*(1), 3–18.

Pennebaker, J. W., Francis, M. E., & Booth, R. J. (2001). *Linguistic inquiry and word count: LWIC 2001.* Mahwah, NJ: Erlbaum.

Pennebaker, J. W., & King, L. A. (1999). Linguistic styles: Language use as an individual difference. *Journal of Personality and Social Psychology, 77,* 1296–1312.

Pennebaker, J. W., Mayne, T. J., & Francis, M. E. (1997). Linguistic predictors of adaptive bereavement. *Journal of Personality and Social Psychology, 72,* 863–871.

Peplau, H. (1991). *Interpersonal relations in nursing.* New York: Springer.

Polanyi, M. (1958). *The study of man.* Chicago: University of Chicago Press.

Polkinghorne, D. E. (1988). *Narrative knowing and the human sciences.* Albany: State University of New York Press.

Reed, P. A. (1995). Treatise on nursing knowledge development for the 21st century: Beyond postmodernism. *Advances in Nursing Science, 17,* 70–84.

Reed, P. A. (1999). Response to "Attentively Embracing Story: A Middle-range Theory with Practice and Research Implications." *Scholarly Inquiry for Nursing Practice: An International Journal, 13,* 205–209.

Rogers, C. R. (1951). *Client-centered therapy.* Boston: Houghton Mifflin.

Rogers, M. E. (1994). The science of unitary human beings: Current perspectives. *Nursing Science Quarterly, 7*, 33–35.

Sandelowski, M. (1991). Telling stories: Narrative approaches in qualitative research. *IMAGE: Journal of Nursing Scholarship, 23*, 161–166.

Sandelowski, M. (1994). We are the stories we tell. *Journal of Holistic Nursing, 12*, 23–33.

Smith, M. J. (1975). Changes in judgment of duration with different patterns of auditory information for individuals confined to bed. *Nursing Research, 24*, 93–98.

Smith, M. J. (1986). Human–environment process: A test of Rogers' principle of integrality. *Advances in Nursing Sciences, 9*, 21–28.

Smith, M. J., & Liehr, P. (1999). Attentively embracing story: A middle-range theory with practice and research implications. *Scholarly Inquiry for Nursing Practice: An International Journal, 13*, 187–204.

Summers, L. (2002). Mutual timing: An essential component of provider/patient communication. *Journal of the Academy of Nurse Practitioners, 14*, 19–25.

Surrey, J. L. (1991). The self-in-relation: A theory of women's development. In J. Jordan, A. G. Kaplan, J. B. Miller, I. P. Stiver, & J. L. Surrey (Eds.), *Women's growth in connection: Writings from the Stone Center* (pp. 51–66). New York: Guilford.

Taylor, D. (1996). *The healing power of stories*. New York: Doubleday.

Van Manen, M. (1990). *Researching lived experience*. Albany: State University of New York Press.

Watson, J. (1997). The theory of human caring: Retrospective and prospective. *Nursing Science Quarterly, 10*, 49–52.

10

Evaluation of Middle Range Theories for the Discipline of Nursing

Marlaine C. Smith

Theories are patterned ideas that provide a coherent way of viewing complex phenomena. Middle range theories have a more limited view of a particular phenomenon than do grand theories. However, because nursing is a professional discipline, all of the theories within it should be evaluated from a perspective that considers the salient elements of the discipline in the evaluation. While there are many sets of criteria for evaluating nursing conceptual models and grand theories (Chinn & Kramer, 1999; Fawcett, 2000; Fitzpatrick & Whall, 1996; Parse, 1987; Stevens, 1984), few focus particularly on theories at the middle range. In addition, there has been little guidance for beginning nursing scholars on the purpose and the process of critical analysis and evaluation of theories. A common course assignment on the evaluation of nursing theory becomes a pedantic exercise, ending in a rather cynical view of theory development. One is reminded of the aphorism "When our only tool is a hammer, all we see are nails." In other words, the tool of critical evaluation taught to students is often weighted toward finding the faults, errors, and inconsistencies within the theoretic structures. It is no wonder that there is evidence of some devaluation of nursing theory and a reticence to engage in its development. The atheoretical measurement of outcomes of practice, while a worthy endeavor, has eclipsed the compelling need to create systems of thought with potential to describe and explain the nature of phenomena of concern to nursing science. The nursing scholars who contribute to the development of theory for the discipline, including those who are featured in this text, are innovative pioneers who courageously offer their ideas for the advancement of the discipline and the betterment of health care for those we serve. It is important, then, to balance the identification of theoretic weaknesses with the aspects of appreciation, recognition, and affirmation of their strengths. The purposes of this chapter are to provide tools for a balanced and reasoned evaluation of middle range theory for the discipline of nursing. Describing the purposes of theory evaluation, articulating a set of criteria to guide evaluation of middle range theory, and elaborating a process for conducting this evaluation organize the chapter.

THE PURPOSE OF THEORY EVALUATION: TOWARD A POSTMODERN VIEW

Evaluation is one of the most popular indoor sports of the organizations in which we live. Because these organizations are accountable to public and private stakeholders, evaluation is used as a measure of assurance and accountability. The meaning of evaluation carries an onerous tenor because of baggage that is often attached to it. Students receive grades that reflect evaluation of achievement in a course. A score or category is received when one is evaluated for job performance. Often this evaluation is attached to some reward. The memory of the evaluation of papers, projects, and practice may be more often marked by the red ink of what was done wrong than what was achieved or done well.

The common, modern definition of evaluation is a process of determining or fixing the value, worth, or significance of something. This definition reflects the anxieties that are experienced surrounding evaluation, connoting the determination of a static and absolute outcome of worth or value. A postmodern meaning of evaluation is quite different. It reflects the presence of subjectivity and contextuality, the diversity of opinions from a community, and, ultimately, the tentative nature of any outcome. It becomes an informed and flawed opinion rendered at a particular moment in time by a person with inherent biases and values. This opinion, which one hopes is not arbitrary or capricious, is based on some sound, reasonable measures or criteria that can be applied consistently. However, it is important to note that the criteria and the evaluator's application of them are value-laden. In this way, they should be viewed not as absolute judgments of worth but as one honest examination by a member of a community.

The evaluation of theory, then, is a process of coming to an opinion about its worth or value. Kaplan (1964), in his discussion of the validation of theory, states that its purpose is to examine a theory's value or worth for advancement by the scientific community. When evaluating nursing theory we ask questions about its worthiness to be used as a guide for inquiry and practice and to be taught to students. Theory, by its definition in any paradigm of science, is a creative constellation of ideas, offered as a possible explanation or description of an observed or experienced phenomenon. In the process of evaluation one is not determining the truth of the theory, but its value for further exploration within the scientific community. History affirms the tentative nature of theory evaluation. Theories that were judged by the scientific community as valid were often later abandoned. Ptolemaic theory on the geocentric nature of the planetary system was abandoned later for the Copernican theory that the earth and the planets revolved around the sun. Many revolutionary ideas of our time were evaluated initially as worthless. Rogers' (1970) conceptual system, describing the integral nature of human-environment energy fields, was an object of ridicule in the early 1970s. Thirty years later, its correspondence to burgeoning contemporary thought is eerie.

Members of a disciplinary community bear the responsibility to participate in authentic dialogue around ideas. The purpose of evaluation of theory in this context is to share in the evolution of the discipline through reflection and comment on the ideas offered up within the community. The greater value of evaluating theory is to participate as individuals in the community's structuring of ideas. While the theory is given to the community, the community re-forms it through critique, testing, and application. The life of any theory is determined by the scientific community's engagement with it. Evaluation of theory is essential to the life of the theory, leading to its extension, revision, and refinement.

Based on the preceding discussion, it is important that the evaluator stay true to the purpose of evaluation of theory. The stance of the one evaluating theory from a postmodern perspective is characterized by intellectual empathy, curiosity, honesty, and responsibility. The empathic stance is the attempt to understand the perspective of the theorist and is defined by Paul (1993) as "to imaginatively put oneself in the place of others in order to understand them" (p. 261). Here, the evaluator listens carefully to the point of view. Listening is being aware of one's own biases but trying to put them aside to really hear ideas, even if the evaluator does not share them. The stance of empathy requires an appreciation of others' points of view and a seeking out of the origin and context of those points of view. Curiosity is the second characteristic of the critical stance. Here, the evaluator raises questions in the process of studying the theory that are born from a quest to understand. The evaluator plays with the theory in different circumstances and imagines ways of testing or understanding it more deeply. The evaluator engages fully in trying to understand and acquire a range of sources on the theory and its application. The third stance is one of honesty. The evaluator trusts individual inner wisdom and recognizes the need to honor that wisdom in sharing the evaluation. Knowing his or her own biases and limitations, the evaluator is still willing to share personal reflections on the theory. One of the major hurdles in learning to evaluate theory is to rely on one's own opinions, rather than jump on the bandwagon of others who are considered wiser or more learned. From the postmodern perspective each evaluation should stand on its own, one voice among many diverse ones in the community. It may be difficult to publish negative comments, but it is important to remember that these may be the needed stimuli to make important clarifications or changes in the theory. Finally, the evaluator must be a responsible steward of the discipline. As a member of the scientific community, the evaluator has an obligation to care about the nature of evolution of nursing knowledge. That responsibility entails a thoughtful and scholarly response to the critique, applying the criteria fairly and drawing conclusions that can be useful in the revision or extension of the theory as others use it. Once a theory is published it no longer belongs to the theorist. The voice of the theorist becomes one of many in the community using the theory to guide processes of knowledge development and practice.

In summary, the purpose of a postmodern approach to the evaluation of middle range theory in nursing is to come to a decision about the merits and limitations of the theory for nursing science. The evaluator approaches the evaluation from a stance of empathy, curiosity, honesty, and responsibility. Evaluation of theory is acknowledged as necessary to the evolution of the theory in the context of the scientific community.

THE ORIGIN OF EVALUATIVE FRAMEWORKS

Theories are the language of science. Science is the process of systematically seeking an understanding of phenomena through creating some unifying or organizing frameworks about the nature of those phenomena. In addition, science involves the evaluation of these frameworks for their credibility and empirical honesty (Smith, 1994). The organizing or unifying frameworks of science are theories. Rigorous and systematic standards of inquiry govern the development and testing of theories. Theories are evaluated for their credibility and empirical honesty by judging them against established standards.

The nature of science, and, therefore, of the theories of science, have undergone change. Philosophies of science have evolved from a sole reliance on the assumptions of logical-positivist views toward expanding philosophies of the postpositivist or postmodern era (Smith, 1998). For example, the traditional or empirical-analytic view of science defines theories as sets of interrelated propositions that describe, explain, or predict the nature of phenomena (Kerlinger, 1986). In the human science view, the purpose of theories is to create an understanding of phenomena through description and interpretation. Therefore, the rules of logic, which apply to traditional science, do not apply to human science. For this reason, the frameworks used to evaluate theories must be inclusive enough to encompass these divergent views.

Kaplan's (1964) perspective on the "validation" of theories is open enough to encompass a diversity of theoretic forms. He emphasizes that the evaluation of any theory is not a matter of pronouncement of its truth. "At any given moment a particular theory will be accepted by some scientists, for some of their purposes, and not by other scientists, or not for other contexts of possible application" (p. 311). The evaluation of theory involves the exercise of good judgment in determining a relative and tentative truth, and is by its nature normative, in that the community ultimately determines the outcome. "The validation of a theory is not the act of granting an imprimatur but the act of deciding that the theory is worth being published, taught, and above all, applied—worth being acted on in contexts of inquiry or of other action" (Kaplan, 1964, p. 312). Kaplan identifies three major philosophical conceptions or norms of truth that can be exercised in the process of evaluating theory: correspondence or semantical norms, coherence or syntactical norms, and pragmatics or functional norms. See Figure 10.1, ladder of abstraction.

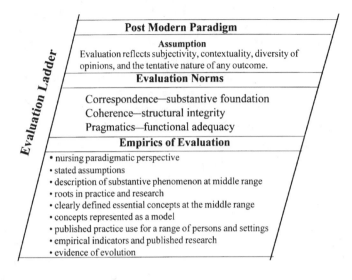

FIGURE 10.1   Ladder of abstraction.

The norm of correspondence refers to the substantive meaning of the theory. Through application of this norm, one judges the degree to which the theory fits the facts. While "facts" are in themselves understood through a theoretic lens, Kaplan argues that this does not necessarily present a tautology. Any theory must in some way pass the test of common sense. While he acknowledges that significant discoveries have flown in the face of common sense, these discoveries in some way could be explained through their relationship to accepted knowledge or some convergence of evidence that supported the plausibility of the theory. Through the norm of correspondence one evaluates the extent to which the theory fits comfortably within the nexus of existing knowledge.

The norm of coherence relates to the integrity of the theory's structure. Kaplan describes the experience of the "click of relation, when widely different and separate phenomena suddenly fall into a pattern of relatedness, when they click into position" (p. 314). This experience of "truth" or wholeness occurs when all the fragments of the theory come together to form an integrated whole. Simplicity is the most widely applied norm of coherence. Descriptive simplicity is the quality of expressing the complex ideas of the theory parsimoniously. Inductive simplicity refers to the phenomenon being described by the theory. The theory must encompass a manageable number of ideas; too many will overwhelm the capacity of the theory to serve its purpose to provide a framework for understanding the phenomenon. Kaplan warns that a theory can be too simple, in that it goes too far in reducing the complexities. Theories should introduce the degree of complexity necessary for clear understanding, nothing more. He quotes Whitehead's axiom: "Seek simplicity and distrust it" (p. 318). Another norm of coherence is esthetics, that is, the beauty perceived upon the contemplation of the theory. The beauty of the theory involves some sense of symmetry and balance, but Kaplan warns, "beauty is not truth" (p. 319). The process of developing theory is creative, and that creativity is expressed in a product that possesses an aesthetic quality.

The final norm is pragmatics and refers to the effectiveness or functional capability of the theory. In a professional discipline, the norm of pragmatics instructs us to consider the degree to which the theory can guide practice and research to advance the goals of the discipline. On the other hand, Kaplan states that the theory is not judged by the extent to which it makes some external difference alone; he acknowledges that other factors might interfere with or enhance the success of application. The theory is also judged by what it can do for science, "how it guides and stimulates the ongoing process of scientific inquiry" (pp. 319–320). So the degree to which the theory has spawned research questions is relevant. "The value of the theory lies not only in the answers it gives but also in the new questions it raises" (p. 320). A theory is validated when it is put to good use in the application of concerns to the discipline. The evaluative framework for middle range theories is based on these norms. Criteria will be clustered into the following three categories: substantive foundation, structural integrity, and functional adequacy.

An abundance of evaluative frameworks for nursing theories have evolved over the past several decades (Chinn & Kramer, 1999; Fawcett, 2000; Fitzpatrick & Whall, 1996; Parse, 1987; Stevens, 1984). Some of these frameworks are applicable to middle range theories while others are not. Liehr and Smith (1999) summarized the literature about the nature of middle range theories. They concluded that middle range theories are identified by their scope, level of abstraction, and proximity to empirical findings. Scope refers to the breadth of phenomena addressed by the theory. Compared to conceptual models and grand theories, middle range theories offer constellations of ideas or concepts about more circumscribed phenomena of concern to the discipline. In this way they are intermediate in scope, focusing on a limited number of concepts focused on a limited aspect of reality (Liehr & Smith, 1999). Level of abstraction locates middle range theories between the abstract level of conceptual models and grand theories and situation specific theories. The language of middle range theory describes concepts and relationships between them more concretely. Finally, middle range theories are more proximal to empirical findings than are conceptual models and grand theories. They are developed through an analysis of empirical findings or at a level of immediate testability. These three qualities of middle range theories should be represented in the evaluative frameworks for them.

The following criteria (Table 10.1) have been developed from Kaplan's norms for validating theories and are informed by the essential qualities of middle range theories to create an evaluative framework specific to theories of the middle range.

Substantive Foundation

Substantive foundation is the first category of criteria for the evaluation of middle range theory in nursing. This category includes criteria that are based on Kaplan's norm of correspondence, and leads to questions about the meaning or semantic elements of the theory. A middle range theory in nursing contributes to the knowledge of the discipline of nursing, and is developed from assumptions that are clearly specified. The theory provides knowledge that is at the middle range level of abstraction. There are four major criteria related to substantive meaning: (1) the theory is within the focus of the discipline of nursing, (2) the assumptions are specified and are congruent with the focus of the discipline of nursing, (3) the theory provides a substantive description, explanation, or interpretation of a named phenomenon at the middle range level of discourse, and (4) the origins are rooted in practice and research experience. Each of these criteria and the questions that guide the application of the criteria in evaluating the theory will be discussed.

The first criterion emphasizes that a middle range theory in nursing is judged by its location in and contribution to the discipline of nursing. The question, "What makes a middle-range theory in nursing a *nursing* theory?" is interesting to consider. Some (Fawcett, 2000; Parse, 1987) assert that nursing theories are only those identified as the conceptual

TABLE 10.1   Framework for the Evaluation of Middle Range Theories

Substantive foundations

1. The theory is within the focus of the discipline of nursing.
2. The assumptions are specified and are congruent with the focus.
3. The theory provides a substantive description, explanation, or interpretation of a named phenomenon at the middle range level of discourse.
4. The origins are rooted in practice and research experience.

Structural integrity

1. The concepts are clearly defined.
2. The concepts within the theory are at the middle range level of abstraction.
3. There are no more concepts than needed to explain the phenomenon.
4. The concepts and relationships among them are logically represented with a model.

Functional adequacy

1. The theory can be applied to a variety of practice environments and client groups.
2. Empirical indicators have been identified for concepts of the theory.
3. There are published examples of use of the theory in practice.
4. There are published examples of research related to the theory.
5. The theory has evolved through scholarly inquiry.

models and grand theories developed by nurses in the 1960s through the 1980s. From this perspective, legitimate middle range theories in nursing are those deduced from or inductively developed within existing conceptual models and grand theories of nursing. This is problematic in that it fixates theory development in what has been considered legitimate in the past. It is important to leave space for the possibility of emergent conceptual models or grand constructions that may be articulated as sets of foundational assumptions upon which middle range theories are constructed. The evaluator should expect that a middle range theory in nursing contributes to knowledge about human–environment health relationships, caring in the human health experience, and/or health and healing processes (Fawcett, 2000;

Newman, Sime, & Corcoran-Perry, 1991; Smith, 1994). It should be possible to locate the theory within a paradigmatic perspective endorsed by nursing, such as the particulate-deterministic, interactive-integrative, unitary-transformative schema (Newman et al., 1991), the totality or simultaneity paradigm (Parse, 1987), or the reaction, reciprocal interaction or simultaneous world-view (Fawcett, 2000).

The second criterion regarding the specification of assumptions in the category of substantive foundations is that the origins and ontological foundations of the theory are specified. The developer of the middle range theory holds philosophical assumptions that are either explicitly stated or implicitly implied by the meaning of the theory. Fawcett (2000) argues that the belief that middle range theory is developed outside the context of a conceptual frame of reference is absurd. She emphasizes the contextual nature of theory building. The assumptions of a middle range theory identify the context for theory building and should be identifiable. A stronger middle range theory would explicate the assumptions.

The ideas of parent theories or models should be clearly identified in the explication of the meaning of the theory. The developers should cite primary sources from any parent theories that may be accessed for greater depth in understanding. While some middle range theories will not be explicitly derived from nursing conceptual models, parent ideas that shaped theory development would be clearly described.

Finally, the meaning of the theory should be consistent with its foundational assumptions. This consistency is essential. If Rogers' Science of Unitary Human Beings (SUHB) forms the assumptions of a middle range theory, the meaning of the concepts within the theory should not violate these assumptions. One would not use the language of "adaptive responses" in a theory purportedly derived from the SUHB. If the assumptions are not derived from an existing conceptual model/grand theory, the synthesized assumptions provide a frame of reference for this analysis. Without this, one is left to analyze inferred foundations and how the middle range theory corresponds to their meaning.

The third criterion related to substantive meaning states that the middle range theory provides substantive knowledge about a named circumscribed phenomenon of concern to nursing. Liehr and Smith (1999) contend that a middle range theory is known by the way it is named and that it should be "named in the context of the disciplinary perspective and at the appropriate level of discourse" (p. 86). Middle range theory is defined by its focus on providing knowledge about a specific phenomenon of concern to nursing. The theory should offer a substantive description, explanation, or interpretation of this particular phenomenon that leads to a new understanding or different way of considering the phenomenon. It is incumbent on the developer of the theory to provide adequate explanation substantiated by logical reasoning and reference to existing knowledge sources that lead to a full understanding of the meaning of the concepts and their relationships to each other. Finally, the theory should capture the complexities of the phenomenon that it addresses. A theory is a map of some aspect of reality; like a map it cannot capture the landscape. However, to the extent possible the theory should approximate the fullest range of conceptual relationships that it addresses.

The fourth criterion deals with the rooting of the origins of the theory in practice and research experience. Middle range theory grows out of the research and practice experiences of nurses, who articulate a set of concepts to describe and explain a phenomenon that they have observed in their work. The evaluator will seek out the practice and research roots of the theory. It may be that one set of roots (practice or research) is sturdier than the other. This assessment may indicate a next direction for further application of the theory. Well-developed middle range theory will have documented development related to both practice and research.

Structural Integrity

A middle range theory is a framework that organizes ideas. Like any framework, it has a structure. The structure provides strength, balance, and the aesthetic qualities that ensure its integrity. Structural integrity is the category that was derived from Kaplan's (1964) norm of coherence. There are four criteria for evaluation of the structural integrity of middle range theories: (1) the concepts are clearly defined, (2) the concepts of the theory are at the middle range level of abstraction, (3) there are no more concepts than are needed to explain the phenomenon, and (4) the concepts and relationships among them are logically represented with a model. The four criteria for structural integrity and their application are discussed below.

The first criterion is that the ideas and the relationships among them are clearly presented within the theory. Concepts are the names given to the abstract ideas that constitute the theory. The relationships among the ideas are developed into statements or propositions. In any middle range theory, the concepts within it should be clearly defined. Any neologisms (newly coined terms) should be adequately defined. The relationship statements, whether called propositions or not, should articulate the relationships among the central ideas or concepts within the theory. Concepts, even within the context of middle range theory, are abstractions, and, as such, it takes some willingness to understand them. However, the definitions should lead to this understanding and provide precise meaning.

The second criterion related to structural integrity is that the ideas of the theory are at the middle range level of abstraction. All concepts should be on the ladder of abstraction at a similar level. For example, health may be considered a concept at the metaparadigm level; adaptation, at the level of grand theory; and anxiety, at the level of the middle range. Mixing these as concepts within one theory would be an example of concepts at differing levels of abstraction. Similarly, the concepts in the theory should consistently be presented at the middle range level, more concrete and circumscribed than concepts at a higher level of abstraction. The deductive or inductive processes of theory development should be transparent in the presentation of the theory. Movement up the ladder of abstraction to paradigms or down the ladder to empirical indicators should be logical, reasoned, and clear.

The third criterion is that there should be no more concepts than are necessary to describe the theory as named. The theory should be organized and presented parsimoniously. That means that the ideas should be synthesized and communicated in the simplest, most elegant way possible. Extraneous concepts or unclear differentiation of concepts creates complexity that confuses rather than clarifies.

The fourth or final criterion is that the ideas of the theory are integrated to create an understanding of the whole phenomenon, which is presented in a model. This criterion leads to consideration of the internal consistency, balance, and aesthetics of the theory. The concepts and statements of the theory should be logically ordered so that they lead to an appreciation and apprehension of the theory meaning. The relationships among the ideas can be represented in a schema, a model, or a list of logically ordered statements. In any case, it is the responsibility of the developer to make these relationships accessible. All ideas (concepts and related statements) in the theory should have semantic congruence, that is, the meanings are not contradictory. Middle range theories are creative products of science. As such, there should be balance and harmony in the way they are presented.

Functional Adequacy

For a professional discipline, functional adequacy is arguably the acid test of a middle range theory. Middle range theories are closely tied to research and practice. They may be generated from research findings and used to develop testable hypotheses. They may have been developed in relation to a practice dilemma, and they can be used to create practice guidelines. Middle range theories build nursing knowledge and are valuable in and of themselves for this contribution. There are five criteria for functional adequacy of middle range theories: (1) the theory can be applied to a variety of practice environments and client groups, (2) empirical indicators have been identified for concepts of the theory, (3) there are published examples of use of the theory in practice, (4) there are published examples of research related to the theory, and (5) the theory has evolved through scholarly inquiry. Each of these criteria will be described below.

The first criterion of functional adequacy is that the theory is able to provide guidance for a variety of practice populations and environments. One would expect literature that documents use of the theory with more than one population and in more than one setting. Because the theory is middle range rather than situation specific, this generality criterion exists. In this case, generality is limited to the central phenomenon of the theory. In this book, individual chapters discuss theoretical structures for phenomena such as self-efficacy, unpleasant symptoms, and uncertainty.

The second criterion is that there are empirical indicators identified for the concepts of the theory. Empirical adequacy is an essential aspect of middle range theory. Empirics are meant to go beyond empiricism and include perceptions, symbolic meanings, self-reports, observable behavior, biological indicators, and personal stories (Ford-Gilboe, Campbell, & Berman, 1995; Reed, 1995). Researchers working with the middle range theory may have selected empirical indicators for measurement of theoretical constructs or they may develop the middle range theory from descriptions and stories. Both of these examples support the theory's empirical adequacy. Empirical adequacy is an indication of the maturity of the theory.

The third criterion is that there are published examples of how the theory has been used in practice. This criterion offers evidence to support that the theory makes a difference in the lives of people. Published reports of the theory should demonstrate that use of the theory enhances well-being and quality of life. When the middle range theory is taken to practice there are expectations about emergent outcomes. These outcomes may be identified and tested by those conducting evaluation studies on theory-guided practice.

The fourth criterion is that there are published examples of research related to the theory. This criterion is a strong indicator of functional adequacy. The research findings can be examined for the level of support of the theory. In addition, middle range theories may generate hypotheses or research questions. Any refinements to the theory based on research findings should be examined; this indicates that the theory is open enough to change through the incorporation of further testing or development of ideas. In the process of evaluating this criterion, it is important to examine the evolution of the theory over time through inquiry and reflection.

The fifth criterion is that the theory has evolved through scholarly inquiry. Theories should evoke thinking, raise questions, invite dialogue, and urge us toward further exploration. This engaging quality of the theory is a hallmark of its potential for advancing the discipline. In order for the theory to grow, a community of scholars must engage with it in practice and research. Middle range theories build the discipline of nursing through expanding knowledge related to specific phenomena. The speculations offered by the theory push the boundaries of what is currently known and will invite continuing systematic inquiry. In this way the theory evolves and contributes to the development of nursing science and art.

APPLYING THE FRAMEWORK TO THE EVALUATION OF MIDDLE RANGE THEORIES

The evaluation of middle range theory involves preparation, judgment, and justification. In the preparation phase those evaluating the theory should spend time understanding the theory as fully as possible through dwelling with it. Dwelling with is investing time in reading and reflecting on the theory. The elements of the critical stance—empathy, curiosity, honesty, and responsibility, as articulated earlier in this chapter—are applied during preparation. It is important to gather a variety of sources on and about the theory, including primary sources written by the author of the theory, research reports, critiques, and practice papers. Reading the theory repeatedly to understand the ideas is the first step. In this process of beginning analysis, it is important to identify the central ideas and the structure of the theory. Middle range theories are developed from parent theories, empirical findings, or practice insights. Depth in understanding a theory may require going to the source documents that were critical to its development. Critical evaluation requires attending to questions and reactions to the theory that surface during the reading. It is important to record these questions and reactions. The next step in preparation is studying the practice and research reports related to the theory. Note how the theory was tested or extended through research. Examine how the theory has been applied in practice and any outcome studies that relate to the application of practice approaches or models based on the theory. Written critiques by others will provide another source of information. Because they may interfere with or unduly influence one's own evaluation, it is preferable to read those critiques or evaluations after one's own is completed.

The judgment phase is the heart of the evaluative process. In this phase the evaluator reads and reflects on the criteria in the evaluative framework. The evaluator trusts self as the instrument of judgment, one who has seriously and rigorously engaged in studying the theory. The evaluator reflects on and refers to the notes and responses created during the analysis process. The criteria in the evaluative framework are a guide toward making decisions about the meaning, structure, and practice and research applications. The strengths and the weaknesses of the theory should receive equal weight in the judgment phase. Both of these elements of the evaluation can contribute to the development of the theory. In the justification phase the evaluator supports judgments with explicit reasons for the decisions and with examples that illustrate points. In this phase the evaluator can refer to other written critiques that may support or refute judgments about the theory. The evaluation is written in a narration structured by the criteria in the framework. Each criterion is addressed through weaving judgments and support of those judgments. A balanced evaluation identifies both the strengths and limitations of the theory and suggests specific recommendations for clarification, extension, or revision.

The goal of this chapter was to explicate the purpose, structure, and process of evaluating middle range theories. Middle range theories are at the frontier of nursing science. The development of substantive knowledge through middle range theories promises movement toward disciplinary maturity. These theories will direct and spawn new inquiry and will stimulate the development of nursing practice approaches to enhance health and well-being. The evaluation of nursing theory is an essential activity within the scientific community. It leads to the advancement, refinement, and extension of substantive knowledge in the discipline. It is a critical skill of any scholar and is honed through practice and mentoring.

REFERENCES

Chinn, P. L., & Kramer, M. K. (1999). *Theory and nursing: Integrated knowledge development*. St. Louis: Mosby.

Fawcett, J. (2000). *Analysis and evaluation of contemporary nursing knowledge*. Philadelphia: F. A. Davis.

Fitzpatrick, J. J., & Whall, A. L. (1996). *Conceptual models of nursing*. Stamford, CT: Appleton & Lange.

Ford-Gilboe, M., Campbell, J., & Berman, H. (1995). Stories and numbers: Coexistence without compromise. *Advances in Nursing Science, 18,* 14–26.

Kaplan, A. (1964). *The conduct of inquiry*. San Francisco: Chandler.

Kerlinger, F. N. (1986). *Foundations of behavioral research* (3rd ed.). New York: Holt, Rinehart & Winston.

Liehr, P., & Smith, M. J. (1999). Middle range theory: Spinning research and practice to create knowledge for the new millennium. *Advances in Nursing Science, 21*(4), 81–91.

Newman, M. A., Sime, A. M., & Corcoran-Perry, S. A. (1991). Focus of the discipline of nursing. *Advances in Nursing Science, 14*(1), 1–6.

Parse, R. R. (1987). *Nursing science: Major paradigms, theories, and critiques*. Philadelphia: W. B. Saunders.

Paul, R. (1993). *Critical thinking: How to prepare students for a rapidly changing world*. Santa Rosa, CA: Foundation for Critical Thinking.

Reed, P. (1995). Treatise on nursing knowledge development for the 21st century: Beyond postmodernism. *Advances in Nursing Science, 17,* 70–84.

Rogers, M. E. (1970). *An introduction to the theoretical basis of nursing*. Philadelphia: F. A. Davis.

Smith, M. C. (1994). Arriving at a philosophy of nursing: Discovering? Constructing? Evolving? In J. Kikuchi & H. Simmons (Eds.), *Developing a philosophy of nursing* (pp. 43–60). Thousand Oaks, CA: Sage.

Smith, M. C. (1998). Knowledge building for the health sciences in the twenty-first century. *Journal of Sport and Exercise Psychology, 20,* S128–S144.

Stevens, B. (1984). *Nursing theory: Analysis, application, evaluation.* Boston: Little, Brown.

Appendix

Ladders of Abstraction

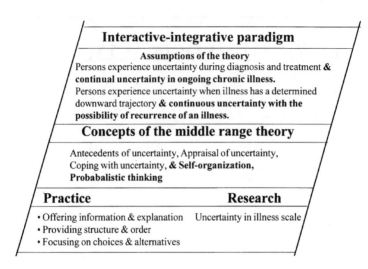

Ladder of Abstraction A: Uncertainty in illness and reconceptualization.

Bold-face and roman type used to differentiate the two theories presented.

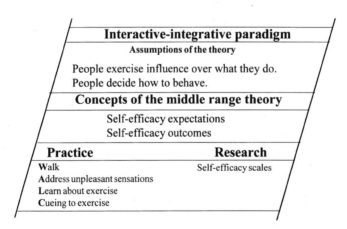

Ladder of Abstraction B: Self-efficacy.

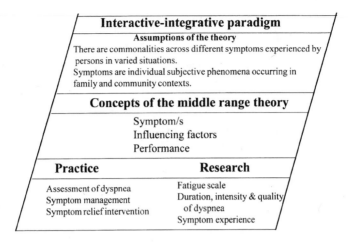

Ladder of Abstraction C: Unpleasant symptoms.

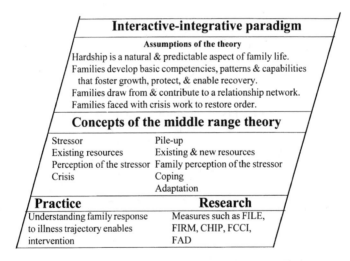

Ladder of Abstraction D: Family stress and adaptation.

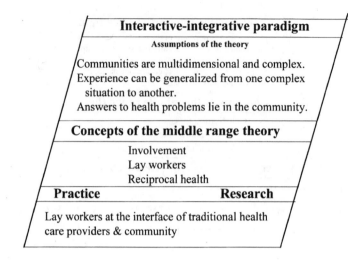

Ladder of Abstraction E: Community empowerment.

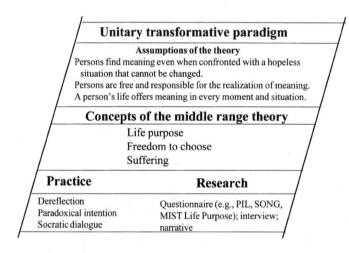

Ladder of Abstraction F: Meaning.

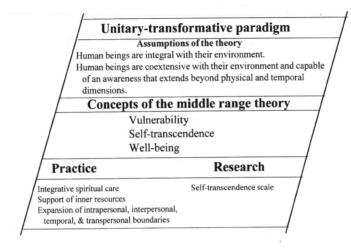

Ladder of Abstraction G: Self-transcendence.

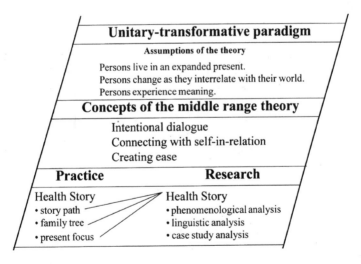

Ladder of Abstraction H: Attentively embracing story.

Index

Comfort Theory and Practice: *A Vision for Holistic Health Care and Research*

Katharine Kolcaba, PhD, RN, C

≋NEW≋

"I am most excited and impressed with the scope and focus of this work. As I began to read it, I had trouble putting it down. It is highly readable, engaging, all-inclusive, and most informative."

—**Jean Watson,** RN, PhD, HNC, FAAN

"I am honored and delighted to recommend this text for all nurses who care for and care about patients."
—from the Foreword by **May Wykle,** RN, PhD, FAAN

This book combines a first-person account of the development of the theory with supporting research, and practical information for its application. Kolcaba analyzes the concept of comfort; describes its physical, psychospiritual, environmental and sociocultural components; evaluates its meaning in the many different contexts that health care occurs; and describes how it can be measured.

Partial Contents:
- Preface
- **The Seeds of Inquiry**
- The Mission
- Measuring Comfort
- Philosophical Perspectives
- Theoretical Explorations
- Attributes of Comfort
- The Experiments
- The Ethics of Comfort Care
- Mission Updated
- Visions of Comfort for the Futrue

2003   288pp   0-8261-1633-7   soft

536 Broadway, New York, NY 10012-3955 • Tel: (212) 431-4370 • Fax: (212) 941-7842
Order Toll-Free: (877) 687-7476 • **Order On-Line:** *www.springerpub.com*

Springer Publishing Company

Nursing Theories
Conceptual and Philosophical Foundations
Hesook Suzie Kim, PhD, RN, and **Ingrid Kollak,** PhD, Editors

This book is designed to help readers gain a deeper understanding of nursing theories, through examining them in their conceptual and philosophical context. Nursing theories have not been developed in a vacuum—each has rich and varied roots in Western traditions, and this book allows readers to view this larger picture. It is organized around major themes in nursing and health care, in which discussion of specific nursing theories is integrated. Theories discussed include: human needs and nursing theory, patient empowerment, holism, existentialism and phenomenology, humanism, the health/illness continuum, and more.

Contents:

1999   240pp   0-8261-1287-0   hard

536 Broadway, New York, NY 10012 • Order on-line: www.springerpub.com
Order Toll-Free: (877) 687-7476 • (212) 431-4370 • Fax (212) 941-7842